INSTRUMENTS OF THE ORCHESTRA

THE TRUMPET AND TROMBONE

THE TRUMPET AND TROMBONE

An Outline of their History, Development and Construction

PHILIP BATE

LONDON · ERNEST BENN LIMITED

NEW YORK · W. W. NORTON & COMPANY INC.

First published by Ernest Benn Limited
25 New Street Square, Fleet Street, London, EC4A 3JA
and W. W. Norton & Company
55 Fifth Avenue · New York, 10003
First published 1966
Second corrected impression 1972

Distributed in Canada by
The General Publishing Company Limited, Toronto

© *Philip Bate 1966, 1972*

Printed in Great Britain

ISBN 0 510 36411 X

TO

Y. M. B.

From a drawing by Walter Trier

Contents

Introduction

IT MAY perhaps be thought a little surprising that of the numerous brass wind instruments used in music today, the Trumpet and the Trombone should have been selected for consideration in a single volume rather than any other pair or group which in their present-day form show a greater superficial resemblance. The reason is that these two, though nowadays often classified as belonging to different families, share the distinctive feature of a mainly cylindrical tube, and can, in their ultimate origins, be traced back to the same parent. Moreover, there are good reasons for believing that the trombone actually developed out of one form of the 'natural' trumpet through the application of the telescopic slide principle.

The ultimate parent of the cylindrical tubed brass instruments is found in the hollow cylindrical stem of a plant, while those instruments of a mainly tapered bore derive from the conical horn of an animal, or from the shell of a mollusc. All three of these occur plentifully in Nature and are still used for musical purposes by primitive peoples. The story of their transformation into the sophisticated art-instruments of today is a long one and there are many gaps in our knowledge of it, but the thread can certainly be traced as suggested later in this book. The very word 'horn' is a constant reminder of the origin of the conical bored brasses, though it is sometimes carelessly used, especially in America, to denote any lip-energised instrument from the true trumpet to the bass tuba. Popular speech in musical matters is often deceptive and the historian must use discretion in the matter of proper names. For instance, the two celebrated instruments found in the tomb of King Tut-ankh-amen are described quite properly in Hickmann's catalogue of Egyptian antiquities in the Cairo Museum, as trumpets. In both instruments the greater part of the tube is cylindrical, but in one of them the expansion at the root of the bell is comparatively abrupt, while in the other it is more gradual and takes up a much greater proportion of the total length, and a casual glance at the catalogue illustration might well lead a purist to call the one instrument a trumpet and the other a horn. In such a case the final distinction would presumably depend on the relative proportions of the cylindrical and conical parts of the tube, but to pursue the matter to such a length would be intolerably pedantic. On the other hand, the use of 'Trumpet' as a comprehensive term for all lip-energised instruments, as in Lavignac's *Encyclopédie*, has, in spite of the contributor's explanation, led to all sorts of confusion and should be discouraged.

Again, consider the Jewish ritual *Shophar*, one of the few instruments regularly used today which afford us an unbroken link with Antiquity. This is by all criteria a *horn* and is, indeed, very little modified from the natural ram's horn from which it is fashioned. It is the instrument with which the Children of Israel under Joshua encompassed the walls of Jericho, and in the original Hebrew account the name *shophar* is specifically used. In the English Authorised Version of the Bible the word is rendered as *trumpet*. Further, according to Jewish tradition, at the New Year, Rosh Ha-Shanah, it is the *shophar* that is sounded; yet this festival, in common English usage, is called the 'Feast of Trumpets'. On the other hand, compare this with another biblical reference, the Book of Numbers x. 1-10. Here we read of 'trumpets of silver' and the original Hebrew word is *hatzotzeroth*. This indicates the existence of a clear distinction in Mosaic times between natural horns and man-made trumpets of metal and, moreover, the Divine ordinance 'of a whole piece shalt thou make them' gives us a measure of the skill of the Israelitish metal workers of that period.

These two cases are typical of the curiosities and inconsistencies which crop up in any piece of musical research, but I think perhaps most frequently in connection with the history of instruments. Here the student's material is drawn from many different sources, some of them apparently remote from the immediate subject, yet all must be compared and evaluated. The work of the historian becomes in a way that of a musical detective, and while it is intensely interesting it is also anxious. In this field it is never possible to say that the last word has been spoken, for much evidence is capable of more than one interpretation, and from time to time fresh clues emerge which may modify long-accepted opinion. This can be readily understood if the reader will look for a moment at the kind of material that is available today. There are three main sources of information about the development of any musical instrument: first, actual examples from public or private collections, with descriptive matter and photographs; second, descriptions, instruction books, fingering charts, makers' lists, etc., and illustrations from contemporary sources; and third, music composed at different times for that particular instrument. Of these the first is clearly the most satisfactory. Here we have actual objects which we can compare, measure, and test in various ways. We may even find quite ancient specimens in playable condition. Of course, the physical characteristics of such specimens may have become altered with the passage of time and the natural processes of decay, though this is perhaps less likely to affect metal instruments than those of wood or other organic materials. We may reasonably expect the original measurements of antique brass instruments to be little altered unless they have been subject to careless handling or very advanced corrosion.

Descriptive matèrial varies greatly in its usefulness, depending as it does on the intention of the writer, his accuracy, and his terminology. Illustrations, too, are of varying value. Such early wood-cuts as those in Praetorius' *Theatrum Instrumentorum*, for example, are crude yet give a much more vivid idea than many engravings from museum catalogues or makers' lists, while the drawings annexed to patent specifications, which one might expect to be authoritative, are often frankly misleading. Photographs would appear to be the best sort of illustration, yet these too present pitfalls, particularly as regards perspective, and they cannot be relied on for finely accurate measurement unless several different views can be compared. There is today a growing tendency for woodwind enthusiasts to employ X-ray photographs and these are useful indeed, but again they form an uncertain basis for measurement unless the distances between tube, subject, and plate and the contained angle of the beam of rays be known. Thus, it will be seen that the scholar must not only collate and compare many sorts of evidence, but he must try when interpreting it to use judgment in the matter of standards.

Thirdly, the music of any period should always be consulted for the light it can shed. It is, for instance, quite possible that an instrument that would be hopelessly inadequate today may have been capable of much more than was required of it at the time it was made. Why, as an example, is it that some of the first writers to describe the trombone appear to disregard the chromatic possibilities which are and have always been inherent in the telescopic slide principle? The music composed shortly before and soon after the earliest accounts of the slide surely provides the answer, which seems to be that the slide made its appearance in response to a desire for a fuller diatonic compass rather than to any implicit need for a completely chromatic brass instrument at that time. In European music the fully developed concept of chromaticism was not complete till a much later period. Today the capacity of the slide trombone to produce relatively indeterminate tones is much valued in a certain class of music.

During the last hundred years or so scholars have increasingly turned their attention to the properties and behaviour of musical instruments, and a great deal has been written on many different aspects of the subject. Much of this material is, however, distributed through the pages of encyclopædias, periodicals, pamphlets, and the like, and is not very easy to find. Moreover, many valuable works are out of print and, due to their specialist nature, are somewhat unlikely to be reissued. A good deal, too, consists of mere statements transferred from one reference book to another by authors who were out of touch with first sources. Writers have quoted writers, often without acknowledgment and without any re-check or verification, and as a result many statements are accepted as proven fact which began as no more than surmise or, at best, well-informed opinion. Tradition plays a great part in our knowledge of musical instruments, and though tradition is to be respected, it should not be accepted blindly and without reasonable enquiry. Throughout this book I have tried to be clear as to the sources of my information.

As to the general lay-out of the volume, a word of explanation is perhaps due. First, I should like to make it clear that the general descriptions presented in Chapters 2, 3, and 4 apply to modern instruments, or to those sufficiently recent that the reader is likely to find them still in use. We should remember that a player who has formed his technique on an instrument that was perhaps the latest thing at the beginning of his musical life and has served him well over the years, is not particularly likely to exchange this for a more modern one without very careful consideration of the pros and cons; and a professional career may possibly last for half a century. Obsolete constructions, though often the parents of present-day ones, belong properly, I feel, to our historical section and I have therefore deferred their consideration as far as possible to these chapters. Again, the various essential features which characterise both the trumpet and the trombone are intimately bound up with certain immutable laws of physics. I have therefore thought it useful to place the chapter on Acoustics at the beginning of the book, as this forms the basis of much that must be discussed later. I have endeavoured to keep this part as clear as possible, though it can hardly be very simple, and to the reader whose interest is purely historical I would suggest that he need not burden himself with it—at least at the outset. I should hope, however, that later on he might come to enjoy the beauties and complexities of this fascinating science. As a result of this decision, which makes the section something of a separate essay, there will be found a few minor duplications between chapters. Other duplications arise inevitably from the consideration of topics from different viewpoints and I hope these will not be regarded as blemishes.

Another matter which I think may require some explanation is the rather arbitrary way in which I have divided the historical chapters. As Adam Carse pointed out, the history of the trumpet in Europe really falls into two periods with a transition occurring during the first half of the 19th century when the old 'natural' trumpet began to acquire valve or other mechanism, and to change into a fully chromatic instrument. A similar division can be discerned in the story of the trombone, for, although it has always by its very nature been chromatic, it also passed through the hands of the reformers at that time, though with somewhat different results. This natural division I have adopted, but I have felt that at least one more is required, and this I have placed at the end of the Roman Era. The choice was dictated rather by convenience than by any distinct historical break or change in the direction of development. What is obvious is that between the fall of the Roman Empire and the 13th century our sources of information become rather meagre. From this period we know more of architecture and the allied arts than of music, though there are accounts of Gregorian Chant in the 6th century, and the first use of an organ in church is reputed to have occurred in the year 757.

In respect of a previous book, I have been both praised and criticised for the number of notes that I placed at the end of each chapter. In the present volume I have again supplied extensive references and comments for the sake of the student, but I have deliberately kept them as notes in the hope that thereby the lay reader will not find the general narrative too disconnected.

Finally, I must say that this book makes no pretence at being an exhaustive treatise. Probably at the present time such a work would only be within the scope of an exceptional man who combined scholarship with musical experience and performing ability of a high order. The Trumpet and the Trombone provide a fascinating subject on which arts, crafts, and sciences all have a bearing. What I have attempted to do is to provide in a moderate-sized volume a conspectus which may interest and satisfy the lay reader on the one hand, and furnish something of a signpost for the potential specialist on the other. I know that there are certain omissions—for one, I have made no attempt to list or criticise the playing literature of either instrument, for there are many others better qualified than myself for this task. I have also avoided extensive references to living players and their performance as I feel that this is the province of the professional music critic. In some places I have presented conjectures and opinions of my own, and I hope it will be clear where I have done so. I am aware that these may perhaps be challenged and in their defence I would only say that I have not set them down lightly.

P. B.

Acknowledgements

THE FRIENDS, fellow students, musicians and musicologists who have given me help and encouragement in preparing this book make a very long list, and I thank them all. In particular my gratitude is due to Dr. Gerald Abraham, Anthony Baines, Dr. Arthur Benade, Geoffrey Brand, Dr. Catherine Brooks, Mrs. Adam Carse, J. A. Christiansen, Horace Fitzpatrick, Brian Galpin, Squire L. G. Grimes, the executors of the late Professor Bernard Hague, Duncan Hamilton, Rex Harris, Rolf Harris, Dr. F. Lloyd Harrison, Dr. R. A. Higgins, Spike Hughes, The Rev. Dr. Louis Jacob, Philip Jones, Dr. Trevor A. Jones, Lyndesay G. Langwill, Bill Lewington, Guy Oldham, Reginald Morley-Pegge, Maurice M. Porter, L.D.S., Steve Race, and William Teske. All these have been most generous in their various specialities; have advised me, lent instruments or documents, or have helped me in practical experiments.

To Eric McGavin I wish to express special appreciation for his laborious researches into the archives of Messrs. Boosey and Hawkes and other establishments now amalgamated with them or under their direction. This firm has been most kind in permitting the reproduction of data from their catalogues and other documents which give a broad view of the brass instrument industry in this country over a period of many years; and I have to acknowledge similar courtesies from Messrs. Butterworths, the publishers of *Research in Industry*; the *British Dental Journal*; and the editor of *Musical Quarterly*.

I am deeply indebted to the custodians of the following museums or specialist departments for facilities of all kinds, and to their various governing bodies for permission to reproduce photographs: The British Museum, Department of Greek and Roman Antiquities; The London Museum; The Wallace Collection; The Horniman Museum; The Ashmolean Museum, Oxford; The Museum of the Conservatoire Royal de Musique, Brussels; The Conservatoire National Supérieur de Musique, Paris; The Kunsthistorisches Museum, Vienna; The Germanisches National-Museum, Nürnberg; The Museum of Fine Arts, Boston, Mass.; The Metropolitan Museum of Art, New York; The Smithsonian Institution; The Lambeth Palace Library; and The Royal Military School of Music, Kneller Hall; also to Odhams Press Limited for the cartoon by Walter Trier from *Lilliput*, and to Penguin Books Limited and R. Harris for the chart from his book *Jazz*.

My thanks go also to Miss Houlgate, Reference Librarian to the B.B.C., and her staff, for many kindnesses; to Neil Badger and Hugh Tosh for much most exacting photographic work; and to Lyndesay Langwill and my wife for easing the labour of collation and proof-reading.

P. B.

The tonality or pitch of an instrument is indicated by a capital, e.g. trumpet in C, or B♭ trombone. To save innumerable musical examples, the following method of staff notation has been adopted.

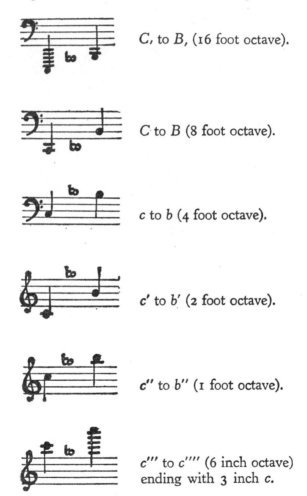

C, to B, (16 foot octave).

C to B (8 foot octave).

c to b (4 foot octave).

c' to b' (2 foot octave).

c'' to b'' (1 foot octave).

c''' to c'''' (6 inch octave)
ending with 3 inch c.

List of Illustrations

The instruments grouped in each of the following plates are reproduced as nearly as may be to the same scale. For reasons of perspective, however, strict accuracy has not always been possible.

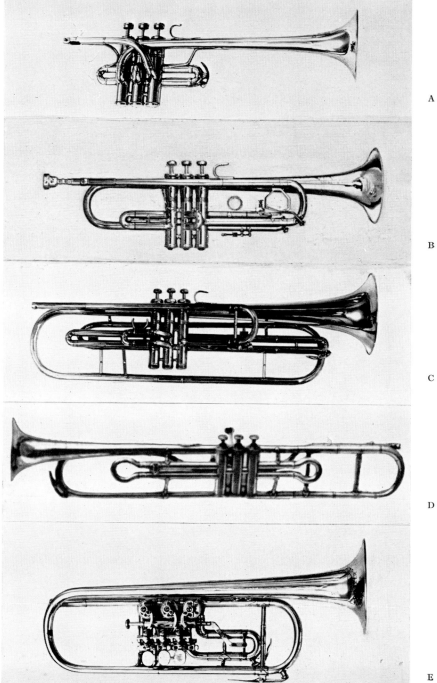

A

B

C

D

E

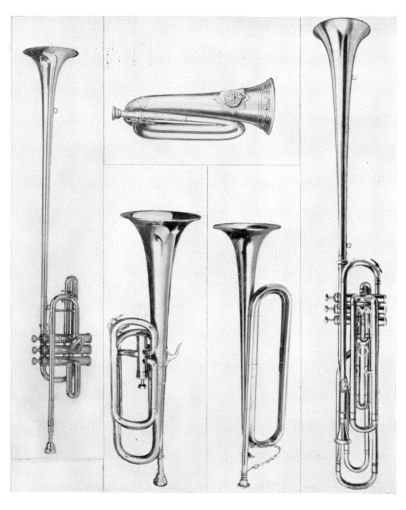

B   C   D   E

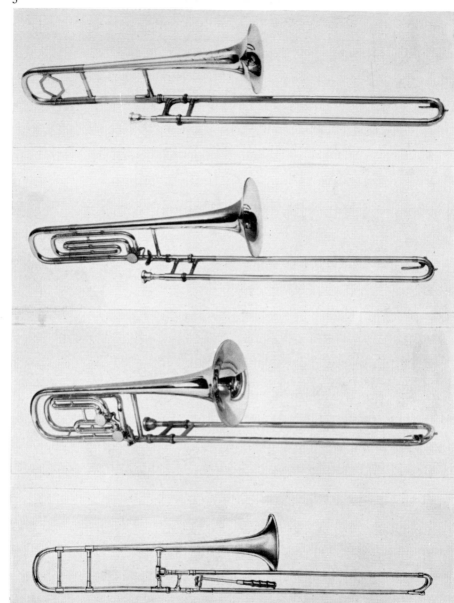

A

B

C

D

PLATE 3   Modern Slide Trombones

A. Large bore B♭ tenor. *Boosey and Hawkes, London.*

B. B♭-F tenor-bass. *Boosey and Hawkes, London.*

C. B♭-F tenor-bass with second valve transposing to E. 10 inch bell model used principally as bass trombone. *Reynolds, Cleveland, Ohio.*

D. Small-bore ('peashooter') bass in G. *Boosey and Hawkes, London.*

[*Ref.* Chapter 3]

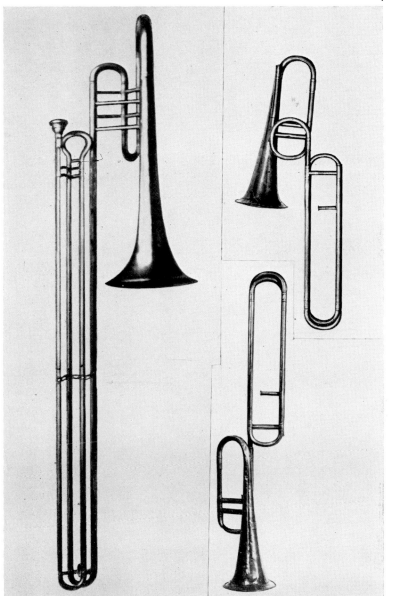

PLATE 4   Double-slide Trombones
    A. Contrabass in C. This instrument, preserved as a curiosity, was at one time known to London orchestral players as 'King Kong'. *Boosey & Co., London. c. 1880.*
    B and C. Bass in G. By means of an alternative coil in the centre the bell may be directed either forward or backward over the player's shoulder. *F. Pace, Westminster. 1834–49. Guy Oldham Collection.*

A B C

PLATE 5 Valve Trombones
   A. Six-valve 'independent' system. *A. Sax, Paris. c. 1852.*
   Archives of Besson & Co.
   B. Tenor in B♭ 'short' model. *John Grey, London.*
   C. Tenor in B♭ 'long' model. *Reynolds, Cleveland, Ohio.*
   B and C by courtesy of Bill Lewington Ltd., London.

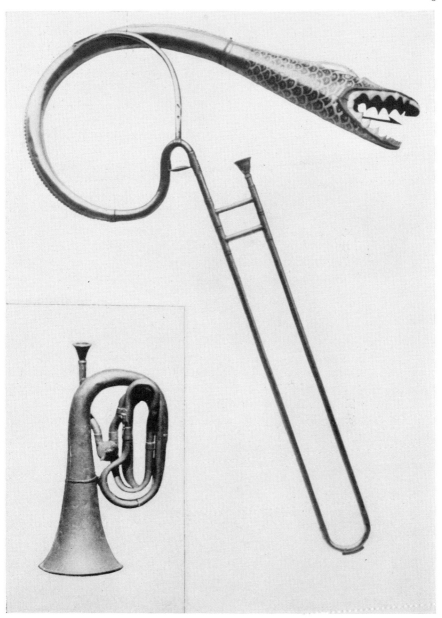

PLATE 6
A. *Buccin* Trombone in B♭. *Ricchi, Rome. Early 19th century. Adam Carse Collection, Horniman Museum, London.*
B. Trumpet-bugle with rotary valve. *Probably French. Royal Military School of Music, Kneller Hall. By permission of the Commandant.*

A. Trumpet in D, Silver. *Anton Schnitzer, Nürnberg, 1581.*

B. Trumpet in D, Brass with silver mounts. An ornament ball has probably been removed from the bell yard in the course of reconstruction. Mouthpiece modern. *Augustine Dudley, London, 1651.*

C. Trumpet in D, Silver. (Shown dismantled, see p. 77.) *William Bull, London. c. 1680.*

D. Trumpet in D, Brass, with silver mounts. *William Bull, London.*

E. Trumpet in D, Brass. The ornamental ball has presumably been removed and permanent metal struts soldered in. *Hans Geyer, Vienna, 1690.*

F. Trumpet in D, Brass. Extensively repaired. Engraved *Johann Wilhelm Haas in Nürnberg* and *I.W.H.* with trade mark (a hare) in the form adopted by W. W. Haas, son of I. W. H. *Post 1723?*

G. Trumpet in D, Brass. Marks similar to F above, but an altogether less ornate instrument. Shows wooden block between yards with cord binding.

[Ref. Chapters 4 and 6]

A and E Kunsthistorisches Museum, Vienna. C, Ashmolean Museum, Oxford. B and D, the London Museum. Reproduced by permission of the Trustees. F, Wallace Collection, London. Reproduced by permission of the Director. (Crown Copyright.) G, Adam Carse Collection, Horniman Museum, London.

7

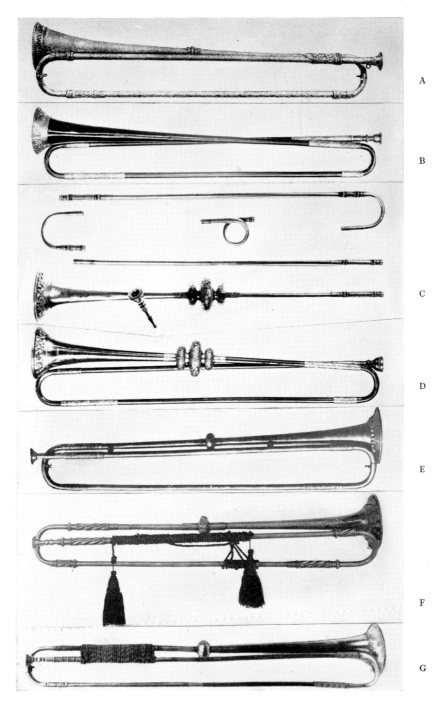

A

B

C

D

E

F

G

PLATE 8 Sackbuts, 16th–18th centuries

A. Quart-posaune in F with transposing slide to E incorporated in the bell bow. *Isaac Ehe, Nürnberg, 1612. By courtesy of the Germanisches National Museum, Nürnberg.*

B. Alt Posaune in F. *Michael Nagel, Nürnberg, 1663. Adam Carse Collection, Horniman Museum, London.*

C. Treble Posaune in B♭. *J. J. Schmeid, Pfaffendorf, 1781. By courtesy of the Museum of Fine Arts, Boston, Mass. (ex Galpin.)*

D. Gemeine Rechte Posaune (tenor) in B♭. *Jörg Neuschel, Nürnberg, 1557. By courtesy of Anthony Baines. (ex Galpin.)*

[*Ref.* Chapters 4 and 6]

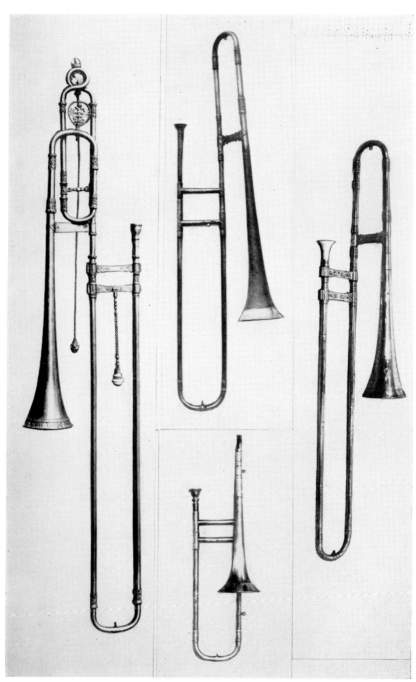

PLATE 10 Buisines, 15th century

A. Buisines depicted in the centre panel of a 'Christ Glorified' by Fra Angelico (1387–1455). *National Gallery, London.*

B. Buisine in D. On the evidence of the bell marks this instrument was formerly attributed to one of the *Sebastian Hainleins* of Nürnberg, although the date engraved thereon (MCDLX) is incompatible with this. Recent re-examination by an expert Medievalist suggests that the bell section is in fact of 19th-century workmanship, though the rest of the instrument is probably very ancient. *By courtesy of the Museum of Fine Arts, Boston, Mass. (ex Galpin.)*

[*Ref.* Chapters 4 and 6]

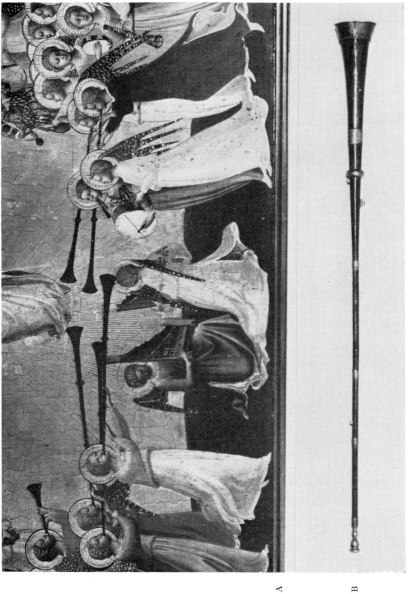

A

B

A

B

PLATE 11 Trumpets in Medieval and Renaissance Art

A. Straight, and unstayed folded trumpets depicted together. Painting of a joust held by Richard II at Smithfield, from the *Chronicle of St. Alban*. Lambeth Palace Library MS 6. *c.* 1400. *Reproduced by permission of the Trustees.*

B. Two details from 'The Worship of the Golden Calf', Filippino Lippi (1454–1507). On the left is a typical 15th-century folded trumpet (unstayed); on the right a Roman *Cornu*, both instruments treated as elements of pictorial composition and ornamented in Renaissance manner. *National Gallery, London.*

[*Ref.* Chapter 6]

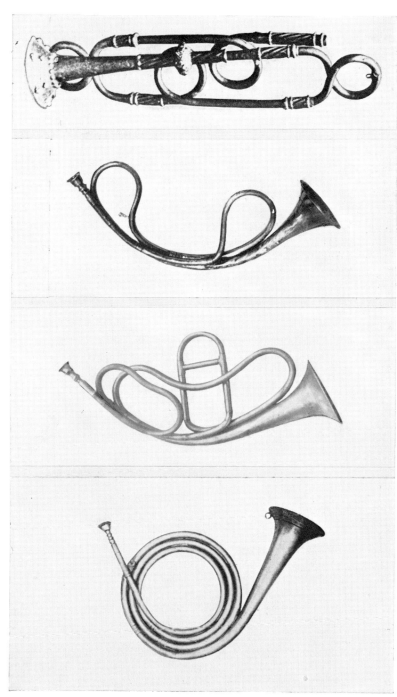

12

A

B

C

D

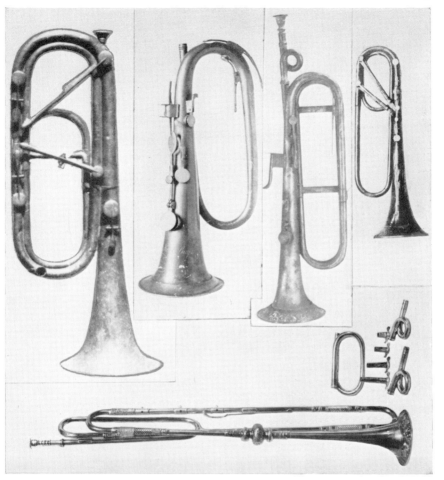

E

A

C

D

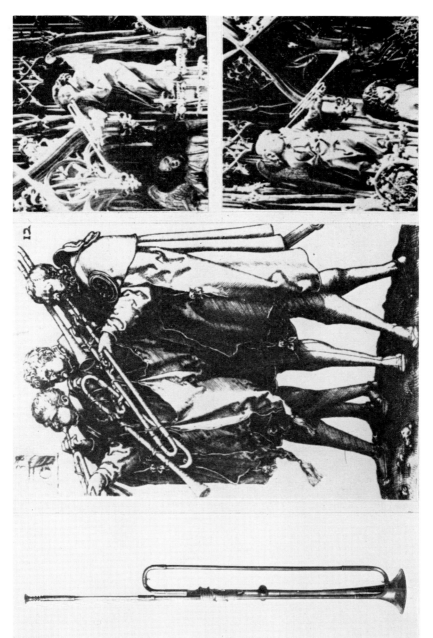

12

B

A

PLATE 15   Slide-Trumpets

A. Lithograph portrait of Thomas Harper, senior, from his *Tutor* of 1836.

B. English Slide-Trumpet by Köhler, London. *c.* 1865. Crooked in D. This is the later model with elastic spring instead of the cased watch springs shown at C. *Adam Carse Collection, Horniman Museum, London.*

C. English Slide-Trumpet, crooked in E♭. (Possibly an older natural trumpet adapted? This was a common fate among cherished instruments.) The push-rod in the centre carries a notched sleeve and pin device to adjust the 'home' position of the slide, and so the basic tuning. *Smithsonian Institution.*

D. French Slide-Trumpet. Dauverné's system. *Archives of Besson & Co. London.*

[*Ref.* Chapter 6]

15

A

B

C

D

PLATE 16   Modern 'Bach' Trumpets

   A. Two-valved trumpet in A. *Silvani and Smith, London (possibly of French make). Post 1884.*

   B. Steinkopf-Finke trumpet in D. *1961.*

   C. Trumpet in F. Menke's model with two rotary valves. *Alexander Gebrüder, Mainz. c. 1934.*

   D. Trumpet in high D. *Mahillon, Brussels. c. 1892.*

[*Ref.* Chapters 6 and 8]

A and D were used by the late John Solomon (see p. 179)

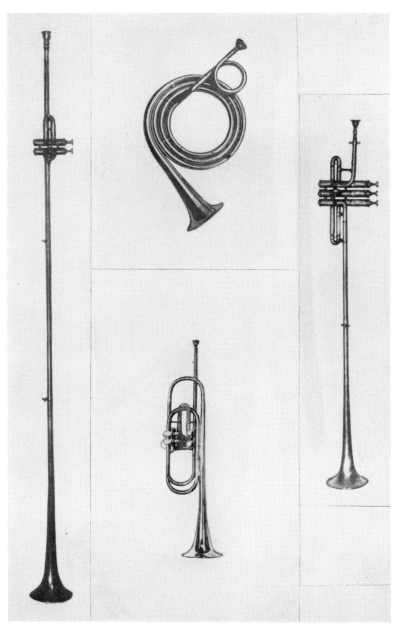

C   D

A

B

C

D

E

F

18

PLATE 18 Manufacture

A. 'Pegging' the bells in the traditional manner.

B. Details of the hydraulic expansion process applied to the bell and first bow of a trumpet. At the top and right are the two mating dies of the press. On the left the raw tube. In the centre the tube ready to be rough bent and brazed to the flare below. At right centre, the finished bell and bow. *By Courtesy of Boosey and Hawkes, London.*

[Ref. Chapter 9]

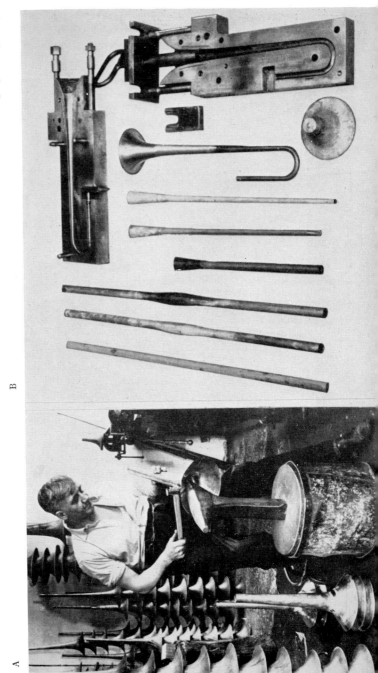

A

B

Acoustics

IT WILL NOT, I think, be unfair to suppose that the majority of readers who take up this volume have some basic knowledge of the nature of sound and its propagation. To those who are not acquainted with the subject but may desire a simple introduction to it, Chapter I of Alexander Wood's book *The Physics of Music* is strongly commended, for it is delightfully lucid and easy to read.[1] For our present purpose, however, we need only bear in mind the elementary facts that a musical sound is always generated by what scientists call a 'system' in a state of vibration and that it is transmitted to the hearer by some intervening *medium*. The system may be a stretched string, as in the piano or violin; a confined column of air, as in an organ pipe; a bar of metal, as in the vibraphone; a bent metal rod, as in the tuning fork, or any of a multiplicity of other devices. The medium between the source of the sound and the hearer may be solid, liquid, or gaseous, and the sound is propagated through this in the form of a series of successive compressions and rarefactions among its component particles which we call *sound waves*. In our common experience the most familiar medium is the air, at the bottom of a great sea of which we all live. It is the impact of these sound waves on the ear-drum that engenders the physiological and mental process that we call *hearing*. The frequency with which the compressions and rarefactions in the medium follow each other determines the *pitch* of the note heard—whether it is a high or a low one. We may also look at this matter in another way. The distance between similar points or phases in any two successive sound waves, say crest to crest or trough to trough, is termed the *wavelength*. High sounds have short wavelengths, deeper ones have longer. Thus wavelength is also a measure of pitch. If the wavelength be halved, the frequency (pitch) is doubled, and vice versa.

It is now getting on for a century since the first really scientific approach was made to the problems of acoustics as found in wind instruments. Certainly the general behaviour of musical pipes in its simpler aspects has been known and more or less understood for hundreds of years, but the first true insight into the structure of complex tones (which include practically every sound known to music) came with the work of Helmholtz in the early 1860s. It was he who by beautifully conceived experiments proved the truth of Ohm's earlier statement that the ear senses, as pure tones, only simple harmonic vibrations in the air, and that the quality of a complex musical sound depends solely on the order, number, and intensity of simple tones which are its components.

Much early tonal investigation could only be qualitative, as, for instance, Helmholtz's classical analyses by means of selectively tuned resonators, and syntheses with tuning forks. It was not till the advent of the telephone receiver and the phonograph in the '70s that the first quantitative work came in sight. At this stage the extreme complexity of the whole affair became evident, and it remained for Dayton Miller with his 'Phonodeik' and later workers with electrical methods[2] to begin to get things formulated. At the present time a great deal of work is going on, though it is still far from complete. All the standard orchestral voices have been subjected to tonal analysis and their characteristics plotted. We can now compare them both qualitatively and quantitatively.

Today the field of orchestral acoustics is ever widening and is clearly too large to be even outlined in these pages. We must, therefore, content ourselves with a few important general statements which will clear the way for a more specialised study of the trumpet and trombone. Today, also, the concepts of classical acoustics are subject to review and probably some revision, but they still remain the most useful starting-point for a short account.

From the point of view of physics all wind instruments appear as highly complex vibratory systems. All have, however, certain easily recognised common features. There is always some form of *generator* or *exciter* which initiates and maintains the sound. Next there is a *resonator*, commonly taken to be the body tube of the instrument, though more accurately it is the air column contained therein, whose size and shape are defined by the tube walls. Together these form a coupled dynamic system and the vibrations of the two are associated in a very intimate and complex way. The resonator is, however, the dominant partner which determines and stabilises the pitch of the sound produced, and, that this may be so, the mass of the air column is made fairly large, and its coupling with the generator tight, i.e. there must be no leakage of air between them. Should the acoustic coupling fail, the generator will take charge and emit its own note.

The structure of the generator is one of the important factors on which the classification of musical instruments is based, but there are many other considerations involved. Indeed, a really comprehensive classification is difficult to formulate in any simple way, if only because there are several different viewpoints from which the matter may be approached. Here, however, a limited generalisation without too much detail will serve. In the orchestral wind instruments used today the generator may be either

(a) The free 'air-reed', a simple jet of air shaped by the player's lips and blown against the sharp edge of a 'mouth hole' as in the transverse flute.

(b) The cane reed, double or single, as in the oboe and clarinet families respectively.

(c) The so-called 'lip-reed' generator which comprises a cup or funnel-shaped mouthpiece together with the player's actual lips as the vibrating part.

This latter is found in all brass instruments and is the only type to concern us here. Whatever form it takes, however, we can regard the generator as a sort of valve which constantly maintains the vibrational energy of the air column in the tube by converting a steady stream of compressed air from the player's lungs into a series of pulses whose frequency is determined by the characteristics of the column itself. The degree of coercion imposed by the resonator on the vibrating element of the generator varies in the different types. The cane reed is almost completely dominated by the resonator which it energises, but the vibration of the lips in sounding a brass instrument, though strongly influenced, is not so dominated. For this reason the generic term 'lip-reed' is not really a good one. There is not complete analogy between the behaviour of a brass player's lips and that of the blades of a cane reed.[3]

A resonating air column may be excited at any point, but in musical practice it is obviously most convenient to do this at one end. It is a popular fallacy that the mere rushing of a stream of air along a pipe will generate a musical sound; this is not so, nor should the 'valve' simile we have just used lead us to suppose that a large quantity of air is involved. Often very little air actually passes through a wind instrument during playing, and the distress sometimes felt by inexperienced players is mostly due to difficulty in getting rid of unused air accumulating in the lungs. Further, for experimental purposes it has been found possible to elicit the characteristic resonances of trumpet tubes without recourse to any actual air stream at all.[4]

The third feature common to all present-day orchestral wind instruments is some provision for altering at will the length of the air column, and the reason for this we shall look into next. It is an immutable law of Nature that the air in any given tube will vibrate only in certain fixed modes, and the frequencies of these modes, and hence the notes produced, depend primarily on the length of tube. For instance, the lowest note which can be produced from a tube effectively open at both ends and

approximately 8 feet long is that which we call C or .

This note is termed the *fundamental* and by referring to the length of the tube concerned we get a useful method of labelling the particular octave within the range of our hearing to which the note belongs. Thus such terms as 'the 4-foot octave' or 'the 16-foot octave' are universally recognised by musicians, and particularly instrument-makers.

In certain conditions, a vibrating body can produce a series of notes higher than the fundamental, and to appreciate how this comes about we must look for a moment at some of the simplest and oldest recognised laws of acoustics. To be capable of vibration any body must possess two properties, elasticity and inertia, as we shall find explained in any elementary textbook of physics. Let us first consider then the familiar case of a stretched cord such as a harp or violin string. When this is twanged we can clearly see that it vibrates in an eliptical loop with no motion at the fixed ends but a maximum displacement at the middle. If, however, we prevent any movement in the middle by gently touching the string with a finger it will divide itself into two loops, end to finger and finger to end, and the note we hear will rise an *octave*. Similarly, if we touch the string at one-third of its length it will divide into three loops and we shall hear a still higher note, the *twelfth*, and so on. These higher notes are called *harmonics* of the fundamental. This phenomenon was observed by Aristotle, was discussed by Mersenne (1636),[5] and was fully investigated by Sauveur of Paris in 1701[6] when he coined the term *partial tones* for the notes sounded by a string when vibrating in aliquot parts. When a stretched string vibrates in this way the points of no motion are termed *nodes* and those of maximum displacement *antinodes*.

Now let us consider an air column in a tube. We have already said that such a body can vibrate. This we are entitled to do since air as a fluid has the required properties of elasticity and inertia. The vibrations of a column of air differ in kind, however, from those of a string. In this case they take the form of a series of periodic compressions and rarefactions among the actual air particles which make up the column. Because of the similarity in behaviour of all elastic vibratory systems we can usefully apply the same terminology to any one of them. Hence, in an air column a point where there is least displacement of air particles (but conversely maximum pressure variation) is called a node, and one where there is most displacement an antinode. Suppose our column is contained in a doubly open cylindrical tube. At each end it communicates with the ambient air, so there can be little or no rise of pressure there. On the other hand, displacement at these points is virtually unrestricted. The two ends therefore become displacement antinodes when the column is energised, and in the first or simplest mode of vibration there will be a node midway between them. In the higher modes the end conditions cannot change; the terminal antinodes persist and symmetrical groups of nodes and antinodes will develop between them. These facts can be both deduced from pure mathematical considerations and proved by practical experiment.[7] By a mathematical

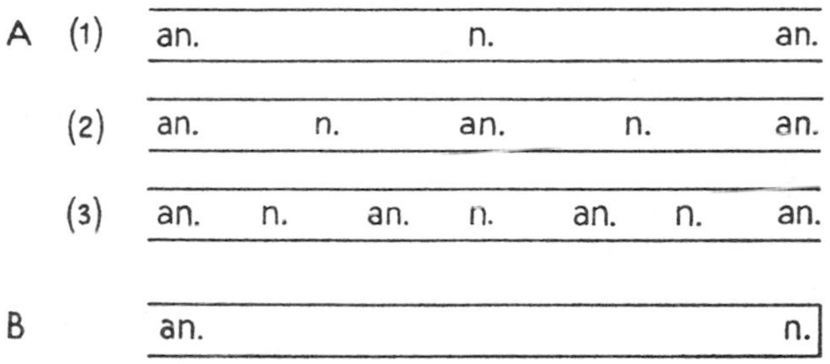

A (1)   an.   n.   an.

(2)   an.   n.   an.   n.   an.

(3)   an.   n.   an.   n.   an.   n.   an.

B   an.   n.

Fig. 1   A   Air column in an open pipe vibrating in
            1. Fundamental mode; 2. 2nd or Octave
            mode; 3. 3rd mode
         B   Air column in stopped pipe. 1st mode

process rather too complicated to be quoted here it can be shown that in a gently tapered tube such as we have in musical instruments very similar conditions occur.[8] Doubly-open air columns have a lowest or *fundamental* frequency of vibration whose sound has a wavelength of twice the length of the tube, and this is where the direct connection between the length of a tube and the sound generated comes in.[9] In the higher modes such columns will generate sounds whose wavelengths are integral fractions of the fundamental ($\frac{1}{2}$, $\frac{1}{3}$, $\frac{1}{4}$, $\frac{1}{5}$, etc.). This is called the *harmonic series* and its components harmonics or *partial tones*, again on the stretched-string analogy.[10] To illustrate this in musical terms Fig. 2 represents the first sixteen sounds theoretically available from our 8-foot open pipe, No. 1 being the fundamental. We can see

1 2 3   4 5 6 7 8 9 10 11 12 13 14 15 16

Fig. 2   First sixteen notes theoretically available on 8′
open tube, No. 1 being the fundamental

at a glance that this is a very curious series. The first octave contains

no intermediate notes; the second but one ; the third has

three ; but in the fourth there are eight running

approximately scale-wise. We should note here also that Nos. 7, 11, and 13 are considerably out of tune according to the diatonic scale now universally used in western music, a point which we shall meet again when we consider the behaviour and use of actual instruments.

The harmonic series does not, of course, end with the fourth octave, it continues into the fifth and higher octaves in semitone and smaller intervals; but here we must take note of that word *theoretically* and be on our guard. In tubes used for musical purposes the ratio of diameter to length (what the instrument-maker calls 'scale') is of great importance, and this too will be mentioned frequently in subsequent pages. Although the entire series of harmonics is nominally available on any tube, in actual practice the range of 'scale' that is useful is rather limited. It is quite possible for a tube to be so wide or so narrow that no musical sound can be extracted from it. Further, within the useful range, a tube narrow in relation to its length will more readily yield its higher harmonics, while a wider one is more generous at the lower end of the series. Tubes of the order usually employed in modern trumpets will not as a rule yield the fundamental at all, so their working compass is founded on the octave harmonic (No. 2 in Fig. 2). On certain instruments with a rather wider bore the fundamental becomes possible but may still be too uncertain or too rough in quality to be musically acceptable. Really wide-scale instruments such as the tubas have a working range founded on the actual fundamental, and although they have corresponding limitations at the upper end of the series they are most valuable as a wind bass, deep toned without being intolerably bulky. The use or otherwise of the fundamental in the working compass of brass instruments is another characteristic which has sometimes been adopted as a basis for classification, and has led to the not very helpful distinction between 'half-tube' and 'whole-tube' instruments.

So far we have examined only the air column in a tube effectively open at both ends (usually called simply an 'Open Pipe'), but in certain musical instruments, notably the clarinet and the 'Stopped' ranks in the pipe organ, the tube is effectively *closed* at one end. What difference does this make? In the first place, there must still be an antinode at the open end where pressure cannot rise above that of the surrounding air, but at the closed end the column will be prevented from moving as a whole, so at that point there will be a node. From this we can argue that in the first mode of vibration the wavelength of the sound generated will be *four times* the length of the tube. In other words, to sound a given note a stopped pipe is only half the length of an open one. Secondly, the first harmonic produced will not be the octave but the twelfth, and the harmonic series peculiar to a stopped pipe will comprise the ratios of $\frac{1}{3}$, $\frac{1}{5}$, $\frac{1}{7}$, etc., of the fundamental. In terms of musical notation Fig. 3 shows the fundamental and the first seven available harmonics of an 8-foot *stopped* pipe. The above facts account for the unique behaviour

octavo

Fig. 3 First seven available harmonics of an 8′
stopped pipe

of the clarinet among orchestral woodwinds, and also its comparative shortness in relation to other reed instruments pitched in unison with it. In this case again both experimental and mathematical proofs could be quoted but here, I think, we may be best served by referring to a demonstration which, like the vibrating harp string, is visible.

Thanks again to the similar behaviour of vibratory systems, we can liken the conditions in an air column to those in a coiled metal spring. If the spring be freely suspended compression waves will travel to and fro along it as they do in an 'open' pipe (Fig. 4 A). If, however, free motion is restrained at one end by firmly clamping the spring compression waves in it will travel as they do in a 'stopped' pipe (Fig. 4 B).

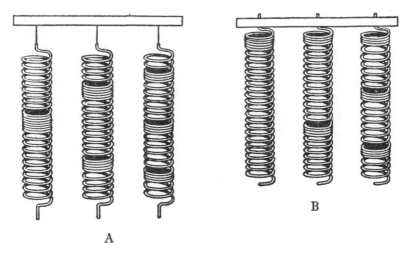

A

B

Fig. 4 A Compression waves in a free spring. Analogous to 'open' air column vibrating in 1st, 2nd, and 3rd modes
        B Compression waves in a spring restrained at one end. Analogous to 'stopped' air column. 1st, 2nd, and 3rd modes

The foregoing paragraphs have, I hope, made clear why it is that in any practical wind instrument (other than the most primitive) we must have some mechanism for changing the length of the air column. Figs. 2 and 3 show that the harmonic series coincides with any of the scales recognised in art music only at a limited number of points, and means have had to be found to fill in the natural gaps. By enabling the player to change the length of his resonator at will he is supplied with a number of different fundamentals, and consequently harmonic series, from which he can select the notes required to build up a scale. The ability to elicit with certainty any particular harmonic from a number of different series is the first essential in the mastery of any lip-reed instrument, and is the basis of all playing technique.

The simplest way to alter the length of the resonator is to make a number of side-holes in the tube, more or less remote from the mouth-piece, such that they can be opened and closed in succession by the fingers either directly or with the help of some key-mechanism. The opening of a side-hole is more or less equivalent to cutting off the tube at or near that point, so the process is effectively one of *shortening* the air column. This is the system employed in woodwind instruments, where it works very well, but with the brass it is not used today. It was at one time, however, applied with some success to wide-bore brasses, as witness the Ophicleide and the Key-bugle, both useful instruments which enjoyed a life of over half a century. Allied to tubes of trumpet proportions the idea has proved less happy.[11]

The principle on which all brass instruments, of whatever scale, are now constructed is the exact converse of the side-hole system. Instead of effectively *shortening* the air column it is here progressively increased by the addition of calculated extra lengths. This is achieved by means of either a movable telescopic section in the main tube, or by a number of spring-loaded valves each of which when pressed down switches in a preadjusted length of supplementary tubing and cuts it out again when released. The telescopic system is today found only in the slide trombone, but it is much the older and simpler of the two. It has certain great musical advantages as well as some drawbacks which are fully discussed on pp. 48 and 49, so here we may consider simply its acoustic behaviour. Fig. 5 is a drawing of a trombone with the slide in its closed or 'first' position. The dotted lines indicate the slide drawn out in six stages or 'shifts' each of which progressively lowers the fundamental sound by one semitone. If we suppose this instrument to be pitched in B♭ (the common pitch for the tenor trombone) then the first shift lowers the fundamental to A, the second to A♭, and so on. The notes below each shift in the drawing show the first six harmonics of each of these fundamentals, and it will be seen that they include a complete

chromatic sequence from a diminished fifth below the

upwards. From this we conclude that a brass player requires a minimum of seven harmonic series spaced a semitone apart, and in the trombone these are given by seven positions of the slide.

The slide of the trombone is a beautifully simple and efficient apparatus, and, indeed, to the acoustician it approaches perfection.

Its only defect from his point of view is that it inevitably introduces two slight but abrupt changes in the diameter of the body tube. These, however, can be made extremely small, and although their effect is probably measurable by modern laboratory techniques, in musical performance they are quite negligible.

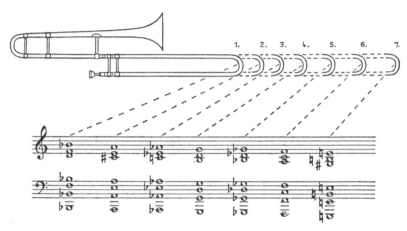

Fig. 5   Compass of B♭ tenor trombone in the seven positions

This being so, we may perhaps ask why instrument-makers and players have nevertheless persisted for nearly a century and a half with the development of valve systems. The answer would appear to be twofold. First, the telescopic principle is by its nature incompatible with taper-bore instruments since it demands a considerable length of absolutely cylindrical tubing.[12] Secondly, the valve possesses one virtue which the slide lacks; it is practically instantaneous in action. This point has always been of great importance to the player, and it seems most probable that the first objective of the early valve designers was not to create a fully chromatic brass instrument, but rather to increase the availability of *natural* instruments by cutting down the time-consuming process of putting on and taking off detached transposing crooks (see p. 73). The full chromatic possibilities of valves and, indeed, of the trombone slide, appear to have been appreciated only after these devices had already gained some footing among performers.[13]

The story of valves and the mechanical ingenuity that has been lavished on their development is so important and fascinating a part of instrumental history that it merits a chapter to itself. The essential

principle of the apparatus must, however, be touched on here. How are
valves made to supply the seven harmonic series which, as we have
seen, the fully equipped player requires? Today, in the light of basic
acoustics, it would appear logical to provide six so arranged that, when
added one after another, each would lower the preceding fundamental
by a semitone. Thus we should get the equivalent of the seven positions
of the trombone. Such an additive or, as the French call it, *dépendent*
system, requiring the simultaneous use of as many as six fingers at
certain times, might have objections from the player's point of view, but
it would satisfy all acoustic requirements.[14] In common with most
orchestral instruments, however, the valved brass in its early stages
developed more or less empirically according to the ideas of many
improvers, and in the face of much opposition and prejudice. Among
the earliest surviving specimens of mechanised brass we find both
two- and three-valved types, and as regards the French Horn, at least,
both sorts were in use as late as the mid-19th century. At this remove of
time it is unwise to be dogmatic, but the consensus of evidence as well
as logic suggests that the two-valved instruments preceded the three
by (at least) a few years. In spite of the claims of some of their sponsors
the former cannot, of course, have been chromatic throughout their
entire range, but they would have been so (less only two notes) in the
third and fourth octaves which, at the time of their appearance, were
the accepted part of the compass for melodic writing.[15] Two transposing
valves, whole-tone and semitone, having proved their worth, it was a
natural step to add another with sufficient tubing for a drop of a minor
third, though exactly when and by whom this was done we do not
know. With these three transpositions combined in different ways the
required seven series spaced approximately at semitone intervals became
possible, and three valves have since remained the common arrangement
on which all additive systems are based. The whole-tone valve is nowadays usually placed nearest to the player and is called No. 1; the semitone next as No. 2: and the tone-and-a-half as No. 3. By using his valves
as in the following table the performer can lower any note in the original
harmonic series of his instrument by any desired interval from a semitone to a diminished fifth.

     1. No valves sound the original series.
     2. 2nd valve sounds a semitone lower.
     3. 1st valve sounds a whole tone lower.
     4. 1st + 2nd valves sound a minor third lower.

5. 2nd + 3rd valves sound a major third lower.

6. 1st + 3rd valves sound a perfect fourth lower.

7. 1st + 2nd + 3rd valves sound a diminished fifth lower.

Unfortunately, this system which at first sight seems so perfect has one inherent defect that is sometimes insufficiently noticed in text books and 'tutors'. This is summed up in the word *approximately* in the above paragraph. When we embark on the lengthening of air columns we quickly come up against elementary mathematics, and we find that for any interval by which we may wish to lower any fundamental there is a fixed mathematical ratio between the length of the original column and that of the supplement. Because this *is* a fixed ratio a valve tube which is calculated to lower the original fundamental by any interval will be too short to do so if that fundamental has already been lowered by another valve. The new air column will be a little too short and the new fundamental a little too sharp. This may be made clearer if we look again at Fig. 5. Here we notice that each successive shift of the trombone slide is a little longer than the previous one though each represents exactly a semitone drop.

This trouble is not particularly serious with short instruments such as the modern four-foot trumpet, although it is inevitably present when two or three valves are used together. The trumpet player who is aware of the problem can do quite a lot to improve matters by subtle adjustment of his embouchure. Also, as indicated in the table, it is customary to use the first and second valves together to produce the minor third which taken this way is only very slightly sharp. This sets free the third valve to be tuned considerably flatter than its nominal interval so that it will to some extent compensate for the deficiencies of the others when combined with them. With longer instruments the defect becomes increasingly serious and more than the average player can deal with by lip techniques without spoiling his tone. Further, the increasing sharpness of the 1 + 2 combination no longer allows this to replace a downtuned third valve. As a concrete example let us take a valved B♭ tenor trombone. As built today to the pitch of A = 440 by a leading British firm, this instrument has an open tube length of 108 inches. We press the first valve down and get the A♭ series by the addition of ⅛th of the open tube, or exactly 13·5 inches. Now we change to the third valve and get the G series by the addition of ⅕th of the open length, or 21·5 inches. Suppose now we want to go a tone lower to get the F series. To do this we must add on ⅛th of the length that is already sounding G, and for this we require 16·2 inches. But the first or whole-tone valve can supply only 13·5 inches so when we add it we come out 2·7 inches short and the F series is woefully sharp.

At this stage the player really does need the help of some special compensating mechanism, and the problem of designing this has exercised the ingenuity of many leading makers and players since the middle of the 19th century. In general we may divide compensating devices into two classes, those which introduce extra tubing automatically, and those which do so only at the discretion of the player, and there have been enthusiastic advocates of both types. Probably the all-round best are those, such as Blaikley's automatic system invented in 1874 (British Patent 6418 of 1878), which make no change in the orthodox three-valve fingering. Compensation has also been obtained by adding a small trombone-like slide to the normal valves, and, indeed, a trombone is known which combined valves with a full compass slide, thus hopefully offering the player the best of both worlds. A few of these special systems we shall refer to later, but in this book generally we have no occasion to go very deeply into the subject since the modern trumpet player with his four-foot instrument manages very well by the methods already mentioned, and the valve trombone is now almost totally eclipsed by the descendants of the classic slide instrument. It is in the field of the large-scale conical instruments, the bugle-horn family, that compensation really comes into its own. For readers who may be interested I have supplied some guiding references in the Bibliography.

We have so far confined our attention to the two most obvious elements of the coupled system which is a musical wind instrument, but there is a third which comes into being, as it were, only during the act of playing. When a wind player blows his instrument the generator is coupled both to the resonator and to the air cavities of the head, throat, and chest so that air in them is also set in vibration. This is easily demonstrated by the use of a stethoscope. It follows that the player and his instrument together form a coupled system of *three* elements each of which he can to some degree control. He can vary the dimensions of the resonator with his fingers; he can influence the generator by lip control; and he can to some extent modify the shape and volume of his air cavities by the use of the throat and chest muscles. This third element is extremely difficult to investigate in any mensurable way but there is no doubt that it plays a great part in artistic performance as distinct from mere mechanical 'blowing'. It is probably the unrecognised basis of the advice often given to the learner—

'imagine you are singing the note you want to produce'. Measurement
of the air pressure exerted while playing has been achieved by introducing a small manometer tube into the corner of the mouth, but in interpreting the readings obtained we must bear in mind the possible
effect of abnormal conditions on the player. Efforts have also been
made to measure the absolute pressure of the lips on the mouthpiece
rim by mounting a trumpet on a spring balance arrangement.[16] The
value of this is, however, open to some doubt unless properly controlled
experimental conditions can be maintained. We can perhaps get some
idea of the influence of the air cavities on the behaviour of a wind
instrument by considering the 'boot' of an organ reed pipe with which
they have some affinity. The matter is complicated, but it is known, for
instance, that if the boot is so large that the mass of air in it has a natural
frequency related to those of the reed itself and the pipe above, it may
seriously interfere with their proper functioning.[17] It seems quite
possible, I think, that the natural frequencies of the air cavities may
sometimes assist and sometimes interfere with the lips in their capacity
as the vibrating part of the generator.

Timbre

It has been recognised from very early in the history of acoustics
that nearly all the sounds we regard as musical—those which are the
most appealing or satisfying to the human ear—are complex and incorporate frequencies which are higher than the fundamental. The first
satisfactory explanation of the origin of these partials, whose presence
can often be detected by the unaided ear, was that given by Sauveur
when he demonstrated that in a stretched string both complete and
segmental vibrations can occur at the same time. The same phenomenon
can be shown to take place in vibrating air columns. This matter was
very fully investigated by Helmholtz, *c.* 1870, when, by means of tuned
resonators applied to the ear, he was able to identify the separate
components of complex tones. He was, however, unable to measure
their relative intensities. Nowadays, through the development of electrical techniques, we have methods by which the displacement/time
relations of air vibrations can be visually displayed in the form of a
graph, and this subjected to analysis by mechanical or mathematical means. We can also analyse sounds directly and measure the
relative intensities of their components by means of so-called 'search
tones'.[18]

It is customary today to refer to the products of tonal analysis as *tonal spectra* by analogy with the line spectra obtained by examining light with the spectrograph. A very useful type of comparative diagram can be made from tonal spectra by plotting each component of a complex tone at its appropriate frequency along a base line. A linear scale of frequency is adopted as this makes it easier to recognise if the partials are harmonic or not. A logarithmic scale is, however, employed for the intensities since the type of microphone now used in such investigations measures the *pressure* of sound waves impinging on it, and this convention allows weaker partials to be more readily displayed.[19] Figures 6 and 7 show tonal spectra for four notes distributed over the working compass of a typical modern trumpet and tenor trombone respectively. They show in both cases highly complex structures with many powerful overtones, especially at the lower end of the range. To this we can attribute the characteristic brilliant 'brassy' tones of these instruments. There is also to be seen a significant difference. In the B♭ of the trombone, out of some forty partials displayed, Nos. 1, 3, 6, 8, 9, 10, 11, 12, 19, and 20 are nearly as powerful as the fundamental. In the f♯ of the trumpet Nos. 3, 4, 5, 6, 7, and 8 approach the fundamental in strength, but beyond this the 'noble retinue' of harmonics, as Richardson has called them, fall off progressively but so gradually that the analysing apparatus has been unable to distinguish between them after about the twenty-fifth. When sounding c″ (512 vibs. per sec.) the trombone shows only three partials, all below the frequency of 3,000, while the trumpet sounding the same note shows five within that range and four more above 3,000 before the analyser fails to differentiate them. These two spectra explain very clearly just what the ear senses when listening to the trumpet and trombone playing the same note, a comparative lack of brilliance and a general smoothing out of tone in the latter case. We also see that with both instruments there is progressive smoothing of the tone as we ascend which is, in fact, true of almost all wind instruments. For comparison Fig. 8 shows the spectrum of b (240 vibs. per sec.) as sounded by a French Horn crooked in F. It shows only four partials in all and of these only the first approaches the fundamental in power. This is a typical spectrum for a suave and rounded tone, and may be attributed to the unbroken shape of the Horn mouthpiece, and the rapid expansion of the bore and bell in relation to length. The factors which influence the timbre of brass instruments have been recognised and exploited empirically for centuries. Today, tonal analysis gives us a quantitative view of some of these and permits of something approaching precision in instrumental design. They are:

1. The scale of the tube, as already mentioned on p. 6.
2. The internal configuration of the mouthpiece.
3. The shape of the tube; cylindrical, tapered, or mixed.
4. The curvature and size of the bell.
5. The thickness, and possibly the material of the tube walls (in so far as these may affect mechanical resonances. See 'Formants' below).

The Function of the Mouthpiece

The mouthpiece of a brass instrument presents us with a remarkable paradox. On the one hand it is to the player the most intimate, personal, and cherished part of his instrument, and is the physical source of some of its most admired qualities. On the other, from the simple point of view of basic acoustics, it is completely superfluous. Almost anyone with a little 'know-how', courage, and strong lips can elicit at least a few musical tones from any tube of convenient size, even a piece of gas-pipe. This, however, quickly becomes a painful process unless the end of the pipe is rounded off or cushioned in some way. Observe also the qualification 'of convenient size'. This means that the diameter/length ratio of the pipe must be within the acoustically practical limits explained on p. 6 and its actual diameter large enough to allow the lips to vibrate when placed across it; say between 16 mm. and 30 mm. This consideration brings us to what may be taken as historically the first purpose of the mouthpiece, to provide a practical coupling between the lips and the body-tube. There is clear evidence that Ancient Civilisations were quite aware of this requirement, though they do not appear to have known the detachable mouthpiece such as we now use.[20] For example, the two famous metal trumpets of Tut-ankh-amen, both big enough in the bore (17 mm. and 13 mm. respectively) to be applied directly to the lips, are cushioned by the application of a short *outer* ferrule with a rolled edge. Today the tubes favoured for most brass instruments are too small in diameter to be blown directly, and a tapered connector of some kind is required. For this purpose a simple funnel merging at its narrow end into the main bore is sufficient, and this is virtually what we have in the mouthpiece of the earlier French Horns. The bore of modern Horn mouthpieces has become rather more sophisticated for various reasons, but their primary function is still to bring down a 'lippable' diameter to that of the end of the main tube.

Though their origin is obscure the ancestors of the detachable mouthpiece made their appearance in Europe, as far as we know, in

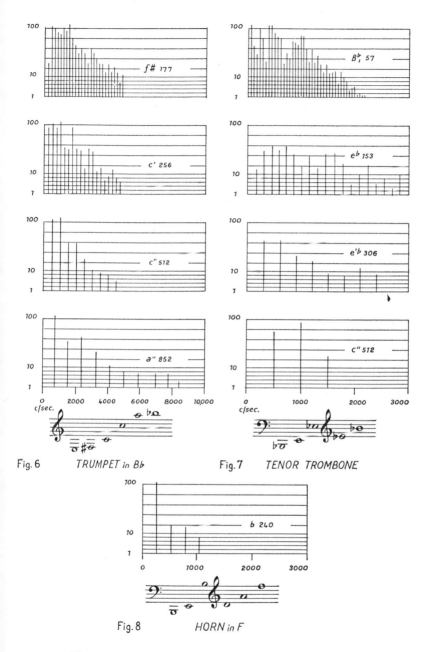

Fig. 6   TRUMPET in Bb

Fig. 7   TENOR TROMBONE

Fig. 8   HORN in F

Figs. 6, 7, & 8   Tonal Spectra (*after the late Professor Bernard Hague*)

C

the early years of the Renaissance, a period when musical interest began to centre on timbre and tonal contrast. From this time we have (1) the simple funnel of the Horns and (2) the cupped mouthpiece that we associate with all other brass families. The former we may regard simply as non-resonant 'adapters', but the latter have resonant properties which make them an acoustic adjunct of great importance. This fact brings us to the second and most valued function of the modern mouthpiece—as a creator or modifier of timbre.

The essential features of the cup-mouthpiece are the cup itself and the throat or orifice at its base which communicates with the bore of the instrument. Both of these are subject to great variation, and readers will find them described in some detail in Chapter 2. Characteristically a shallow cup and a sharp-edged throat tend to emphasise upper partials and produce a brilliant tone, while a deeper cup and rounded throat make for a milder one. When such mouthpieces are allied respectively with mainly cylindrical or mainly conical resonators whose own characteristics tend the same way the effect is much increased and we get the very distinctive contrast between the true trumpet and, for example, the cornet. Different combinations of mouthpiece and resonator produce the individual tone colours of different instrumental families. All this has, of course, long been known from practical experience, but until comparatively recently anything like a scientific explanation has been lacking. In the 1920s, however, Richardson sought to account for the behaviour of trumpet mouthpieces on the grounds of certain recognised acoustical facts, and he presented some very persuasive arguments and figures in support.[21] To judge by the tone of some subsequent writers his ideas are not universally accepted, but they certainly merit serious consideration. The basis of Richardson's concept was the well-known phenomenon of 'edge-tones'. It is recognised that a flat jet of air projected through a slit tends to break up into curls or vortices, but without any orderly sequence. If, however, the jet be directed against a more or less sharp edge the vortices are marshalled into regular cyclic order, and the jet + edge system becomes a form of tone generator. This is now recognised as the operating principle of organ flue-pipes.

Since it is known that, in similar way, a jet of circular section directed against a circular orifice produces an edge-tone, Richardson suggested that the jet of air from the player's lips impinging on the throat of a trumpet mouthpiece might do the same, and so contribute to the characteristic timbre of the instrument. It follows that it is part of the trumpet player's art to get the 'reed' tone of the vibrating lips, the edge-tone of the mouthpiece throat, and one of the natural frequencies of the tube into resonance with each other. When this happens a tripartite coupled system comes into being and the note 'speaks' with great power and brilliance. Richardson indicated that such a dual generator is very efficient, but calls for subtle control by the player and allows

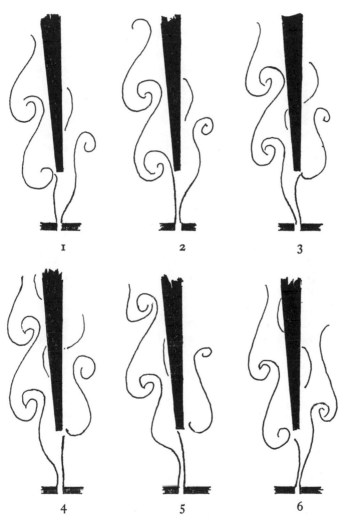

Fig. 9   Generation of Edge-tones (*after Carrière*)

him little latitude.[22] With the virtually 'throatless' mouthpiece of the Horn the player can do more to 'pull' a note in or out of tune since the lips alone are involved.

In offering his hypothesis, in his book, Richardson presented the simple edge-tone formula in this form:

$$\text{Pitch} = \frac{\frac{1}{2} \text{ (Velocity of issuing breath),}}{\text{Distance from lips to mouthpiece throat}^{23}}$$

He also worked out quantities for the condition when the presumed edge-tone equalled the lowest frequency employed in playing various different instruments (not necessarily the actual fundamental of the tube. See p. 7, *ante*). In the case of a trumpet sounding a nominal f♯ (174 vibs.) the required depth of cup appeared as 42 mm. which is rather over four times the depth of an average good modern mouthpiece. But if we work Richardson's equation backwards substituting mouth-piece depths of 10 mm. and 8 mm. (as representing the limits of good modern practice), the edge-tone frequencies go up to 1,460 and 1,825 respectively. These, in round figures, approximate to the 8th and 10th partials of the f♯, both of which are extremely prominent in the tonal spectrum of that note as sounded by the trumpet. Although Richardson's proposition is not today accepted by all acousticians, we may perhaps surmise that edge-tones generated at the throat of the mouthpiece reinforce the power of certain partials already present in the lip-generated sound.

While considering the mouthpiece as a source of tone colour we should examine briefly one obsolete pattern which is of particular interest to the musical historian. This is the extremely shallow type used by the 'Clarino' players of the 18th century. These men, for the sake of the scale-wise disposition of the harmonics, made a specialised study of the fourth octave, and above, of the old long trumpet, commonly the 8-foot C or the 7-foot D instrument. From surviving examples it appears that the players who took charge of the highest parts, ascending at times as high as the 20th or even the 23rd harmonic of the fundamental, used a mouthpiece with a sharp throat, a cup sometimes no deeper than 6 mm., and a proportionately rather large diameter—generally between 18 and 20mm. According to the edge-tone hypothesis —at first sight—trumpets with such mouthpieces would seem bound to yield sounds loaded with very high partials and therefore harsh and strident. We have, in fact, no evidence that they did so. The true Clarino technique did not survive the 18th century, but one or two modern players have, by special study of old instruments, been able in some degree to reproduce it.[24] The late Walter Morrow did so in a demonstration before the Musical Association in London in 1895, and a member of his audience on that occasion has assured the writer that the tone was warm and rounded. It seems possible that high edge-tones *were* strongly generated by the Clarino players' special mouth-piece, but, as tonal spectra show, there are comparatively few partials in the fourth octave resonances of the trumpet air column which these could have influenced at all powerfully.

As one further illustration of the dual nature of the 'lip-reed' mouth-piece we may look at the obsolete family of Cornetts or Zinken which has recently been subjected to something of a revival. These were a group of wooden instruments with a narrow tapered bore, lip energised, and furnished with side holes. Although they were made in various sizes the bore at the top was always too small to be applied directly to the lips. The problem was met either by providing a small detached cup mouthpiece of hardwood or ivory, or by coning out the top of the bore to a diameter convenient to the lips. In this way a more or less throatless 'mouthpiece' was created out of the actual substance of the tube wall. Both arrangements provided a satisfactory 'adapter' for the lips, but with a tonal difference so marked that by the time of Praetorius the coned-out type was regarded as an instrument *sui generis* under the title of Mute Cornett or Stille Zink.

Irregularities in the Bore – 'Steps', Bends, Perforations

A gentle and well-regulated expansion in at least part of the tube is an essential feature of all brass instruments, Trumpets and Horns alike. If, however, we examine a large number, both antique and modern, we come to the conclusion that makers have almost always regarded *sudden* changes in the size of the bore as undesirable. In brass instruments the only quite unavoidable sudden changes of bore are found at either end of the trombone slide, or in valve tubes when drawn out for tuning purposes. Both of these can, of course, be made very small, no greater indeed than a difference in diameter of twice the thickness of the tube wall. In contrast to the brass men, many woodwind makers in the 18th and early 19th centuries appear to have introduced deliberately quite large changes in bore at the joints of their instruments. This seems to have been connected with the principle of tuning employed.[25]

It is now recognised that in the case of a nominally cylindrical pipe a bulge in the bore near an antinode of the note sounding will raise the pitch of that note, and, conversely, will lower it if near to a node. We must consider also that an irregularity in the bore which is near an antinode when the fundamental is sounding may be approached by a node when the air column breaks up to give a harmonic. In this way it is possible for some harmonics in a given series to be out of tune with their *prime tone* (as well as mathematically incommensurate with each other (see note 10, p. 33)), and it is easy to imagine what effect this might have in an instrument such as the trumpet all of whose notes are harmonics of but seven basic tube lengths. It also seems possible that with an irregular tube some of the higher overtones which influence characteristic timbre might appear at frequencies other than those predicted by simple mathematics. Further, it is known that in instruments of mixed cylindrical and tapered bore the actual spacing out of the harmonic series is much influenced by the shape of the tapered sections. Changes in internal tuning caused by different tapers are not confined to individual tones, but may affect whole ranges. Thus, one type of taper may flatten a group of higher tones and sharpen the lower ones, while another type may selectively sharpen the middle region while flattening both extremes. In the trumpet the particularly influential sections are the bell expansion and the mouthpiece-mouthpipe combination; though some research on these features has been done more is required.[26] Some ten years ago the American firm of Olds were prepared to supply a selection of bells and mouthpipes of different tapers which could be incorporated into otherwise standardised instruments to meet the views of individual customers. It is perhaps open to question whether the average player with a good ear and lip would be prepared to face the inevitable expense of such 'tailoring', but the provision of the facility by a commercial firm clearly indicates the importance of the matter.

The obvious inconvenience of a slender tube 7 or 8 feet long has from very early times been met by folding or coiling. Experience shows that such bending has in general no appreciable effect on the tone of a trumpet, provided that the curves are of reasonably large radius. The first valves produced, however, involved quite sharp bends and even when these did not amount to actual constriction of the bore they undoubtedly led to some deterioration of tone. This was one of the chief objections urged by conservative players against the new-fangled valved instruments—the valve notes were 'stuffy' compared with the open ones. Most brass instrument makers today would deny that with the refined valves now supplied there is anything to choose between valved or open notes, but there still remain some players who are unconvinced. At one time it was supposed that sound waves are guided round curves in a tube like the flow of gas along a conduit, but there is much evidence to show that in fact they proceed by a series of reflections with some loss of energy at each. Because the walls of a metal tube are so rigid the actual loss of energy is very small, but it is not necessarily the same for all frequencies. Consequently, the bends in a trumpet tube may exert a small but selective filtering effect on the components of a complex tone. The conclusion is that in designing a practical instrument it is best to keep the radius of the bends as large as circumstances will permit.[27]

Concerning brass instruments, one of the writer's earliest recollections is of overhearing a blasphemous query by the then senior Director of Music of the British Army as to how his band could be expected to do themselves credit when, through the niggardliness of Government, they had to appear at a concert with instruments full of cracks and pin-holes stuffed up with soap. No doubt there was exaggeration on this occasion, but even with the best care corrosion or the accidents of daily use can result in actual perforation of brasses, and sometimes this can be an acoustic disaster. Remembering that in a vibrating air column a node is a point of maximum variation of *pressure* it is evident that any communication with the surrounding atmosphere at that point must prevent the node from forming. Thus any hole in a resonator tube will kill any harmonics that may require a node at that point, and for the trumpet player this may be fatal.

As we have already said, the influence of a side hole in effectively shortening an air column depends very largely on its size in relation to cross section of that column (see note 11). Fig. 10 illustrates this in a rather exaggerated way, but from it we can see that until the hole gets relatively large its shortening effect is small. Quite a tiny hole, however, is sufficient to prevent the formation of a node and this is why it is so important for detachable crooks and the moving parts of valves to fit with absolute accuracy (note 25, ref. 2). The principle of inhibiting a node, or conversely of encouraging an antinode, by opening a very small hole at a calculated position in the wall of a resonating tube has been part of the second register technique of woodwinds for several centuries. It is found in the 'pinching' of the thumb hole in the Recorder and in the register or 'speaker' key of the Clarinet and the Oboe, but until quite recently we have had no evidence of its use by brass players. About 1959, however, some interesting though minor information came

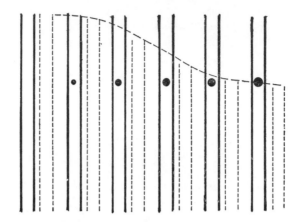

Fig. 10 Illustrating the effect of progressively
enlarging a side hole. The effective sounding length
indicated in broken lines in each case.
(*Adapted from Benade*)

to light. One of the great difficulties of melodic playing on the natural
trumpet has always been to separate with certainty the closely placed
harmonics of the fourth octave and above. Take for example the 12th
and 13th of the 8-foot C trumpet. The former represents a good g
(first space above the stave), but the latter is by nature less than a full
tone higher. It is too flat to serve as an a♮ yet too sharp to be used as a
g♯. No doubt the skilled Clarino player could 'pull' the 13th harmonic
one way or the other sufficiently to make it acceptable at least as a passing note, but how much more often must the average player have been
embarrassed by landing squarely on it when trying for the 'in tune'
12th or 14th. In the course of some research connected with the reproduction of old instruments for the Capella Coloniensis group the
instrument-maker Otto Steinkopf discovered in Germany two late 18th-
century natural trumpets each with two pin holes which were clearly
there by design and were not merely due to corrosion. On investigation
these instruments yielded their complete harmonic series when the
pin holes were stopped with the fingers, but when one or other hole was
opened certain of the 'defective' harmonics were suppressed. Clearly
some thoughtful player had appreciated the principle of 'nodal venting'
and had applied it as an aid to security in performance. It seems
equally clear that the idea was never in use among clarinists for, of the
very many old natural trumpets that survive today, only two or three

are known with the pin holes. Furthermore, clarino playing had died out by the date of these examples. We may wonder a little that a point of technique which appeared useful in the hands of one player, or even of several, did not quickly find widespread acceptance, but we must remember that in 18th-century Europe communication was not so easy as it is today, and there is also much evidence that professional jealousies often prevented the exchange of technical ideas.[28] It seems probable, too, that the conservative clarinist might have found a serious objection to the practice of nodal venting in its effect on tone colour. As J. A. Christiansen, the London trumpet authority, once pointed out to the writer, a vent that will suppress any particular harmonic must do so quite unselectively whether the frequency in question appears as a pure note or as part of a complex tone. Thus, notes sounded with the pin holes open might differ quite markedly from those produced when the holes were closed. This matter of tonal homogeneity throughout the compass of an instrument is further touched on in a later section of this chapter.

The Influence of the Bell – Mutes

The effect of the bell, in so far as it forms one of the tapered elements in a brass instrument of mixed bore, has already been mentioned in a previous paragraph, but the matter really goes rather farther than this. With the exception of the Orchestral Horn, and possibly of some Basses made in Bohemia c. 1880, which may perhaps still be found in certain parts of Europe,[29] all modern brass instruments are provided with bells ending in a short section or 'skirt' (more or less marked) which expands much more rapidly than the tapered portions of the main tube. This is of considerable acoustic significance. The main taper of the majority of brasses develops in approximately 'exponential' form; i.e. the ratio of successive radii at unit distances

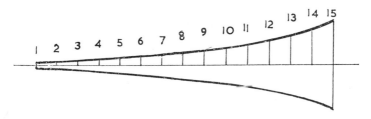

Fig. 11   Profile of an exponential horn of ratio 14/17

apart along the tube is a constant quantity.[30] Fig 11 shows the section along an 'exponential horn' in which this constant quantity is $17/14$. Richardson has called this ratio the 'flare coefficient' and it can be regarded as a measure of the expansion of such a tube.

The following table shows approximate flare coefficients for four actual modern instruments calculated by Richardson from their measurements and it is interesting to note that (disregarding the extreme terminal sections of the Trumpet, Trombone and Cornet) three show the same figure.

Instrument	Flare Coefficient
French Horn	1·25
Cornet	1·25
Trumpet	1·25
Trombone	1·3

This seems to be hardly fortuitous and it suggests that the coefficient of 1·25 for such instruments has been arrived at by makers as a result of practical experience. In the French Horn, although at first sight it appears to have proportionately a very wide bell, the exponential flare is in fact unbroken from one end of the instrument to the other, except, of course, through the valve supplements.[31]

In trying to picture the effect of a brass instrument bell we must bear in mind that when a series of compression waves passing down a resonating tube reach the open end they suffer some degree of reflection owing to the inertia of the air beyond the tube. Not all their energy is passed on to the ambient air. Also the degree of reflection is not necessarily the same for all frequencies, so that a complex tone may be selectively 'filtered' at the end of a tube. Sound waves passing down a tube on reaching the atmosphere assume the form of spheres diverging from a point a little beyond the open end (see note 9, 'terminal antinodes') and the advantage of a flaring tube is that in passing down it they have an increasing curvature imposed on them which makes for a less abrupt transformation at the end. In other words, in passing down a flared tube pressure waves develop a 'spherical wave front'. In consequence of this a flaring horn sends out its sounds more efficiently into the surrounding atmosphere. Even a comparatively small flare at the end of a cone increases its efficiency as a sound transmitter quite markedly. This is well known from experiments with the resonators of certain organ reed pipes. Or, to take a more familiar illustration, consider the cylinder phonograph whose feeble output required to be conserved and nourished in every possible way. How early in the commercial life of this machine was the plain conical 'horn' replaced by one with an everted rim? To sum up so far, then, we may say that the rather sudden terminal expansion of the Trumpet and the Trombone, which was developing empirically well before the time of modern acoustics, is mainly concerned with the efficiency of sound radiation.

While on the subject of the exponential flare there is another point we should consider and this is one which may contain a note of warning to the instrument-maker. A property of the exponential, as distinct from any other form of tapered tube, is its comparative lack of marked resonances, especially when developed to a terminal diameter fairly large in relation to its length. In the early days of loudspeakers, exponential horns of wide flare were commonly employed by radio engineers because of their more or less even response over a wide range of audible frequencies. Distortion of reproduced music due to the false reinforcement of particular frequencies was minimised, yet they made fairly efficient sound radiators. In Fig. 12, which is derived from the behaviour of an exponential horn of only moderate flare, the dotted line indicates the flat response which would be ideal in a loudspeaker, while the solid line represents the natural responses of the particular horn investigated.

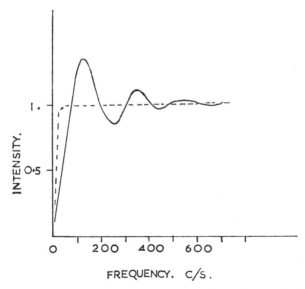

Fig. 12 Frequency response behaviour of a typical exponential horn

It shows very clearly how the peaks fall off and the resonance evens out above a frequency of about 400 cycles a second—say from a♭ up.

Such characteristics are the very opposite of what the instrument-maker usually requires. His need is for strong resonances at certain specific frequencies. Moreover, the farther we depart from the simple cylindrical form in a resonating tube the less intense are the higher partials. It follows that the instrument-maker must beware lest in the pursuit of efficient sound radiation he should adopt too large a flare and so make the tone of his instrument dull and the natural frequencies of the harmonic series difficult to elicit with certainty. It is generally conceded that the mellow sounds of the French Horn, which from tonal analysis we know to be less complex than those of the Trumpet or Trombone, are also more difficult to pitch on surely. By means of an 'exponential formula' well known to mathematicians, an instrument designer can calculate the most suitable flare for a tube of given length.[32] Whether it will pay him to do so now, when the industry possesses a wealth of accumulated empirical 'know-how' is another matter.

Finally in this section, we must look at one other property of the bell which is connected with its dimensions—*directivity*. As long ago as 1940 Northrop pointed out that the tonal spectra of some organ pipes appeared to vary with the relative position of the sound source and the analysing microphone, and he concluded that a single-point tonal analysis may not truly represent the harmonic output of an instrument.[33] It is common experience that a brass instrument at a distance sounds somewhat different when played 'at' or 'across' the listener. In the differing conditions of the open-air concert, the large auditorium, and the recording or broadcasting studio, the matter assumes considerable importance. During the last twenty years a good deal of research has been devoted to this point and it has become clear that the directivity of brass instruments varies in different parts of the audible range. The explanation (somewhat over-simplified perhaps) appears to be that with the lower tones whose wavelengths are large compared with the circumference of the bell, the final section exerts a sort of scattering effect which simulates the all-round radiation of a point sound source. At the other end of the scale, where the wavelengths are shorter than the circumference, the spherical wave front expands less rapidly than the skirt of the bell itself so this has little influence. The sound is then propagated mainly along the axial line of the instrument. Between the two extremes there is a range of frequencies in which directivity begins to show, but with much less certainty. These regions in the compass have been plotted quantitatively for different instruments, and it is clear that their position and extent depend on the dimensions of the bell.[34]

Having considered the principal aspects in which the shape of the normal bell is important, we may look briefly at the implications of muting. The use of a detached mute inserted into the bell is no new thing—it has been known to musicians for several centuries—but it is only since about the 1920s that, through the popularity of dance and 'show' bands, it has become really familiar to the layman. In modern orchestral music it has become quite common for composers to specify muted trumpet or trombone, or even, as in *Petroushka*, muted bass tuba, but until very recently the actual effect sought has seldom been indicated in the score. The type of mute to be used has been left largely to the discretion of the player or perhaps of the conductor. In these circumstances it is hardly surprising that, although mutes in bewildering variety are supplied by commercial music houses, little systematic investigation of their individual properties seems to have been done. A general description of modern mutes and some illustrations will be found on p. 74. The *Concise Oxford Dictionary* defines a mute as a 'pad for deadening [the] sound of a wind instrument'. This description, however, does not tell the whole story. It is a common idea that the sole purpose of a mute is to reduce the *volume* of an instrumental sound but, while this may happen incidentally, the true function is to modify a complex tone by disturbing that distribution of its partials which is accepted as normal. By muting some partials may be reduced in relative intensity while others (very often the dissonant ones) are rendered more prominent. This the mute does, we may say, by altering the physical character of the bell which, to a great extent, governs the normal sound. Any object, a pad of cloth, or even the player's hand inserted in the bell has some effect in this direction. This is the basis also of the practice of 'hand-stopping' which was formerly an important part of the technique of the French Horn, and was at one period tried also in connection with the natural trumpet. We should bear in mind, however, that in Horn technique muting and hand-stopping are not quite the same thing, and for the following reason. The gradual advance of the hand or a stopper towards the throat of the bell progressively flattens the pitch as we might expect (note 25), and in this fact *trumpet* players may have found a means of bringing their 11th and 13th harmonics more nearly into tune (see also p. 109). There then comes a point where, with some slight change in 'attack', flattening ceases and instead an overall rise of pitch occurs. On the Horn in F this rise is almost exactly a semitone, so by hand-stopping, players on that instrument could command a second and very useful harmonic series, albeit of a somewhat different quality. To the horn player, then, 'muting' refers to tone colour, but 'hand-stopping' implies a method of filling in gaps in the harmonic series without the use of valves.[35]

The earliest information we have about trumpet mutes leads us to suppose that these were no more than conical wooden stoppers with a hole bored through the centre. These would have been quite efficient as bell-modifiers, and no doubt served their purpose, as it was then understood, well enough.[36] Incidentally, these appear always to have had the property of raising the pitch like the fully inserted hand. Modern mutes, basically hollow conical or pear-shaped structures more or less completely closed at the wide end, are a rather different matter, and their behaviour may, I think, be divided into two aspects. Evidently they will modify the physical character of the bell just as did the old wooden plugs, but, as hollow bodies, they may be expected to have their own internal cavity resonances. These resonances will tend to reinforce to some extent any partial tones whose frequencies are directly related to them. Thus the modern mute appears as an acoustic apparatus of considerable efficiency. The bizarre sounds that some of them produce are easily understood if we remember that the natural resonances of a cone closed at the base form a curious inharmonic series in the ratios of $1:43$, $2:45$, $3:47$, $4:47$, $5:38$, etc. Unlike the primitive plugs, modern mutes do *not* as a rule raise the pitch, probably because the re-entrant tube which most of them carry acts as an extension of the instrument itself. For the best results a mute must be matched to the instrument with which it is used, and for this purpose the inner tube is sometimes made telescopic with a screw adjustment.

Formants

The power of discrimination possessed by the ear is one of the marvels of Nature which we are only now beginning to understand. From the dawn of human intelligence Man has had to 'believe his ears' and through them he has become aware of many curiosities in the behaviour of sounds which he has simply had to accept. It is only during the last hundred years, with the advance of tonal analysis and the use of electrical analogies, that acousticians have been able to offer some explanation. Two facts which are quite apparent to the unaided ear and which are now confirmed by tonal spectra are that the higher over-tones are more prominent in loud than in soft notes, and that successive notes on any instrument vary more or less in quality from one to the next. If we listen to a steady upward scale played throughout the compass of a trumpet it is not difficult to distinguish these changes even though the total impression is one of homogeneity and there is a feeling of 'trumpet', as it were, through the entire range. This may be purely subjective, and perhaps it is due to the listener becoming conditioned to accept any quality of sound within certain previously experienced limits as characteristic of the instrument. It seems however to go much deeper. We suspect, in fact, that running through the entire compass of the trumpet there is some factor which is not explained by the classical acoustic concepts which have so far served us.[37] The theory of *Formants* seems to supply the explanation.

It appears that throughout at least the most distinctive part of its compass each instrument shows a fixed group of prominent frequencies which are always present in the tonal spectrum whatever the nominal note sounded may be. This phenomenon was observed as long ago as 1837 during Sir Charles Wheatstone's investigation of vowel sounds, and it led to his 'fixed pitch' theory of vowels, later to be established by Helmholtz. Briefly, the Wheatstone-Helmholtz concept was that every vowel, no matter on what note it may be uttered, is determined by certain fixed frequencies that are invariably present.[38] To a great extent experiment has confirmed this theory, and the very sensitive methods devised by Dayton Miller have revealed the presence of these characteristic frequencies even in whispered vowels quite un-phonated. Further, it has been shown that certain vowels contain more than one outstanding permanent frequency. This can be explained by the existence of *selective resonances* in the air cavities of the head. In 1897 these distinguishing frequencies were named 'formants' by the physicist Hermann-Goldap. Now we know that the body-tube of a wind instrument, whatever its material, cannot be *absolutely* rigid and unyielding. Indeed, the stiffer we try to make it the more likely it is to develop mechanical resonances of its own. A proportion of the energy applied to the generator is used up in making the walls of the body vibrate in their own natural frequencies, and these frequencies may be passed on.[39] We have seen (note 11) that a thick-walled tube with side holes has certain frequency-filtering properties as do the bells, etc., of brass instruments. Together these facts seem to offer some analogy with the human voice apparatus. Assuming this analogy Hermann-Goldap analysed the tones of a number of orchestral instruments and satisfied himself that each showed a characteristic array of frequencies always present throughout the compass. He therefore announced that orchestral instruments, like the voice, possess formants, and in them he claimed to have identified the source of *timbre*. To the acousticians of his time Hermann-Goldap's theory appeared quite revolutionary and, in spite of early corroboration by Dayton Miller and by Stumpf in 1926, it proved rather slow of acceptance.[40] Today the theory is gaining ground, though a few authorities are still sceptical. We shall, I think, be wise to recognise that it still requires further extension, and in fact some of the originator's own findings show this clearly. For example, two instruments of very different character which he investigated, an oboe and a clarinet, both showed the same formant range, but in the oboe it proved to be more powerful than the fundamental tone, while in the clarinet the fundamental was predominant. The conclusion is that the mere presence of a formant is not the *sole* determinant of timbre. In woodwind spectra the formants are very clearly distinguishable, but in the brass, with the notable exception of the horn, they are not nearly so easy to recognise because their effect is often masked by the large range of other closely packed harmonics.

Beyond its application to single instruments the idea of formants can be extended to an infinite degree and opens up vast fields of speculation. Just as some simple tones will 'beat' together to produce a 'difference tone', so, we conceive, may the components of a formant range. Perhaps we may find that the formants of two different instruments playing together will unite to give a new formant characteristic of the combination. Consider, too, that instruments playing in unison with each other may yet perhaps have formants whose components are dissonant. Multiply these simple cases by the number of individual instruments which now appear together in the symphony orchestra, and the complexity of the resultant sound almost baffles the imagination. Yet it is probably in this very complexity—in what Bonavia-Hunt has called 'the clash of myriads of formants'—that we find the brilliance of the full orchestra or the grandeur of the organ chorus; brilliance and grandeur that no single instrument possesses.[41]

NOTES

[1] Alexander Wood, *The Physics of Music*, London, Methuen & Co., Ltd., third edn., 1945.

[2] Wegel and Moore, 'An Electrical Frequency Analyser', *Trans. Amer. Inst. of Electrical Engineers*, Vol. 42 (1924). E. Meyer and G. Buchmann, 'Die Klangspectren der Musik Instrumente', *Sitzungsberichte der Preuss. Akad. der Wissenschaft*, 1931, pp. 735–78.

[3] Arthur H. Benade, 'The Physics of Woodwinds', *Scientific American*, Oct. 1960, p. 146. Haward W. Henderson. 'An Experimental Study of Trumpet Embouchure', *Journal of the Acoustical Society of America*, Vol. 13 (1942), pp. 58 *et seq.*

[4] John C. Webster, 'Internal Tuning Differences due to Players and the Taper of Trumpet Bells', *Journal of the Acoustical Society of America*, Vol. 21, No. 3 (1949).

[5] Marin Mersenne, *Harmonie Universelle*, Paris, Baudry (1636).

[6] Joseph Sauveur (1653–1710). Born a deaf-mute, Sauveur learnt to speak at the age of seven. In later life he became a most distinguished acoustician and wrote a number of original and important works on this subject.

[7] Alexander Wood, *op. cit.*, p. 11. P. M. Morse, *Vibration and Sound*, New York, McGraw-Hill (1948).

[8] It is known that a conical tube continued to the vertex behaves as if it had an antinode there, as it has at the open end. For a *node* to appear at the vertex the pressure would have to be infinite, since the cross section there is zero—an unrealisable condition. A node does, however, appear near the middle, so we have a state similar to that in the doubly open tube, and the same harmonic series will be generated by successive modes of vibration. This agrees well with the observations of practising musicians.

[9] In practical conditions the terminal antinode of an air column occurs slightly beyond the open end of the tube. In determining wavelength or pitch from the dimensions of a tube it is therefore necessary to add on to the length a small but constant 'correction factor' whose absolute value depends on the cross section. For a cylindrical pipe with a clean cut end 0·6 of the radius is the usually accepted value, but this will be modified if the end be either contracted or belled out (see *The Physics of Music*, p. 126). This is the basis of an age-old method of tuning open metal organ pipes. Furthermore, the correction factor is not identical for all the harmonics of any particular air column. Hence, in attempting to design a practical musical instrument from first principles some compromise will be called for.

[10] It will be seen from the above that it is possible for some partial tones to be mathematically incommensurate and therefore mutually 'out of tune'. They can, in fact, be 'inharmonic'. The noun *harmonic* is quite commonly used as a synonym for *partial tone*, and the British Standard Institutions *Glossary of Acoustical Terms and Definitions* (1936) recognises this. French acousticians, however, make the definite distinction that a harmonic is a pure tone while a partial may contain its own array of overtones. There are also differences in accepted usage between physicists and musicians. To the former the nth harmonic implies a frequency equal to n times the fundamental, whereas in music it means a frequency of $(n+1)$ times the fundamental.

[11] In practice the opening of a side hole is not exactly equivalent to cutting off a length of tube. The air in the section *below* the hole exerts a sort of 'loading' effect on the remaining air column which to some extent slows down its vibration. Moreover, the diameter of the hole in relation to that of the tube, and the thickness of the tube wall penetrated, must be considered. A hole through a thick wall, as in a woodwind, can be regarded as a very short wide tube, so in any practical calculations the 'end correction' factor should be applied to it. There are also viscosity and other effects to consider which tend to impede the free vibration of the air mass in the hole. The net effect is that a note 'spoken' by a side hole is generally rather flatter than one might at first suppose from the casual examination of an instrument, and this in turn affects the positioning of holes when designing a woodwind.

D

[12] Even with the most advanced modern valve designs it is not possible to preserve absolutely unaltered the theoretical conicity of taper-bored instruments under all conditions, but certain specialised systems, such as Webster's, have gone a long way towards it. In comparatively short and wide-scale instruments, such as the cornet, the amount of cylindrical tubing introduced by the common valve system makes little difference to the characteristic tone.

[13] Of the older musical historians Speer (1697) seems to be the first to reveal an understanding of the true nature of the trombone. In describing its technique he certainly regards it as a diatonic instrument and quotes only four shifts (*zug*) of a full tone compass each, but he does mention the possibility of flattening or sharpening notes by means of a smaller shift of about two fingers' breadth.

[14] As we shall see in Chapter 8, six and even seven valves have been used in some of the more specialised systems but these are employed *independently*.

[15] The eminent authority, R. Morley-Pegge, in his book *The French Horn*, in this series, p. 26, refers to the work of Kölbel, who *c.* 1760 seems to have devised a horn with two closed *keys* which *raised* the pitch by a semitone and a tone respectively, as an attempt to render the horn chromatic. We must consider, too, that to a horn player two valves are sufficient if he is prepared to borrow only a little from the traditional technique of hand-stopping, with which, until quite recently, he would be expected to be familiar. The trumpet player would probably take a different view. Circumstances alter cases.

[16] Constant Pierre, *La Facture Instrumentale à l'Exposition Universelle de 1889*, Paris, Librairie de l'Art Indépendant, 1890, p. 246. Haward W. Henderson, *op. cit.*, p. 60.

[17] W. and T. Lewis, *Modern Organ Building*, London, W. Reeves. second edn., 1923, p. 119.

[18] Bernard Hague, 'The Tonal Spectra of Wind Instruments', *Proc. Roy. Mus. Ass. London*, Session 1946–47, p. 72. This article also includes a valuable specialised bibliography of the subject. A. Damman in *Comptes rendus*, 1929 (208), 1283.

[19] The investigation of tonal spectra is by no means a simple process, and must be conducted under very strictly controlled conditions. In the case of woodwinds, for instance, since some of their frequencies are radiated more or less evenly all round the instrument while others are propagated in a linear manner, the placing of the recording microphone to register true relative intensities may be critical. With brass instruments the varying directional effect of the bell on different frequencies must be allowed for. Both these effects operate even when the investigation is made in a truly anechoic chamber and the lack of full appreciation of such factors has sometimes led to contradictory findings by different investigators.

[20] Curt Sachs, *The History of Musical Instruments*, London, J. M. Dent & Sons Ltd., 1942. On pp. 145 *et seq.* the writer mentions mouthpieces of horn and bronze in connection with the Roman 'tuba'. He does not, however, indicate whether these were detachable in the modern manner. Of the Danish 'Lurer' he says: 'Their mouthpieces resemble those of the modern tenor trombones', but again he is not specific. In the same paragraph Sachs draws our attention to the pitfalls of terminology, and he points out that these particular instruments were strictly speaking not trumpets but horns.

[21] E. G. Richardson, *The Acoustics of Orchestral Wind Instruments*, London, Edward Arnold & Co., 1929, pp. 71 *et seq.* At the time of writing, A. H. Benade is occupied in devising some very sophisticated apparatus designed to record and analyse resonance characteristics of brass mouthpieces. It may well be that when his investigations are complete much re-thinking on these matters will be called for.

[22] This is a point which some experienced trumpet players would probably challenge. After all even a moderate player is expected to bring the sharp 1st + 2nd valve combination into tune. In a very interesting study of the resonance characteristics of a cornet, published in the *Journal of the Acoustical Society of America*, Vol. 13 (1941), J. G. Woodward cites an experiment showing that on the first five open notes the frequency can be forced by lip action alone over an average range of 21 cycles per sec. We note that Woodward describes this as 'changing the tension of the lips', but it does not rule out the possibility that in changing his tension the player may alter fractionally the effective depth of the mouthpiece cup by projecting or withdrawing the actual lip tissue. In the *J.A.S.A.*, Vol. 13, January 1942, Daniel W. Martin of the University of Illinois describes a technique by which, with the aid of a special transparent mouthpiece, he was able to obtain serial photographs, both frontal and lateral, of the actual motion of a player's lips while blowing a cornet in the normal manner. It would be interesting if such photographs could also be obtained with the player deliberately 'forcing' the pitch. If Richardson's application of the simple edge-tone equation to cup mouthpieces holds, it is clear that a very small change in the effective depth will influence the pitch considerably when the blowing pressure is kept constant. When we come, however, to very deep cups as in the larger tubas the necessary lip adaptation gets beyond the capacity of any but exceptional players and compensation of the valve tubes becomes a necessity. A reference to some very interesting experiments directed towards determining the functions of the individual lips in trumpet sounding will be found in a short but admirably lucid article by Dr. W. H. George in *Hi-Fi News* for August 1965, pp. 214–16. See also Hadland, 'The Mechanics of Trumpet Blowing', in *The New Scientist*, 1 January 1959.

[23] Readers are advised that in Richardson's book there are certain inconsistencies of terminology. On pp. 74 and 75 he uses the term 'flange' to mean both the mouthpiece rim and the orifice at the throat. His intention is, however, quite clear.

[24] The prolonged study of obsolete techniques is a matter which, for economic reasons, few modern professional trumpeters can undertake. Clarino playing in the 18th century was confined to certain specialists who in the first place had the physical attributes necessary for it, but this is not to say that there are not plenty of modern players capable of it were the need still present. Consider certain jazz players today, and the compass they can command.

[25] Recently F. C. Karal has published an investigation into the effects of abrupt changes in the cross section of circular tubes. He sums up as follows: 'The constriction inductance can . . . be interpreted physically as an increase in the equivalent length of the tube'. The converse appears to hold good also. Readers familiar with the more advanced aspects of alternating current electricity will recognise the electrical analogy used. In 1960, also, A. H. Benade compared the conditions in a lumpy duct, such as the tube of a woodwind with the holes closed, to the electrical state of a coaxial cable loaded with shunt capacitors where the bulges occur. This analogy might also be applied to irregular brass tubes. F. C. Karal, 'The Analogous Acoustical Impedance for Discontinuities and Constrictions of Circular Cross Section', *Journal of the Acoustical Society of America*, Vol. 25, No. 2 (1953), pp. 327 *et seq.* A. H. Benade, *op. cit.* October 1960.

[26] John C. Webster, *op. cit.*, also J. Igarashi and M. Koyasu, *Journal of the Acoustical Society of America*, Vol. 25, No. 1 (1953), pp. 122 *et seq.* As long ago as 1929 Bouasse pointed out that in a cylindro-conical tube the vibration rate of the fundamental mode is rather higher than in a uniform tube of the same

length, and that the ratios of the higher mode frequencies to the fundamental
are rather greater. The implication of this in connection with brass instruments
as now constructed is well discussed and simply illustrated by Benade in his
Horns, Strings, and Harmony, Doubleday & Co., Inc., New York, 1960, pp. 174
et seq. This characteristic of the mixed bore is one that greatly concerns the
modern designer of trumpets, and is complicated by the fact that, as different
lengths of supplementary tubing are switched in and out by the valves, so the
relative proportions of cylinder to cone in the total bore will be altered.

[27] For a simple explanation of the mechanics of wave fronts progressing along
curved tubes see *Modern Gramophones and Electrical Reproducers*, by P. Wilson
and G. W. Webb, London, Cassell & Co., 1929, pp. 104 *et seq.* The actual case
discussed is that of an acoustic gramophone horn, but the principles apply
equally to brass instrument tubes.

[28] Rockstro states that the celebrated London flautist Florio on reintroducing
the C and C♯ keys which had fallen into disuse (on the flute), appeared in the
orchestra with a small curtain attached to the end of his instrument to conceal
the mechanism from his neighbours. In order to secure the supposed 'secret'
to his own workshop he taught the manufacture of these keys to his daughter only.
R. S. Rockstro, *A Treatise on the Flute*. London, Rudall Carte, 1890, 1928, p. 244.

[29] See an account of instruments introduced by Cerveny of Königgratz in
Constant Pierre, *La Facture Instrumentale*, Paris, 1890, pp. 241 *et seq.*

[30] E. G. Richardson, *op cit.*, p. 75.

[31] E. G. Richardson, *op cit.*, p. 76.

[32] For the mathematical theory of exponential horns, see Crandall, *Vibrating
Systems and Sound*. Mass. Inst. Tech.

[33] P. A. Northrop, *Journal of the Acoustical Society of America*, Vol. 12, p. 90
(1940).

[34] Daniel W. Martin, 'Directivity and the Acoustic Spectra of Brass Wind
Instruments', *op. cit.*, Vol. 13, pp. 309–13, 1942.

[35] This statement is again an over-simplification of the true situation. The
degree of pitch raising obtained with the fully inserted hand varies with the tube
length and therefore nominal pitch of the instrument. A really satisfactory
explanation of the phenomenon has not so far been forthcoming though at least
three eminent acousticians, Mahillon of Brussels, Blaikley of London, and
Bouasse of Paris, have all presented theories. A controlled investigation which
would nowadays be possible with modern laboratory equipment would only be
of academic interest since the practice of hand-stopping is now obsolete—
though much regretted by older players, who feel that it should be preserved
for the correct performance of much older music. Composers as recent as Wagner, and even Debussy, have been most careful to indicate where they required
open, hand-stopped, or muted notes. The whole question of hand-stopping is
fully discussed by a brilliant exponent of the technique in a companion volume
in this series. See R. Morley-Pegge, *The French Horn*, London, Ernest Benn
Ltd., 1960.

[36] Anthony Baines in his *Woodwind Instruments and their History*, London,
Faber and Faber Ltd., 1957, p. 284, states that the military signal trumpet was
used muted when close to the enemy at least as early as the 16th century.

[37] The simple assumptions of classical acoustics are, unfortunately, seldom
fully satisfied by practical orchestral instruments. They take no account of the
way in which vibration has been initiated in the air columns; of the effects of
coupling between generator and resonator in modifying the intensity, range,
and pitch of overtones; or of 'filtering' effects due to side holes or irregularities
in the bore.

[38] As an illustration, if I, a baritone, sing the vowel *ah* on every note in the range of my voice, measurements show that there is always present a dominant vibration of around 824 cycles a second. Now let somebody else, say a soprano, sing the the same vowel on her complete range of notes. We shall again find the outstanding 824 cycles. This is because when we sing *ah* the lips, tongue, and soft palate take up a definite position and the mouth and other air cavities become a resonating chamber which responds chiefly to a frequency of 824. See also G. Mackworth-Young, *What Happens in Singing*, London, Newman Neame, 1953, pp. 20, 25, and 98–99.

[39] Sir James Jeans, *Science and Music*, London, Macmillan & Co., 1937, p. 144. H. P. Knauss and W. J. Yeager, 'Vibration of the Walls of a Cornet', *Journal of the Acoustical Society of America*, Vol. 13, pp. 160–62, 1941. It is on record that the famous Glenn Miller trombones, whose smooth and rounded ensemble were so justly admired in the mid-1940s, used to apply a pad of velvet to the bells of their instruments when playing *piano*. This, if it was anything more than a trick of showmanship, could have had little effect beyond damping out mechanical vibrations, for the pad was not used in any way like a conventional mute. I suspect that the unique effect these men produced was due mainly to the natural qualities of a wide-bore large-belled trombone played with superb artistry. See also Appendix 3, p. 255.

[40] E. Hermann-Goldap, 'Uber die Klangfarbe einige Orchester-instrumente', *Ann. der Phys.*, Vol. 23, pp. 979–85 (1907); C. Stumpf, 'Splachlaute und Instrumentalklänge', *Zeitschrift für Physik*, Vol. 38, pp. 745–58 (1926).

[41] N. A. Bonavia-Hunt, 'What is the Formant?' *Musical Opinion and the Organ World*, December 1948, p. 151, and January 1949, p. 209.

CHAPTER 2

General Considerations: Definitions and Descriptions—The Trumpet

THE TRUMPET (Fr. *Trompette*; Ger. *Trompete*; Ital. *Tromba*)

THE FAMILY of trumpets used today for ceremonial, military, and orchestral purposes comprises a considerable number of instruments of different sizes and pitch. Within this family, moreover, we can distinguish two main groups: (*a*) the so-called 'natural' trumpets whose tube length is fixed, and whose only notes are those of the harmonic series peculiar to that tube length, and (*b*) those instruments whose tube length is instantly variable by means of some form of valve mechanism and supplementary tubing, and which, in the hands of a player of average ability, have a fully chromatic compass of some thirty notes.

The ingenious juggling with the laws of physics by which this result is achieved has been discussed in the chapter on Acoustics, and we need only note here that while a minimum of three valves is required, no more than this number is essential on any of the smaller brass instruments. Special systems employing four to six valves have been designed, but the three-valved trumpet will certainly be the most familiar in appearance to the non-specialist reader. This is the ordinary trumpet of the symphony orchestra, the dance band, and the 'military' wind band, and on the country of its origin will depend the type of mechanism fitted. In Britain, France, and America piston type valves, sometimes termed 'pumps',[1] are usually employed, while in Germany and Eastern Europe generally some sort of rotary action is preferred. Both of these, as well as certain obsolete devices, will be considered in a later section.

Historically the natural trumpet is, of course, the parent type and is of great antiquity, while the mechanised chromatic trumpet is a comparative new-comer not much more than a century old. The important thing to remember is, however, that both instruments are fundamentally the same and possess certain *essential* features in common. These are, first, a body tube narrow in proportion to its length and basically cylindrical. Second, a 'bell' section in which the body of the instrument expands in gentle curve to form a marked terminal flare. Third, a mouthpiece (almost always detachable) broadly in the form of a hemispherical cup with a thickened rim. These features together can be regarded as definitive of the true Trumpet, and the name should properly be reserved for those instruments only which show them. In the classic Orchestral trumpet the bell section usually amounted to something near a quarter of the total length of the tube, and these proportions were maintained in the earlier forms of the valved instrument (the supplementary valve tubing being disregarded). In modern trumpets, however, things are somewhat different. Today several inches of the 'mouthpipe' into which the mouthpiece fits are nearly always slightly tapered. This is, physically, quite a minor deviation from theory, but it does have the effect of easing *legato* playing in certain parts of the compass, and is therefore welcomed by some players. In instruments made fifty years ago this feature is hardly to be discerned at all and it has made its appearance over a period during which ideals of trumpet technique and tone have changed greatly. In addition, the bell expansion in many modern trumpets begins much earlier and in some examples this section may occupy as much as half the total tube-length. In a typical American instrument recently measured the bell represented 50 per cent. of the tube-length, the tapered mouthpipe 21 per cent., and the cylindrical bore (disregarding valve tubes again) only 29 per cent. We therefore have today an instrument tending towards 'cornet' proportions, and the characteristic tone has changed accordingly.

For the sake of convenience in handling, all but the smallest trumpets have from very early times been folded back on themselves two or more times, occasionally even coiled in circles, and sometimes very beautiful forms have resulted. Today the shape is more or less standardised with two primary bends or 'bows' uniting three lengths of straight tubing, and within this general plan individual makers adopt their own relative proportions. These three main sections can conveniently be termed the 'mouthpipe', the 'middlepipe', and the 'bellpipe'. Older makers called these straight sections 'yards'. Provided that the bows are of fair radius, bending or coiling the tube does not seem to have much effect acoustically. Occasionally the type of valves adopted has some effect on the general lay-out and handling of the instrument. Most German trumpets with rotary action, for instance, appear to English eyes as very wide across the parallel sections of the main tube, and they are played with the plane of the coils horizontal instead of vertical as with piston instruments. Otherwise there is little difference except that German players in general seem to prefer a slightly larger over-all bore and a wider flare to the bell. Both of these tend to foster a weightier and perhaps less brilliant tone than is favoured in England or France (see p. 6.)

Although it is probable that when the word 'trumpet' is mentioned nine out of ten of the general public will visualise the valve instrument, so common is it in dance and popular music combinations and in the windows of music shops of all kinds, yet the natural trumpet is by no means unimportant today. It is found, for instance, in the Cavalry Trumpet of the British Army, in the various 'State' and 'Herald' trumpets, and in the American pattern 'Bugle'. All these are of course military types, and indeed, the trumpet has from the earliest times been the instrument of war and pageantry.

The British 'regulation' pattern cavalry trumpet has for many years been traditionally built 'short', being folded upon itself four times and in this form it is very convenient for its purpose as a signal instrument in the field. Recently some makers have introduced a longer model in a higher pitch folded only twice, which is catalogued also as conforming to 'regulations'. I have, however, been unable to find any written official description of either type except in respect of material and pitch. With the modern mechanisation of armies the usefulness of this instrument would appear to be waning, but at the time of writing it is certainly still 'on the strength.'

State and herald trumpets, as the names imply, are used chiefly in ceremonial and lend dignity and colour to State occasions by the sounding of flourishes and fanfares, though even this function is being encroached on nowadays by the ubiquitous valve trumpet. In 1928 the Royal Military School of Music at Kneller Hall acquired a set of specially designed fanfare trumpets furnished with three valves each and pitched in high E♭, B♭, B♭ tenor, and G. These were all built with the main tube straight, the two higher members being somewhat similar to the 'Aida' trumpets which will be mentioned later. The deeper instruments were tailored to the same over-all length as the E♭ with the ancillary tubing closely folded and kept to the rear of the long bell section from which depend embroidered banners. The whole group of instruments thus presents an appearance of complete symmetry when played in consort, and they both sound and look very effective. Today military bands in many parts of the world are regularly using them. The advantage which such instruments offer to the composer of ceremonial music need not be stressed, but in the writer's opinion some care should be taken lest their melodic possibilities be allowed to obscure the true nature of a fanfare.

The simple State Trumpet is also a 'long' instrument, bent twice only, and sometimes arranged to carry a banner. Modern examples vary from the plain and utilitarian to the highly ornate with chased and engraved mounts and bosses. Although differing in some important respects from surviving early specimens this instrument probably represents the nearest approach we now have to the normal trumpet of the late 16th century—the instrument which under Monteverdi and his contemporaries added to its war-like duties the gentler pageantry of the *Dramma per Musica*.

With the American 'Bugle' we meet one of those curiosities of terminology which sometimes bedevil musical research. In Britain and most English-speaking countries the word Bugle means quite unequivocally a short (4 to 4½ feet) widely conical instrument with comparatively little bell expansion.[2] It is by definition a *Horn* (see Introduction), and in this connection we may note that no less an authority than Adam Carse has used the term *Bugle*-Horn in a comprehensive sense to distinguish brass instruments of wide bore and pronounced conicity from the fundamentally narrower and more gently tapered orchestral horns and their precursors. The American pattern instrument is, on the other hand, essentially cylindrical up to the origin of the bell and, indeed, one well-known maker has described it in a recent catalogue as 'in general size, shape and bore—like a fine trumpet without valves'. In the United States most makers supply these 'trumpet bugles'[3] in both long and short models and in various pitches as well. This seems to be in response to the ideas of many drum-and-bugle corps, physical culture societies, etc., who require a much fuller harmony than is available to the elementary 'bugle band' in Britain. Carrying the idea even farther some American style bugles are fitted with a single valve which instantly transposes the instrument from its normal key of G to that of D, thus increasing its scope still more. This valve can usually be locked in the 'off' position for competition playing when G instruments only are permitted. It may be of interest to note in passing that the single transposing valve has occasionally been applied in this country to the true bugle, but its use can hardly be regarded as common. Some forty years ago a leading British firm supplied a number of such instruments, soprano, alto, tenor, and bass, to the Italian Army under the title of 'Bersagliere Horns'.

To round off this short survey of the present-day trumpet, here is a summary of the most important varieties in use. No doubt, to be consistent, these should have been presented in order of size and pitch, and 'natural' instruments first. The familiar B♭ valve trumpet has, however, for many years now been treated as the type instrument of the family and the reference point for comparison and modifications, so I have thought it more useful to place this first. The story of how it attained its present position and ultimately displaced from the orchestra the F valve trumpet—in many ways a finer instrument which itself displaced the natural trumpet—belongs to our historical chapters.

Thus we have today:

Valve Trumpets (Fr. *Trompette à pistons*; Ger. *Ventiltrompete*;
Ital. *Tromba-ventil, Tromba cromatica*)

(1)   Orchestral Trumpet in B♭ (English and French models). Tube length 53 inches (134·6 cm. approx). Main tube 0·45–0·465 inches in diameter, coiled in a single loop. Normally three piston valves. Mouthpipe slightly tapered for the first 5–9 inches. Bell expansion begins in, or just after, the last U bend. Bell diameter averages 4·6 inches.

(1*a*)   The same instrument is exceptionally built with the main tube between the valves and the bell straight for show purposes: e.g. the soprano B♭ of the Kneller Hall fanfare group, or the 'stage' trumpets now used in *Aida*, Act II (where, incidentally, the original score calls for the rather unusual pitches of B♮ and A♭). The late W. F. H. Blandford held the view that this part properly requires only a single valve. The original stage instruments constructed to Verdi's requirements were, of course, valveless.

(1*b*)   A similar instrument in C is sometimes preferred as the standard trumpet in certain French and Dutch orchestras. Introduced in Britain in 1905, the C trumpet has found a more limited popularity among British orchestral players.

N.B. Both (1) and (1*b*) are to be found with some form of built-in 'quick-change' device which transposes the whole instrument down by a semitone or tone. Thus, certain makers offer trumpets in B♭–A or C–B♭.

(1*c*)   Orchestral Trumpet (German models). Similar in pitch to the above, the main tube of these instruments is usually slightly larger in diameter. The bell of the B♭ instrument averages 5·5 inches across. Three rotary valves are the usual complement, and the body coil is generally rather wider across the parallel sections than in (1).

(2) Trumpet in D. Tube length 42 inches (106·7 cm. approx). First devised by the Belgian maker Mahillon in 1892 for the performance of Bach and Handel parts as written. Provided with two or three valves, it was originally built in 'straight' form. Modern examples coiled in the conventional manner. The first of the so-called 'Bach' trumpets of the late 19th century.

(2a) A similar instrument in E♭ is also used for special performances.

(2b) Another similar trumpet in E♭ with a special 'built in' tuning slide to lower the basic pitch to D is also known.

(2c) The E♭ 'Kneller Hall' soprano.

(3) Trumpet in F (one octave above the obsolete F orchestral trumpet). Designed primarily for playing unaltered the trumpet part in Bach's second Brandenburg concerto. Originally a 'straight' trumpet it is nowadays coiled.[4]

(3a) Rotary valved trumpets also pitched in F and D have been produced by a number of German makers, notably Alexander Bros. of Mainz. It has been claimed that with their instruments any good orchestral trumpeter can, with a little practice, successfully essay the formidable Bach solos.

(4) Antedating (2) and (3) a trumpet in high G was produced by Besson of Paris for use in Bach's 'Magnificat'. This instrument is seldom seen today.

(5) A sopranino B♭ trumpet (one octave above the orchestral instrument) has been constructed, but appears to be even more rarely used today than the high G.

(6) In German and Italian Military music a large trumpet in low E♭ or F is often employed. This instrument is seldom seen except in the German model with rotary valves.

(7) Orchestral Bass Trumpet. This instrument was designed to meet the requirements of Richard Wagner. His first concept was that of a sub-octave version of the F orchestral trumpet of his day. Practical difficulties, however, resulted in a compromise, and a wide-bore instrument of trumpet proportions was constructed in C, with detachable supplementary sections or 'crooks' (see below) to lower it to B♭ or A. Nowadays B♭ and C are the accepted orchestral pitches. The construction of the bass trumpet is still not quite standardised, singly and doubly coiled examples being regularly seen. Three or four valves are fitted. In some forms the

bass trumpet admittedly approximates to a valved trombone, but a good example, well played, has a truly individual tone which is well worth preserving in the large orchestra.

(7a) A three-valved B♭ bass trumpet is sometimes employed in pairs in the larger Italian military bands.

(7b) The B♭ 'tenor' of the Kneller Hall group. Same pitch and compass as the B♭ tenor trombone.

(8) The G 'bass' of the Kneller Hall group. Equivalent in pitch and compass to the G bass trombone.

Natural Trumpets

(1) State or Herald Trumpet in D. Coiled once. Over-all length, 28 inches approx.

(1a) The same instrument in E♭. Over-all length 26 inches approx. This is the more usual pitch as used on State occasions by H.M. Household Cavalry. Examples fitted with a transposing slide to D in the front bow are occasionally seen.

(2) Cavalry Duty Trumpet. British Army Regulation model, in E♭. Twice coiled.

(2a) Certain makers now produce a cavalry trumpet in B♭ which they list also as a 'Regulation' model. This instrument corresponds in pitch with the Regulation Infantry Duty Bugle.

(3) American pattern 'Bugle' in G, built in Soprano and Baritone registers. Once coiled. (Sometimes provided with tuning slide to F.)

(3a) As above, 'short' model twice coiled.

(3b) As above, sometimes provided with a single transposing valve to D. Also built as 'Tenor' in unison with Soprano, but of wider bore.

N.B. Measurements quoted in this summary are based on instruments built in modern 'Flat' pitch, A = 439 vibs. at 20° C. This is the 'New Philharmonic' pitch sometimes called in America 'International' Pitch. Instruments built to the common French pitch of A = 435 vibs. (Diapason Normale) would be slightly longer than stated, but in any case tube lengths are only an approximate guide as other factors are involved (see p. 33, note 9).

NOTES

[1] The term 'pump' is often, and perhaps more properly, applied to the inner piston rather than to the whole valve itself. Throughout this chapter the word 'valve' is used comprehensively and implies the valve mechanism plus its associated supplementary tubing.

[2] It should be stated in fairness that this description applies in most respects to the French military 'Clairon' (not to be confused, as in some popular dictionaries, with the English Clarion), except that this instrument has a more developed bell flare. Although to some extent resembling a previously known pattern, the modern clairon was designed in 1823 by Courtois of Paris in response to instructions from the then Minister of War, and was adopted as the official signal instrument of the French Infantry. The chromatic 'Keyed Bugle' or 'Kent' Bugle, introduced by the Irish bandmaster Halliday (c. 1810), corresponded more nearly in general proportions to the clairon than does the British duty bugle. In France today the equivalent valved instrument, the Flügelhorn, is sometimes called 'Grand Bugle'. The reader is reminded that the terminology of the various families of 'horns' which arose in the mid-19th century as a result of successful experiments with valve systems is very confused.

[3] The compound word 'trumpet-bugle' is here used generically. In fact actual compound Bugle-Trumpets have occasionally been made. A drawing of one such incorporating one of his 'Equitri-lateral' piston valves was published in 1851 by Dr. J. P. Oates of Lichfield. This appeared in the *Expositor*, a paper called into existence by the Great Exhibition. A somewhat similar instrument with a rotary valve is in the collection at the Royal Military School of Music, Kneller Hall. This example, in its normal state, approximates to an ordinary bugle, but the use of the valve introduces a considerable length of cylindrical tubing which transforms it into what is virtually a natural trumpet. It is presumed that the idea was to have a single instrument that would serve for either infantry or cavalry duties.

In France duplex instruments of a more complicated sort have from time to time been produced. In these the exit tube from a single mouthpiece and valve assembly can be connected at will by means of an additional valve to either of two sets of body tubing and bells of different character. Thus a military bugle-trumpet with chromatic possibilities has been provided though it has found little if any acceptance. In the main such instruments have been purely exhibition pieces, except in the case of the so-called 'Echo Cornet' used by some soloists, in which the supplementary valve is used to substitute a constricted bell for the normal one. The London firm of Besson employed the same principle near the beginning of the present century in their 'Doublophone' which combined Trombone and Euphonium characteristics, and in the 1930s the American maker Conn advertised a similar hybrid under the impressive title of 'Wonderphone'. Such instruments would appear to find their place only in the 'show band'.

[4] While considering short trumpets designed primarily for modern performances of Bach and Handel parts, we should note that in the 1930s Werner Menke of Leipzig approached the problem from another direction. He had Alexander Bros. of Mainz make for him trumpets in D and F of the full length used by players of Bach's period. These he had fitted with two valves so that modern players might employ their accustomed technique in dealing with the 'defective' natural notes. The choice of mouthpiece was left to individual users. It was not pretended that these instruments obviated the need for special study but they did afford something that the present-day orchestral player could use to replace one part of the technique of the 18th-century Clarino trumpeter. These instruments were not, I believe, available outside Germany and I have therefore not included them in the above general summary. They are further discussed on p. 122.

CHAPTER 3

General Considerations: Definitions and Descriptions—The Trombone

THE TROMBONE (Fr. *Trombone*; Ger. *Posaune*; Ital. *Trombone*. Formerly Eng. *Sackbut*; Fr. *Saqueboute*)

FOR WELL OVER 300 years, at any time, indeed, between the beginning of the 16th century and the first quarter of the 19th, the trombone, under whatever name it may have appeared, must surely have been the most easily recognisable of all brass instruments. As we shall see later, there is considerable evidence of its existence as early as the 14th century, but from 1551 on we have surviving dated specimens. During the whole of that long time any brass instrument, roughly trumpet-like, bent into a flattened S shape, *and provided with a freely movable U-shaped telescopic slide connecting the mouthpipe and the middlepipe* could be simply and positively identified as a Trombone.[1] Then, about 1820, with the appearance of fairly satisfactory valve mechanism, the beautiful simplicity vanished for ever, and the telescopic slide, once the indispensable feature of the trombone, could no longer be regarded as such.

Today the only characteristics which can be accepted as positively diagnostic for all trombones are broadly the same as for the trumpet, i.e. a mainly cylindrical body-tube, narrow in relation to its length; a bell section expanding in a gentle curve to a wide terminal flare; and a deep mouthpiece with a well-developed 'throat'. The essential distinction between the two instruments lies in a different arrangement of relative proportions in these three elements. Length for length the cylindrical diameter in the majority of trombones is rather greater than in the trumpet—to borrow a term from the organ builder, their 'scale' is larger. This matter of scale is, nevertheless, to be considered with some caution in respect of orchestral instruments, for the ratio of diameter to tube length in the different-sized members of any family is not necessarily a constant factor. We shall return to this a number of times later. The bell section in the trombone takes up approximately one-third of the total length (closed length in the Slide instrument) as

46

against one-fourth in the classic Trumpet. These proportions appear to hold good generally in trombones from the late 17th century to the present day. It is, however, in the character of the mouthpiece that we find the greatest divergence between the two instruments and the most important source of their different tone qualities.

In common with several of our more ancient musical instruments, the trombone quite early in its history came to be constructed in various sizes, forming a choir of voices of different pitch from contrabass to high soprano. Not all of these are in use today, even exceptionally, and in this section we shall refer only to those that are so, leaving obsolete forms to be dealt with in the historical chapter. We shall be wise also, I think, to consider the Slide and the Valve Trombones separately, since there are certain musical as well as structural differences between them. They are not, in fact, in every respect interchangeable, as we shall see under the heading of 'Technique and Capabilities'. There are also certain hybrid types which need not concern us here either, but which will be noted in the appropriate place later.

In dealing with the modern trumpet I have described the most familiar first. With the trombone I do the same, with the rather curious result that this time the older and simpler form takes precedence. To the majority of people the slide trombone is by far the better-known instrument, and, indeed, to very many it is the only trombone.

The body of the modern slide trombone, as indicated above, consists of two straight cylindrical tubes, the mouthpipe and the middlepipe, and a bellpipe which may incorporate a small cylindrical length but usually includes the expanding part of the instrument only. These three sections lie parallel to each other and are connected by two approximately semicircular bows (Fr. *potences*). In the more remote past these bows were almost always of purely cylindrical bore owing to problems of manufacture, but with the advance of modern machinery this limitation no longer exists and many makers prefer to use a tapered bell-bow so that the expansion of the bell actually begins somewhere in the bend. Sometimes, indeed, both bell and bow are produced in one piece (see 'Materials and Manufacture'). The greater part of the mouthpipe and the middlepipe form the inner of two pairs of closely fitting telescopic tubes, the outer members of which are connected by the second bow and thus make up the U-shaped *Slide*. The slide is freely movable and by drawing it out the overall length of the body may be extended by nearly two-thirds. Thus the player has at his disposal the notes of a number of Harmonic Series (see p. 10, Fig. 5) proper to tubes of any length between the extremes given when the slide is closed or fully extended. In practice seven are required and hence seven 'positions' of the slide. To the acoustician such a body is probably the nearest approach to theoretical perfection found in any orchestral instrument, its only defect in his view being the slight irregularity of bore inseparable from the use of telescopic tubes.[2] With modern thin walled tubing this can be very small and its musical effect virtually negligible, as is that of the gently curved bows between the straight sections.[3]

Musically, the free-slide principle has endowed the trombone with a refinement which is found nowhere else in the orchestra save among the unfretted strings. As every position of the extended slide is finally determined by ear (quite instinctively by the experienced player) extremely subtle degrees of inflection are possible, and the trombonist can temper the intervals between notes to an extent beyond the reach of other wind players. Indeed, it has been said that the trombone is the only wind instrument that can be played completely in tune all the time. The converse is, of course, unfortunately also true. On the other hand the free slide has certain drawbacks, mainly mechanical. In the first place, the telescopic tubes must fit with great nicety and slide upon each other without appreciable air leakage. They also require for musical reasons to be quite long in relation to the whole instrument, and in these two features we find a considerable source of friction which tends to reduce flexibility of performance. The shift from a fully extended slide to a closed one can hardly be as quick as the pushing down of a piston. In spite of this, however, modern trombonists, spurred on by modern composers, have attained prodigies of agility which would have surprised 17th- and 18th-century players, and which these might well have pronounced as 'foreign to the nature of the instrument' had they been able to hear them. The problem of friction in the slide has always been much in the minds of trombone-makers and one, at least partial, solution has been found in fitting over the ends of the inner tubes a pair of short sleeves of very thin metal, called in the trade for some reason 'stockings'. The stockings alone make contact with the outer tubes, thus markedly reducing the rubbing surfaces (Fig. 13). The price exacted, a slightly greater inequality in the body diameter, appears to be well repaid in greater facility. More recently the stocking has been largely discarded, for modern metallurgy has furnished the instrument maker with low-friction bronze alloys, as well as methods of surface plating so as to take advantage of the gliding properties of dissimilar metals. Thus the simpler form of slide is now almost completely satisfactory and only its natural inertia cannot be eliminated.

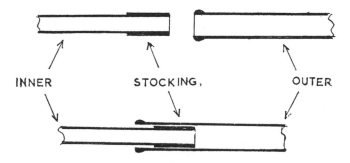

Fig. 13   Trombone slide 'stocking'

A second though minor drawback in the slide comes from its necessarily rather delicate construction. However well designed it may be mechanically, its rather thin tubes are easily put out of adjustment by an accidental blow or twist. The slightest dent can completely lock a slide, so some care is called for in day-to-day handling. The whole trombone too, though beautiful in its lines, is rather ungainly in the larger sizes and therefore most examples are made to take apart just above the slide for convenience in packing.

The need for absolute parallelism between the two limbs of the slide virtually dictates the general shape of the trombone and leaves little scope for freedom of design such as the natural trumpet offers. Only the bell section is susceptible to any great variation of treatment. Most of the more notable makers, from the late 18th century on, seem to agree in arranging this so that the rim of the bell lies slightly forward of the middle of the instrument when the slide is closed. This would appear to be the best average position for comfort and control in playing, for we must remember that as the slide is drawn in and out the centre of gravity of the instrument will naturally shift. The writer has measured a considerable number of trombones, alto, tenor, and bass, made between 1800 and the present day, and of British, French, and American manufacture. In the French examples the tendency is for the bell to be set slightly more forward than in the other makes. All the altos show the bell a little farther back than in comparable tenors and basses. Nevertheless, throughout quite a large series investigated the average position of the bell rim varies surprisingly little and divides the over-all length

E

almost exactly in the ratio of 3 : 2. Of course such figures are in themselves of no great significance, but they do show clearly that the trombone settled down into a stable form round about three centuries ago. In the 17th century, matters were far from stabilised, as surviving examples prove. The celebrated plates in Praetorius' *Syntagma* of 1618[4] show the higher trombones with the bell set much farther forward, but it is interesting to note that one of the earliest-known dated specimens—a tenor made in 1557 by Jörg Neuschel of Nürnberg—shows the 3 : 2 ratio exactly. With the optimum position for the bell thus settled, the modern instrument-maker would appear to have little opportunity to improve this part of the instrument, but one firm at least has recently produced a model expressly designed for dance and show band work in which the bell is very much set back in order to facilitate hand shading and the rapid changing of mutes. During the 19th century some military band trombones were made with the bellpipe coiled in a loop so that the sound was projected back over the player's shoulder, and in others the bell itself was replaced by a grotesque animal mask with open mouth and bared teeth. This fearsome instrument was favoured chiefly in French and Belgian Army bands where it went by the name of *Buccin*. One rather wonders if its sound bore any relation to its appearance. The backward-directed bell is not, as far as I have been able to find out, in use today, but I am informed by one well-known London maker that it could be produced to special order without any difficulty.[5]

We have so far in this section perhaps rather stressed the limitations imposed on the instrument maker by the traditional form of the slide trombone. There is, however, one matter in which his ingenuity is much called for, and has been since the earliest times. This is the disposal within manageable dimensions of the very long tubes required in the bass and contra-bass instruments. The present-day tenor trombone in B♭ has a tube length (closed slide) of some 9 feet. The bass in F is about 12 feet long. Of this total nearly 8 feet form the U of the slide which therefore when closed projects about 4 feet in front of the player, and when fully extended nearly double this distance. When the slide of a conventional bass trombone is fully opened the cross bar at the top is beyond the reach of a player of normal stature and he has therefore to be supplied with a hinged rod and handle to control its two or three lowest positions. The whole arrangement is somewhat awkward and, clearly, in the bass we have gone as far as we can with the conventional design. What then is to be done with the even longer tube of the contrabass?

The answer to this question has, in fact, been known since the great days of the Nürnberg makers in the mid 16th century.[6] Assuming that the F bass represents the maximum over-all length that is practical —not necessarily convenient—in the conventional trombone, and that we wish to preserve the accepted proportions and handling, it is evident that the additional tubing required to make a contra-bass will have to be distributed partly on one side of the point of balance and partly on the other. In the bellpipe this will be no problem for a coil can easily be accommodated there. At the slide end, however, the case is very different. The simple addition of an extra loop will not do here because, for acoustic reasons, the 'telescopes' themselves must be lengthened in the same proportion as the total tube. But if we fold the slide on itself and introduce *four* 'telescopes' we have a practical solution, and this is exactly what the Nürnberg makers did.[7] Since then deep-toned trombones with the double slide have been produced till well on in the present century. The names of Halary, Schott, Sax, Besson, Distin, and Boosey have all been associated with such instruments, showing the wide interest they have aroused in various parts of Europe. Some of these makers went so far as to claim the double-slide principle as a new 'invention' or 'system' though it is, as Carse has pointed out, nearly as old as the trombone itself. The great disadvantage of the double slide, even when subject to the best modern musical instrument engineering, is, of course, its considerable inertia. This was probably of no great moment in the older trombone music; but with Wagner and his successors who recalled the contrabass from a period of comparative obscurity the case is rather different. On the credit side the double slide has a secondary benefit to offer in addition to its relative compactness. With four 'telescopes' instead of two sharing the extension between them the actual distance the slide has to be moved is halved. Thus the 'shifts' on a contrabass trombone in B♭ are the same size as those on a normal B♭ tenor one octave higher in pitch, and are shorter than those on a normal bass in F. This makes possible the provision of a slide long enough for nine positions instead of the necessary minimum of seven, and greatly extends the capacity of the instrument. This point was seized on by Schott of Mainz who in 1817 produced a complete family of double-slide trombones to the design of Gottfried Weber.[8] These, however, failed to displace the regular instruments, possibly because the shifts on the higher members were now inconveniently *small*.

It has already been said that the elongating and coiling of the bellpipe in the trombone involves no great difficulty, but this does not mean that it can be done without careful thought. From very remote times makers have been deeply concerned with the physical as well as the musical beauty of their instruments, wind no less than string or keyboard. The richer examples have often been lavishly decorated, and the ornament applied has faithfully reflected the changing taste of successive ages. The great brass makers of the 16th and 17th centuries found opportunities for decorative treatment in the tubes of their uncomplicated instruments as well as in the stays and mountings. Today, no doubt, the best makers are equally aware of the beauties of good line and balance, but it is unlikely that any of them would indulge in such a fantasy as that shown in plate VI of Praetorius. There are nowadays other overriding considerations to which they must submit.

Fig. 14 Bass Trombone; ornamental treatment of bell bow. (*From Praetorius, c. 1620*)

Acousticians in recent years have learnt a great deal about the effects of constrictions and other irregularities in the walls of resonating pipes. Gentle bends, we know, do not cause much bother, but abrupt or narrow ones are often thought to give rise to 'sensitive' or uncertain notes, and are therefore to be avoided if possible. As an illustration let us take Fig. 15. Here both A and B are drawn from double-slide trombones sold commercially by two well-known French makers about the end of the last century. Both incorporate four 'telescopes' of the accepted type, but the two lay-outs are different. In A the three bows are as large in radius as circumstances permit, but in B—presumably to look different from the other firm's product—they are cramped. It is in such points of design that the difference between a good and a not-so-good instrument often lies, and it is to be feared that very often commercial considerations take first place. Probably the ideal way of dealing with an inconveniently long tube is by coiling it in circles but this is seldom more than partly possible.[9] When, as in the natural trumpet, the air column is of fixed length and is only required to provide the notes of a single harmonic series, it is probably not difficult to arrange necessary bends in the tube where they are acoustically innocuous. But in chromatic instruments such as the trombone, where the tube length is constantly varied whilst playing, it is quite possible for a bend that is harmless with one position of the slide (or combination of the valves) to give trouble with another. Modern instrument-makers are thus constantly up against the need for practical compromise.

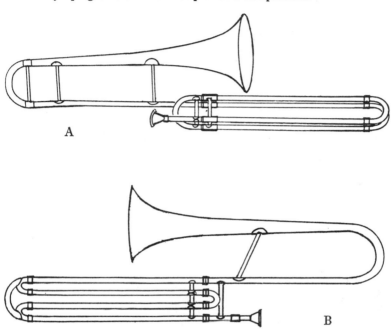

Fig. 15   A Double-slide Bass trombone, system of
             Halary
          B Double-slide Bass trombone, system of
             Fontaine-Besson

Fig. 16 shows two ways in which the problem of stowing away the long bellpipe of the contra-bass trombone has been attacked. A shows plain but carefully calculated folding accommodated within the accepted shape. This model is, in general, the better known of the two and follows a design introduced by the Paris maker Halary about 1885. B is an exclusively English instrument produced by Roosey and Co., probably to the designs of the late D. J. Blaikley, a distinguished acoustician who was technical adviser to the firm for some 60 years. Here the bellpipe is reflected on itself only once (a good feature), the rest of the length being taken up in a large hoop passing under the player's left arm. I have been unable to find out how this rather unorthodox construction was received by players on its introduction, but it would appear to be not uncomfortable in use.[10] This instrument disappeared from the

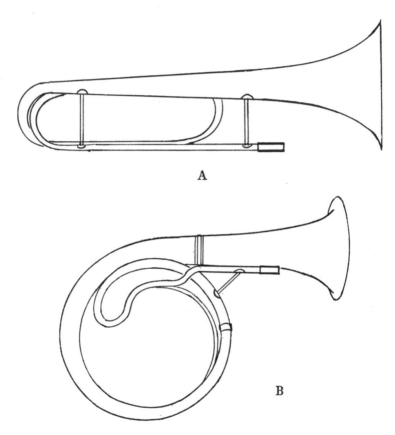

Fig. 16   Bell and bellpipe of contrabass trombones:
A Halary (Paris) model *c.* 1885. B Boosey & Co.
(London) model *c.* 1890. Note the unusually large
'scale' of this instrument

maker's catalogue shortly after 1902, but it is not the model (built in C) which is recorded by Baines as having failed to satisfy Richter for the first London performances of *The Ring* in 1882.[11] (Plate 4 A).

It is perhaps only fair to warn the casual concert-goer that he is not very likely to find either of the above models in current use. The need for trombone tone in the contrabass register is nowadays usually met by a rather different type of instrument—when the Tuba, with or without a modified mouthpiece, is not sneaked in as a somewhat shame-faced substitute. I refer to what may best be described as a duplex or transposable trombone. This is essentially a normal slide trombone of rather large bore, with an additional coil of tubing attached to the bell-pipe which can be quickly switched in and out by a single valve conveniently placed for the left thumb. The principle is the same as in the A–B♭ trumpet already noticed (p. 42) but in the trombone the supplementary tubing lowers the pitch of the instrument by a fourth, thus virtually transforming, for example, a B♭ tenor into an F bass. Such instruments had appeared tentatively (c. 1850) in France, where a piston valve was usually preferred to a rotary one. It was, however, in Germany that the idea really took root and flourished at the beginning of the present century (almost to the exclusion of the simple bass) and there the now generally accepted name of *Tenor-bass* was coined. At that period German ideas in wind playing were influential in America, and German-style instruments were in demand, so manufacturers, in whatever country, had to provide them if they wished to share in that growing market.

As with the trumpet, German players had long preferred a trombone with a larger scale and relatively wider bell than that generally used in France or England. For many years English trombonists used exclusively a narrow-bore instrument, now rather contemptuously dubbed the 'peashooter'. The scale of this, in the B♭ tenor size, is the same as that of the B♭ bass trumpet (p. 43) and its tone is brilliant but of no great weight in the *mezzo-forte* or less.* The peashooter bore is still employed in certain quarters in Britain, but by 1923 it could be safely said that all the notable British symphony players had adopted the 'medium' or the 'large' bore. Today British trombones of the highest excellence are produced in all three scales. I am informed by one leading firm of makers that the three standard bore diameters for the B♭ tenor are related as 1 to 1·07 to 1·11, and that bell diameters preserve about the same ratios, varying from 6 to 9 inches. To be quite fair it should be stated that as early as 1892 some English makers listed both small and medium-bore tenors, though the large bore became a stock model only considerably later. Modern American makers now list medium, medium-large, and large bores, but I have failed to find the small mentioned in any of their up-to-date catalogues. With the

* See Appendix 3, p. 255.

increasing break-down in recent years of national barriers and prejudices in music, the same trends are now to be found in France, where, not so long ago, some of the most celebrated soloists used a bore even smaller than the peashooter.

The reasons for these different national preferences, as far as we know them, belong partly to the indefinable realm of 'taste', and partly to musical history which we must defer to another chapter. Here we shall only notice that the larger bore does beyond doubt tend to a more solid tone, and in proof of its recognition cite two celebrated British players of the early 20th century, Jesse Stamp and Arthur Falkner. Both these men habitually used the narrow bore, but when playing such works as the Symphonies of Brahms they would change over to wide-bore instruments as being those for which the parts were originally conceived. It has been reported that in certain American symphony orchestras it is now customary for first-desk men to use a medium-bore trombone while the second and bass players use the large bore. This certainly reveals an admirable concern for tonal colour, but, as the internal balance of any orchestral group must ultimately rest with the wishes of the conductor as well as with the musical sensibility of the players, it would surely seem to be somewhat pedantic.

During the period when in German-speaking countries the tenor-bass was finally displacing the older F instrument, English opinion was settling in favour of a smaller bass in G. This became the standard third trombone in Britain, and still is so, though now also threatened by the duplex instrument. When the G bass also had acquired the supplementary tubing and quick-change valve it became the G–D bass and, by means of 'pedal' notes, covered the whole range of the B♭ contrabass except for the two lowest semitones. The substitution of an alternative C section in the supplementary tube will, however, make up this lack and furnish even the lowest notes required by Wagner. This magnificent instrument, therefore, carries the genuine trombone tone right through both the bass and contrabass registers, albeit with a somewhat different technique from that of the simple version.

As with all modifications to a basically satisfactory instrument, the B♭–F and the G–D trombones have certain weaknesses which to some extent off-set their manifest advantages. In the first place in both instruments the supplementary coils must be well designed and as little constricted as possible where they enter and leave the valve. This requirement, which is common to all valves, is not always easy to meet without making the barrel rather large and clumsy and so slowing its action. Again a good working compromise is wanted. Comparison of makers' catalogues, nevertheless, shows that cramped designs are to-day nearly as common as good ones, and there are many players who regard too much clever 'plumbing' with some suspicion. Secondly, as the length of the shifts must be increased proportionally as the basic length of the tube is added to, slides which are adequate for the B♭ and G simple instruments respectively will not be long enough to allow of a seventh position when these have already been lowered to F or D by means of the valve. The loss of the seventh position is, how-ever, compensated for by increased facilities in other directions.

Finally in this section we should notice one more very important point concerning 'scale'. Admittedly the duplex trombones 'grew up', as it were, among players who for tonal reasons preferred a large bore, but there is one much more fundamental reason why these instruments are constructed only in the larger scales. In any resonating tube the lowest note of which it is theoretically capable can, in practice, be sounded only if that tube is of a certain minimum diameter in relation to its length. In the lowest four positions on the simple narrow-bore trombone these notes—called by players 'pedal' notes—are either ineffective or are impossible to elicit, but in the extended compass of the duplex instrument some of them become essential. Hence it is necessary for the scale of the B♭–F and G–D trombones to be such that certain pedal notes are good and effective.

From the foregoing paragraphs the reader has no doubt gathered that there is today wide divergence of opinion regarding ideals of trom-bone tone. In Britain there are many highly respected players who feel that the modern German-American school has deliberately sacri-ficed something of the individual character of the instrument, and that the tone cultivated, especially in the softer dynamics, approaches too nearly to that of the wide-bore Horns which they also prefer. On the other hand, British players, too, deplore the bad period when stridency was a common characteristic of the trombone in Britain. This phase has been doubly unfortunate, for accounts of it still tend some-times to colour the foreign view of British brass playing which has for many years been second to none. If the matter be looked at quite objectively it must, I think, be conceded that the modern German tone is probably nearer to that of the ancestral instrument, for we learn from many sources that the sackbut was originally valued for its grave sonority and its ability to support and blend with voices in the Offices of the Church. Thereafter it became the accepted bass to consorts of cornetts and shawms. The scale of the trombones so employed was not, as a rule, large by modern standards, yet we may judge from contemporary music that a mellow and full-bodied tone was looked for. One can hardly imagine, for instance, the highly vocal trombone parts of Schütz, or, two centuries later, the 'Statue' music in *Don Giovanni*, menacing though this is, played with the blare of a modern marching band. We come then, once again, to the mouthpiece as a most important source of tonal character (see pp. 17 *et seq.*).

The production in the early 19th century of the first satisfactory valves paved the way for revolutionary changes among the brass wind. Not that 'natural' instruments were immediately and universally superseded by mechanised ones—that took time, and there was much opposition and prejudice to be overcome before the new devices had been perfected and had conclusively proved their worth. Nevertheless, from that time on it became possible for horn and trumpet players to transpose their instruments from one key to another in no more time than it took to push down a piston, instead of plugging in or taking off supplementary lengths of tube (*Crooks*, see pp. 73–4) as previously. Very soon it was realised that with *three* valves, used either singly or in combination, players on these instruments could within a certain range command a complete chromatic scale. With the trombone the situation might perhaps be thought rather different, for here was an instrument that had always been inherently chromatic. Still, it was hardly to be expected that it alone would escape the attentions of the innovators, and, in fact, one of the earliest English valve patents[12] specifically mentions the trombone, although it seems probable that in this case the instrument was included merely for the sake of completeness in coverage. Whatever the truth of the matter, however, it seems clear from Press notices etc.[13] that by about 1818 in Germany valves had been applied to instruments of trombone proportions. That *crooks* were sometimes employed *c.* 1620 to change the basic pitch of the slide trombone is manifest from Praetorius but I have no evidence that the 19th-century player used them.

At this period Military Music in Europe was making great advances with the formation and standardisation of regular Service bands in a number of countries, and in these the trombone proved of great value in spite of the obvious inconvenience of the telescopic slide under Duty conditions. The availability of valves at once removed this inconvenience and made the instrument as handy as any other for marching or mounted bands. Even so the valve trombone failed to supplant entirely the ordinary instrument in military bands, and although it still has some place in this field on the Continent and, to much lesser degree in America, it has never been really accepted in England. In Continental Concert and Opera orchestras the valve trombone did have a short and rather uncertain vogue, possibly more as a novelty than anything else, but it seems to have been the general opinion in these circles that, in spite of its agility, it lacked something in tone. The same criticism was levelled at early valve *trumpets* and perhaps not without reason. Writing in 1855 von Gontershausen tells us that the best German players were by then getting rid of their valve trombones and reverting to the classical slide instrument.

It is an unfortunate thing that all simple systems using two or three valves together have an inherent defect in intonation (see p. 12). On the shorter instruments the player corrects this almost instinctively by *embouchure* (and perhaps some compromise with the length of his third valve slide) but with increasing length the fault becomes more and more intractable unless compensated by other means. With the application of valves the trombone inherited the trouble, particularly noticeable in the bass instrument, and this weakness also has undoubtedly weighed against its quite considerable advantages. The slightly equivocal position occupied today by the valve trombone is clearly suggested by the number of minor variations in form depicted in different makers' catalogues during the last sixty years. Among these, however, we can distinguish two main types. The first, which we may conveniently call the 'long' model, is built to the general shape and dimensions of the standard instrument with the slide *closed*. The valves are placed about the middle, and all the supplementary tubing is kept to the rear, rather as in the fanfare trumpets mentioned on p. 40. Thus the appearance of the classical trombone is largely preserved. The 'short' model, though also based ultimately on the flattened zig-zag of the ancestral sackbut, shows a remarkable variety in treatment of both the main and the supplementary tubes. These are folded and looped in all sorts of ways, and every single maker seems to have had his own ideas about them. For example, in one so-called 'Cavalry Model' listed in 1938 by a British firm, the fore-and-aft length of the instrument has been so reduced that, in the B♭ tenor size, the front bow projects no more than five or six inches beyond the bell rim, while the bell bow can hardly be seen behind the player's head when looked at in profile. Admittedly this is an extreme case, but many Continental makers have run it very close.

The continued adherence to basic sackbut lines by most makers of valve trombones is surely a remarkable illustration of the force of tradition. 'Valves or no valves' they seem to say 'a trombone must have three long parallel sections'. In fact there is no 'must' about it. The musical characteristics we recognise as essentially *trombone* are due to *the proportions* of the tube and the internal configuration of the mouthpiece and, once the telescopic slide has been eliminated, the tubing can be quite freely arranged in any appropriate form.[14] Thus, about the middle of the 19th century, some undisputed trombones were produced in an upright, tuba-like form, while others, sometimes still to be seen in Continental military bands, employed a horizontal bell with most of the other tubing more or less angled downwards so as to be comfortably carried under the player's arm on the march. It should be noted, however, that this break with tradition was by no means always just a matter of the players' convenience. Often it was absolutely dictated by the mechanical needs of certain specialised valve systems which arose at this period in the course of a continual search for better intonation among the larger brass instruments. Some of these we shall examine in detail in a later chapter. To close this section then we may just mention what is perhaps the most curious of all orthodox 3-valve trombones. This is the 'Helicon' model, coiled in a large hoop and carried round the player's body under the right arm and with the bell over the left shoulder.[15] In the first decades of the present century circular Bass Tubas were commonly to be seen in military bands, and they figure, though in a somewhat secondary place, in British instrument-makers' lists as late as the 1920s. With the exception of the popular Sousaphone, however, the Helicon form seems to be out of fashion at the present time. Circular trombones are indeed rare but certainly deserve notice if only on account of their almost unique place in the remarkable cycling regimental bands of the Netherlands.[16]

The following is a summary of the principal trombones which the reader may find in use today. Not all of them are at all common, nor is nomenclature entirely standardised. For instance, M. Flandrin of the Colonne Orchestra writing in Lavignac's *Encylopédie* in 1927 and supported by Adam Carse calls the high B♭, octave to the tenor, a *treble*, while Anthony Baines in the fifth edition of *Grove* uses the term *soprano*. To M. Flandrin the soprano is pitched in F, an octave above the usual Continental bass, while his alto is in D♭. Here I have used the names most commonly accepted in English-speaking countries, and, as with the trumpet, I have grouped the instruments according to general familiarity rather than in order of pitches.

Slide Trombone (Fr. *Trombone à coulisse*; Ger. *Zugposaune*;
Ital. *Trombone à tiro, Trombone duttile*)

(1) Tenor Trombone in B♭. Tube length 107 inches (271 cm. approx). Built in *small, medium,* or *large* bores averaging 0·45 inches, 0·49 inches, and 0·52 inches respectively. At the time of writing there seems to be a tendency for bores to increase again, the latest sizes quoted by a leading British maker being 0·485 inches, 0·523 inches, and 0·555 inches. A bore much smaller than the least of the above was at one time popular in France for solo work and may still be seen there occasionally. Bell expansion takes up about *one-third* of the total (closed) tube length. Bell diameters vary between 6 inches and 9 inches.

(1a) A similar higher-pitched Tenor in C may sometimes be seen in France (occasionally made with 'quick-change' to B♭).

(2) Bass Trombone in G. Tube length 130 inches (330 cm. approx). Similar to (1), but provided with a jointed handle to control the slide in the lower positions. This is the standard Bass in Great Britain.

(2a) Bass Trombone in F or E♭. Similar to the above, but built in the larger scale bores only. The standard Bass in Germany and where German influence predominates.

(3) Contrabass Trombone in B♭. Details of construction vary a great deal between different makers. The constant feature is the *double* telescopic slide which is about the same length as that of the tenor in the same pitch one octave higher.

(4) Alto Trombone in E♭. Similar in general appearance to (1) though proportionately smaller. After a decline in popularity in the third quarter of the 19th century, this instrument has recently been revived with some success for the performance of classical parts originally written for it.

(4a) Alto Trombones in D♭, E, or F, similar to the above may still occasionally be found in France, though probably not in general use. M. Flandrin writes (1927) of the D♭ instrument only as *Alto* and regards the higher ones as *Sopranos.*

(5) Treble Trombone in D♭, sometimes also called Soprano. This member of the family, after nearly a century of oblivion, was revived in the 1930s as a 'special effects' instrument for the Dance

Band. Often erroneously called the 'Slide Cornet' it seems to have made little impact. Sometimes also provided with 'quick-change' to A♭.

Duplex Trombones

(1)   Tenor Trombone in B♭ with rotary valve transposing to F (Ger. *Tenorbass Posaune*). Built only in the larger-scale bores, this instrument is nowadays more or less the standard for bass trombone parts on the Continent and in America, and is rapidly gaining a foothold in Great Britain. It is to be noted that most American makers now list this instrument simply as *Bass Trombone* and no longer make the plain slide Bass. In this case the bell is sometimes as wide as 10″. Early French specimens may be found with a piston rather than a rotary valve. In some models the F slide may be pulled out to give E.

(1a) The above instrument is also to be found with a second valve which converts the transposition to B♭–E instead of B♭–F. (See also under 'Quick-change Cylinder', p. 74.)

(2)   Bass Trombone in G with rotary valve transposing to D. General construction as (1) above. An alternative longer valve slide is sometimes provided which lowers the transposition to C, thus, with its modified technique, covering the full compass of the simple B♭ Contrabass.

The above transposable trombones can nowadays be regarded as the regular instruments of the class, but special models have also been made to meet the ideas of individual players.

Valve Trombones (Fr. *Trombone à pistons*; Ger. *Ventilposaune;* Ital. *Trombone Ventili; Trombone a cilindri*)

For reasons in the foregoing text, valve trombones do not today fall into a neat classification. The hopes once entertained that they might be useful as a homogeneous group of voices like the ancestral sackbuts have not been realised.[17] The following list may, however, be useful:

(1)   Tenor Trombone in B♭. Built in either 'long' or 'short' form as described in the text above. Three piston valves.

(1a) Similar Tenors to (1), but provided with a fourth valve designed to correct certain faults of intonation. Such instruments are used particularly in French and Italian military bands.

(1b) As (1) or (1a), but provided with rotary valves.

(2)   Bass Trombone in G. Three piston valves.

(2a) Bass Trombone in F. Three or four piston valves.

(2b) Bass Trombone in F. Rotary valves.

(3) Contrabass Trombone in B♭. Three or four rotary valves. Such instruments are notably employed in the larger Italian military bands for whom, together with (2b), they are built with all except the bell tubing angled downwards.

(4) For the sake of completeness this list should also include trombones constructed according to the six-valve 'Indépendant' system of Adolphe Sax. These instruments can hardly be regarded as in common use although they have had extensive trials in Concert work as late as the 1920s—notably under the late Sir Henry Wood at the Queen's Hall, London. The underlying theory of the 'Indépendant' system is quite opposed to that of all other valve arrangements, and its discussion is reserved for a later chapter.

NOTES

[1] I am aware that some readers may think this a very bold statement, but, on the balance of evidence, I believe it to be true. There are written references from the mid-16th century to 'draw' or 'slide' trumpets, and pictorial representations even earlier. These appear, however, to be instruments with a *single* telescopic section in the mouthpipe. Morley-Pegge (*The French Horn*, in this series, p. 10) takes the early 16th-century draw-trumpet to have been a sackbut, but certain inventories surviving from 1573 make quite a clear distinction between sackbuts and trumpets furnished with slides. The late Canon Galpin (*Old English Instruments of Music*, p. 210) specifically refers to 'the Treble Sackbut—wrongly called the Slide Trumpet (Tromba da tirarsi) of Bach's scores'. The evidence is discussed more fully in the historical chapters.

[2] For the sake of completeness we may note here a bass trombone much publicised in the 1930s by a well-known American firm. In this instrument the limb of the slide nearer to the bell was made fractionally larger in bore than the other. Great tonal virtues were claimed for this innovation, but I have been unable to find any player who can speak of it from personal experience. The idea is in fact not at all a modern one. Before 1890 George Case of London had devised such a slide in which the limb nearer the bell telescoped *inside* the corresponding fixed tube. This was on view at the Royal Military Exhibition of that year.

[3] The acute bending of tubes in relation to their diameter is sometimes unavoidable in certain valved instruments. In the opinion of many players this reduces freedom of blowing, or leads to tonal irregularities. On the other hand, most makers who also play their instruments deny this.

[4] Praetorius, Michael, *Theatrum Instrumentorum*, Wolfenbüttel, 1620. Reprint Trautwein, Berlin, 1884. See particularly Plate VIII and compare with figures below the centre panel of the title page.

[5] According to *Grove's Dictionary of Music and Musicians*, 5th edition, London, 1954, Vol. VIII, p. 558, Sir Michael Costa at the Sacred Harmonic Concerts of 1848 insisted on the use of reverse bell trombones in an attempt to ameliorate

their tone as heard in the auditorium. At this time apparently 'overblowing' and stridency were common among English players.

[6] F. W. Galpin, in *Proceedings of the Musical Association*, London, 1906–7.

[7] A *bass* trombone with a double slide marked 'Jobst Schnitzer, Nurnb. 1612' belonged formerly to the de Wit Collection, Leipzig. It is not known if it survived destruction during the War.

[8] Gottfried Weber, composer and acoustician, born at Freinsheim near Mannheim in 1779. He died at Kreuznach in 1839.

[9] The ancestral French 'Trompe de Chasse' and the early orchestral hand horn were, of course, coiled in circles and there are examples of natural trumpets so treated. An unmarked 19th-century example is No. 100 in the Carse Collection in the Horniman Museum, London.

With the invention of body-crooks, and then valves, unbroken circular coiling became impossible, though in a limited way it has survived in orchestral horns, some saxhorns, etc.—in the latter probably more for show than for any particular advantage it affords with such wide-scale tubes.

[10] Certain surviving examples of the 'Buccin' are coiled in this way, but are, of course, nothing like so bulky. See Carse Collection No. 227.

[11] *Grove's Dictionary of Music and Musicians*, London, 5th edition, article 'Trombone', Vol. VIII, p. 554. But why create a C contrabass at all? The original contrabass made by Moritz of Berlin to Wagner's ideas was in B♭.

[12] Patent No. 5013 granted in 1824 to John Shaw, farmer, of Mill Town in the county of Derby. The title in the Official Records is 'Transverse Spring Slides for Trombones, Trumpets, French Horns, and other Instruments of Like Nature'.

[13] *Allgemeine Musikalische Zeitung*, Leipzig, May 1815, November 1817, and July 1818.

[14] This statement is, of course, subject to the same reservations which have already been made regarding *sharp* or *constricted* bends.

[15] It should be noted that with these instruments this is the actual *playing* position. The old French 'Trompe de Chasse' was *carried* in this position in the chase but was not so played. Much misapprehension has been caused by fanciful pictures published by sporting print sellers, etc., who were unacquainted with the real shape of the old wide-coiled instrument.

[16] Excellent photographs of one of these bands were published in a full-page 'spread' in the *Illustrated London News* for September 25th, 1937.

[17] That such hopes were indeed once entertained may justifiably be inferred from the makers' catalogues published near the beginning of the present century. For instance, in 1902 the London firm of Boosey & Co. offered Valved Altos in F and E♭, Tenors in C and B♭, and Basses in A♭, G, F, and E♭. All these could be had with either simple valves or Blaikley's automatic compensating valves. By 1923 only B♭ Tenors and Basses in E♭, F, and G were on offer.

In 1902 the same firm also listed a *Baritone* slide trombone in B♭. I have been unable to get any first-hand information about this instrument, but I think it may be assumed that it was made in unison with the B♭ Tenor, but with a bigger bore to furnish a more robust tone at the lower end of its scale.

CHAPTER 4

Mouthpieces, Tuning Devices, Mutes, Ancillaries

A. Mouthpieces

IT WILL have been realised from what has been said in Chapter 2 that, without any loss of their essential characteristics, the tube and bell of the trumpet lend themselves to a considerable variety of treatment. We now turn to the mouthpiece (Fr. *Embouchure*; Ger. *Mundstücke*) which is the most sensitive, and in some respects the least constant, part of the whole instrument. In this case, however, the variation is dictated neither by occasion nor by the whim of a designer, but by much more subtle considerations. In the first place, in brass playing the actual lips of the performer form the vibrating part of the tone generator; without them the instrument is in fact incomplete. In a measure the lips function as do the reed blades in a woodwind, and for this reason instruments with a cup or funnel-shaped mouthpiece are often classified as 'lip-reeds', although, as we have seen, the analogy is not quite perfect. It is, nevertheless, evident that the rim of the mouthpiece to which the lips are applied must have a considerable influence on the freedom or otherwise of their vibration, not to mention the comfort of the player. For the best results the rim of the mouthpiece must be designed with reference to several anatomical features, viz. the thickness and length of the lips themselves, and the conformation of the supporting structures, the teeth and jaws.[1] The wearing of dentures sometimes creates a problem for the mouthpiece maker, as does the player who habitually places the trumpet to one side rather than in the middle of the lips.[2] The matter is important, and most reputable makers carry a large stock of standard patterns from which the majority of players can be accommodated. The sectional drawings in Fig. 17 will give some idea of the diversity of rim profiles in use today. A, B, and C are modern trumpet mouthpieces, while E and F are for the Cornet. All are taken from the regular catalogues of well-known makers. C is unusual in the way in which the cushion of the rim is offset in relation to the axis of the bore. This is a form of mouthpiece which might be adopted by, for instance, a player with some dental problem. It can hardly be called common, but it is

F

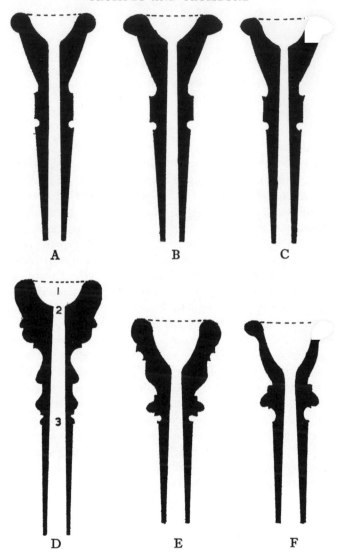

Fig. 17   Trumpet and Cornet mouthpiece in section

interesting to see that the maker has evidently found sufficient demand
to warrant its production as a standard line. All these mouthpieces are
regularly supplied in three different diameters of cup. D represents to
the same scale a mouthpiece of the old type as used commonly till

about 1890. Beyond the limits of the rim itself the external ornamentation of a mouthpiece is really of no significance, though we may note in passing how much superior the older ones usually are in general balance of design. The substance of which cup mouthpieces are made also seems to matter comparatively little. They are, as a rule, turned up from castings, and brass or one of the white bronzes, either plain or silver-plated, are the common materials. Occasionally some players have shown a personal preference for solid silver, but it would appear to have no special virtue. Formerly, ivory, horn, or even hard woods were sometimes used, and recently some makers have tried to introduce plastics. The only advantage here would seem to be to the manufacturer, for a moulding process might well be quicker and cheaper than casting, turning, and plating metal. In his article on the Trumpet and Cornet in Lavignac's *Encyclopédie de la Musique* (1927), M. Franquin mentions an attempt to cushion the rims of metal or glass mouthpieces with india-rubber, but gives the opinion that the lips should be able to slide freely upon a hard polished surface which the rubber does not afford.

The second, and probably more important, of the variable features of a trumpet mouthpiece lies in its internal configuration. The bore of the mouthpiece has three components: the cup itself, the 'throat' or orifice at the base of the cup, and the tube of the externally tapered shank which connects with the body of the instrument. These sections are frequently referred to by the French names *bassin*, *grain*, and *queue*. The first two in particular have important acoustical effects which have been discussed in the appropriate chapter, and in this descriptive section it will be enough to note their characteristics and properties in a general way. The bore of the shank—the 'back-bore'—is of necessity somewhat conical since it forms the correspondence between the throat and the main tube of the instrument, and its angle of taper will be dictated by the relation of these two diameters. There is no doubt that ideally the shank bore should merge imperceptibly into that of the mouthpipe, a point that is not always remembered. It is quite common for players to adhere to a favourite mouthpiece and to 'plug it in' to different instruments whose dimensions do not always match.

At the present time some trumpet-makers who themselves are, or have been, professional players, are doing very interesting work in the matter of matching individual mouthpieces to individual instruments, as well as to the personal needs of instrumentalists. Such specialisation is probably beyond the economics of the moderate-price commercial manufacturer, but it is encouraging to find that such *'artiste-ouvriers'* exist today as in the past, and that there is some market for their special skills. Some of the most refined mouthpieces made today, especially in America, are constructed in two sections which screw together with a fine thread so that the player can at will unite the cup of his choice with rims of different size and curvature. The pioneer in this has been Vincent Bach, formerly 1st trumpet in the Boston Symphony Orchestra, and now a leading consultant on the trumpet and head of a large manufacturing organisation.

Looking at Fig. 17 let us first consider the old trumpet mouthpiece represented in sketch D. Here we have a shallow hemispherical cup and a sharply defined angular throat. The former characteristic favours the sounding of the higher notes in the series, while the latter makes for brilliance and incisiveness of sound. A small cup diameter likewise favours the higher notes, and a larger one the lower. The diameter of the throat is also influential, and one too small in relation to the diameter of the cup will reduce the over-all fullness of tone. The traditional mouthpiece is now obsolete, and for the section of a typical modern one we must turn to drawings A, B, or C. Here the cup is rather deeper and with a distinct element of the cone in it. The constriction at the throat is still marked, but its angularity is now rounded off. The effect is to reduce somewhat the incisiveness of the tone and to make easier the slurring of notes over wide intervals. This feature seems to have developed more or less concurrently with the adoption of the tapered mouthpipe. In the course of the last century the throat of the mouthpiece has been subject to a great deal of trial-and-error experiment, and at times some quite bizarre forms have appeared. Two of these are illustrated in Fig. 18. In example A a series of nicks has been filed out round a normal circular throat, giving a star effect.[3] In B the throat

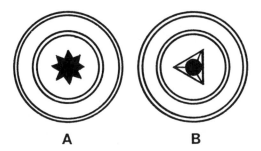

A   **B**

Fig. 18   Trumpet mouthpieces: A nicked throat; B
triangular throat

has been opened out in the shape of an inverted triangular pyramid. This latter is, in fact, not at all a bad mouthpiece and attached to a modern trumpet gives a tone that is both full and incisive. This we might expect since the edge where the cup and the superimposed pyramid meet is quite sharp, and the actual area of the throat is considerably larger than the particular back-bore used would have provided if not so modified. It is interesting to note that one modern specialist is now providing a mouthpiece with very similar tonal characteristics to example B, only he simply cones out the throat leaving the junction with the cup fairly sharp.

There is no doubt that during the last thirty or forty years the 'accepted' tone of the orchestral trumpet has tended more and more towards that of the cornet whose typical bell-shaped mouthpiece with a rather ill-defined throat is illustrated in drawings E and F, Fig. 17.[4] The limit in reduction of the throat is reached in the mouthpiece of the French Horn, some typical sections of which are shown in Fig. 19. In

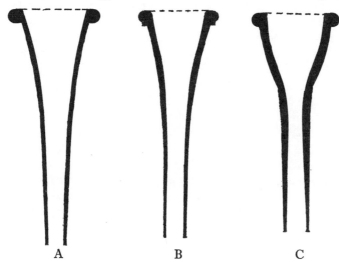

A   B   C

Fig. 19 Horn mouthpieces: A Classic French. B Modern French (military band). C Modern German (orchestral)

theory, and at one time in practice, this mouthpiece was strictly a truncated cone, and was made out of sheet metal rolled up and soldered, the rim being formed by turning over the edge. Later the common practice of turning from the solid was adopted and some slight degree of curvature was applied to the walls (Fig. 19 A.). A modern military French Horn mouthpiece is shown at B and here it will be noticed that there is a slight element of the 'cup' to be seen. This example has also the slightest trace of a back-bore, difficult to show without exaggeration in the drawing, but quite distinguishable with the aid of callipers or a set of plug gauges. There is, in fact, a vestigial throat. These characteristics are even more developed in modern German examples designed for use with the wider-bored orchestral horns now universal in that country, and increasingly favoured in England and America.

The modern tendency to reduce the brilliance of trumpet tone has been deplored by many critics, especially in Britain by those old enough to remember the noble playing of such as John Solomon, and before him Walter Morrow. Fashions, however, change in music as much as in other arts, and it is not impossible that a reversal of opinion may occur some time in the future. After all, we should remember that there was a time not so long ago when in England the technically easier cornet nearly ousted the trumpet from all but the largest metropolitan orchestras, and it was largely due to Morrow that the older instrument was restored to a proper regard.[5] What *is* important is for conductors and players to bear in mind when performing music of the Classical or Baroque periods the quality of sound that composers then expected to hear. This is not to say that it is sacrilege nowadays to play the magnificent *obbligati* of Bach or Handel on valve trumpets. We should hear them seldom indeed if we did not; but we do know with some certainty what the best trumpets of Bach's time sounded like, and we can now reproduce this sound reasonably well (see pp. 177–9). Equally, in the writer's opinion, is it futile to speculate about what one or other of the great composers of the past would have done had modern instruments been available to him, and to re-score his works accordingly. Surely one measure of a composer's genius lies in what he accomplished with the resources of his own time. The introduction of a so-called 'Bach' trumpet with valves in the 1890s and the misunderstandings which followed, make a fascinating chapter in trumpet history, and this we shall examine in detail hereafter.

The foregoing paragraph, though perhaps something of a digression, indicates some of the considerations that influence the choice of a mouthpiece today. With the trumpet, as with any musical instrument except perhaps some keyboards, tone production is, in the ultimate, an intensely personal thing. It begins in the ear of the mind. It is for the player, first, to conceive the quality of tone he admires and wishes to cultivate, and then, in the light of acoustical knowledge and awareness of his own physique, to select the mouthpiece that will help him most. For this reason mouthpieces present a tremendous variety of detail, and the student, were he to measure a score in current use, might well not find two identical.

There is no brass instrument mouthpiece that has changed more with the passing of centuries, or which today shows greater variation, than that of the trombone. The earliest surviving sackbut mouthpieces whose date is unquestioned[6] show a plain conical bore, not quite so deep as that of the orchestral Horn, and with a fairly definite throat. This type is still in vogue with some French players, as witness Lavignac's *Encyclopédie* of 1927, from which Fig. 20 A has been redrawn— the typical 'embouchure' of an instrument of rounded and mellow tone. During the 19th century, however, with the entry of the trombone into the military band and then the opera house where a more penetrating sound was desired, a more cup-like shape developed and what was virtually a new orchestral colour appeared, firm and brilliant when well produced, yet without the 'clash' of the military trumpet. That did not necessarily mean that discerning musicians could not still produce the old warmth, and in 1844 Berlioz was able to write that the trombones might 'chant like a choir of priests', but could also 'take part in the wild clamour of the orgy'—a fine example of Gallic extravagance, but none the less true! This, at its best, noble tone was that cultivated by the leading English players towards the end of the century, and was based on a mouthpiece such as that shown in Fig. 20 B, which is taken from Victor Mahillon's *Éléments d'Acoustique* of 1874.

B. *Tuning Devices (Bits, Shanks, Crooks, and Slides; Quick-Change Arrangements)*

At the beginning of Chapter 2 we spoke of 'so-called "natural" trumpets whose tube length *is fixed*, and whose only notes are those of the Harmonic Series peculiar to that tube length'. This is a perfectly valid generalisation, but we can easily see that, from the point of view of practical music-making, it implies serious limitations. At the period when the trumpet began to find a regular place in the orchestra and had to submit to the disciplines of ensemble playing, standards of pitch were indeed variable[7] and any instrument that could not adapt itself to them suffered a grave disability. The problem was, however, overcome by providing the player with a selection of short lengths of tubing, slightly tapered externally, called *bits* (Ger. *Setzstücke*), which could be inserted between the mouthpiece and the main tube. This method of fine adjustment was used extensively on all types of brasses up to the end of the 19th century. It is still employed in certain circumstances but the modern, and more stable, way is to introduce a short U-shaped telescopic slide, just friction tight, at some suitable bend in the main tube. In the trombone this is usually applied at the bell bow where it

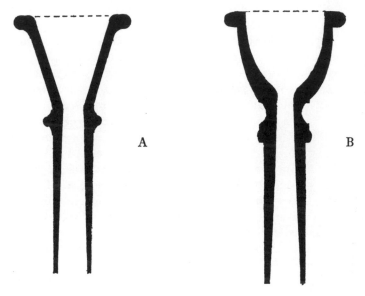

A   B

Fig. 20   Trombone mouthpieces. Extreme variations
of profile

does admittedly interfere a little with the regular expansion of the tube. There would seem, therefore, to be some acoustic advantage in the late George Case's system of placing the tuning slide at the bow of the main slide. This idea has not, however, found general favour. In the trumpet a single telescope at the end of the mouthpipe, with a binding screw to retain it, is sometimes though rather rarely found.

The composers who first brought the trumpet into the realm of Art-music had, of course, to accept the limited offering of the Harmonic Series, though they did not regard this as in any sense a defect in the instrument (see Chapter 11). It is, however, only a step from short tuning bits to longer accessory tubes designed to lower the pitch by recognised intervals such as the semitone, whole tone, or minor third. These, according to Praetorius, made their appearance round about 1600 and greatly extended the scope of horns and trumpets.[8] Thereafter composers were no longer confined to a single Harmonic Series from any one instrument, and it even became possible for a change to be made in the course of a piece if adequate time were allowed. Such accessory tubes when straight are termed *shanks*, or when curled up to reduce their over-all length *crooks* (Fr. *Corps de Rechange*; Ger. *Krummbogen* or more commonly just *Bogen*). Crooks could, of course, be combined with tuning-bits to effect both a basic change of pitch and a minor tuning adjustment at the same time. Indeed, there seems to have been no objection, other than mechanical instability, to using two crooks together. The great disadvantage of crooks with the trumpet (and even more with the horn) was the number and therefore weight that a fully equipped player, in the later years, had to carry. Gerber reports that by 1757 the maker Werner of Dresden was supplying horns with no less than nine, and by the end of the 18th century the possible complement of crooks and couplers had gone up to fifteen. The wish to get rid of such luggage may well have stimulated early experiments with valves quite as much as the desire for quicker transposing facilities in the orchestra.[9] The old natural trumpet, however, died hard, and even after the third valve had been added it long remained customary to provide crooks also.

The association of crooks and valves on the same instrument introduces an important aspect of tuning—what we may call 'internal tuning'. In a brass instrument the function of a valve is, quite simply, to change the fundamental pitch through a specific interval by adding on or cutting off a piece of supplementary tubing, and thus giving rise to a new Harmonic Series. For any given interval there is a fixed mathematical ratio between the length of the main tube and that of the supplement. But, because this ratio *is* a fixed one, if the main tube has already been lengthened by a crook, the supplementary one when added will be too short and the new Harmonic Series too sharp. This is in fact just the same difficulty which occurs when two or more valves are used together as mentioned in Chapter 1, and it will be considered again when we come to look at modern valve systems. The matter did not long escape the notice of brass-makers, and very few old instruments are known which do not have some provision for tuning the valve-tubes themselves. This was effected by bending them into parallel-sided loops and introducing the U-shaped telescopic slide. By these means the problem was more or less solved, but the device takes an appreciable time to adjust, and the marriage of crooks and valves remained rather an unhappy one.

In due time detached trumpet crooks passed out of use altogether, but valve tuning slides remain an essential feature of all well-designed instruments. The favourite general-purpose trumpet today is pitched in B♭, but it is sometimes convenient in orchestral playing to lower it to A♮. A shank for this purpose is nowadays quite out of fashion, and the necessary extra length is inserted in the mouthpipe either as a U-slide which can be quickly opened and closed by means of a touchpiece, or as a small loop switched in and out by a rotary valve with no return spring (Fr. *Barillet*). These devices are usually catalogued as 'quick changes'— somewhat of a misnomer, we may think, since they do not remove the need to adjust the valve slides also.

C. *Mutes*

The acoustic properties of mutes inserted in the bell of a brass instrument have already been touched upon in Chapter 1, and we shall consider their musical significance later. Here, then, it will be sufficient to give a general description of them, and perhaps to clear up one or two common misconceptions. The first is that the muting of brasses is a modern device originating in the world of trivial music and only recently admitted to respectability by serious composers. Nothing, indeed, could be farther from the truth. Trumpet mutes for musical purposes as distinct from military have been known at least since the early 17th century, and a drawing of one is to be found in Mersenne's *Harmonie Universelle*. The identity of the first of the major composers to write for muted trumpets has been a source of controversy among musicologists; Mozart and also Berlioz have been credited with the innovation, but a passage calling for mutes in Alessandro Scarlatti's *Mitridate Eupatore* of 1707 antedates both.[10] The appetite of the restless twenties for new sensations of every kind led to the use of a bewildering variety of mutes in the dance band, and this has perhaps given a false impression.

The other common misapprehension regarding mutes is that their primary object is to reduce the *volume* of sound. It is true that a certain mute on a trumpet played *pp* may give an effect of *distance* but it does so by modifying the harmonic content of a complex tone, rather than by any marked reduction of over-all dynamic. The same mute used in a fortissimo may have a very different effect. We may note here that the second and constricted bell of the Echo Cornet mentioned in note (3), p. 45, is nothing more than a mute incorporated in the permanent structure of the instrument.

Today a mute or two will be found among the equipment of almost every trumpet and trombone player, 'straight' or dance band. They are made in endless variety, from the simple conical plug bored down the centre to the dance band man's bowler hat, though, as with the proverbial old man's potatoes, there are probably 'more names than sorts'. The materials used are wood, glass, metal, fibre, or cardboard, the latter covered with leather-cloth. Probably the commonest form is a hollow truncated cone served at the narrow end where it enters the bell with a ring of cork—if there is a clear through passage—or with detached strips of cork if the base is completely closed. The average mute has little or no effect on the pitch of the instrument but some are provided with a so-called tuning slide. The internal arrangements again vary a great deal, but the majority of mutes have some sort of re-entrant tube. Fig. 21 shows the outer appearance of a selection from recent catalogues, and it may be said that these are by no means the strangest that are to be seen.

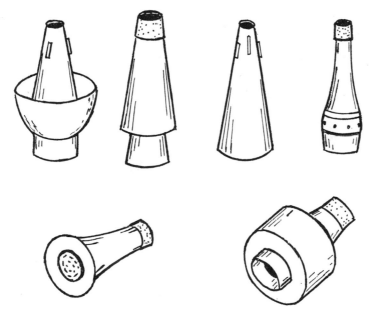

Fig. 21   Mutes sketched from recent catalogues

To round off this descriptive section we must notice briefly a number of ancillary features which are today part and parcel of both the trumpet and the trombone. Some of these date back to the earliest entry of the instruments into organised music, while others represent mechanical improvements or reflect changes in musical usage that developed subsequently.

D. *Stays, Guards, and Strengthening Pieces*

Today rigidity of the whole structure is regarded as a *sine qua non* in brass instruments, but this has not by any means always been so. The earliest bent trumpets, if we can rely on the evidence of 14th- and 15th-century painters, were simply folded in a flattened S shape with the yards and bows all in one plane and no stays or girders of any kind. In the next phase, which seems to have become stabilised during the 16th century, the trumpet was further compressed by, as it were, twisting the two bows in opposite directions so that the bell and mouth-pipes were brought parallel to each other and only about an inch and a half apart. Some support was then provided by placing a shaped block of wood between the two tubes and wrapping them with a strip of cloth, or ornamental cord which also formed a carrying sling. This block of wood is described in the Koch *Lexicon* as late as 1802. The characteristic of the arrangement was its essential *looseness* and a similar feature appears in early trombones also. Here, of course, at least two stays were absolutely necessary, one across the top of the slide, and one between the middlepipe and the mouthpipe near the socket. Even these, however, were quite loosely fitted, being made of flat metal with a hinged clasp at each end which surrounded the tube and was kept

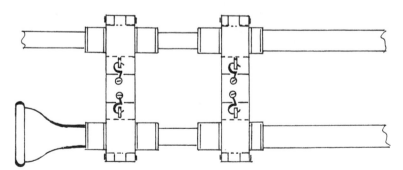

Fig. 22   Principle of loose stays on sackbut

closed by a hasp with a turn-hook or a peg (Fig. 22). Between the clasp and the tube was a cloth or leather packing. In the great majority of antique trombones a third stay was fitted between the middlepipe and

the root of the bell. Pictures dating from the early 16th century occasionally show sackbuts without this third stay, but actual specimens are
extremely rare. The Jobst. Schnitzer instrument already mentioned
(p. 64 note 7) is one such, but even here we cannot be certain that a
detachable stay has not been lost. The woodcuts in Praetorius (1618)
certainly suggest detachable stays in all three places, but in the celebrated Neuschel sackbut of 1557 we find a *fixed* bell stay which appears
to be contemporary with the other two which are movable. The reason
for this deliberate looseness in the staying of early brasses is not, as
far as I am aware, to be found in any contemporary writings, and we
can only surmise that it arose from a (possibly erroneous) idea that
such instruments would sound more easily if the tube itself had some
freedom to vibrate.[11] It was certainly not due to any lack of technical
ability among the old metal workers. Furthermore, it is known from
some few early instruments that have come down to us in an unaltered
state that these were originally made with all their components, bell,
yards, and bows, separate and dismountable. The various sections were
simply held together by well-fitting sleeves or *ferrules*, and the whole
affair kept reasonably rigid by the above-mentioned cloth binding or
loose stays. Still, one cannot be altogether surprised by such an entry
as the following from the Lord Chamberlain's accounts for February 20th,
1685, 'Received Thomas Barwell's trumpett, all broke to peeces, which
was Culthrop's, weight 16 oz.'[12] Sometimes a link of wire was passed
through a small hole in the bell rim of a trumpet and passed around the
upper yard.[13] On the inner curve of the bows we often find soldered
small rings through which, no doubt, a string or thong was passed.
These, clearly illustrated in Virdung (1511), should not be confused
with the larger rings sometimes found on the middle pipe of modern
State Trumpets and which are intended to keep a tied-on banner spread
out. Such a construction, rickety though it may seem to modern eyes,
speaks highly for the skill of the old makers for, of course, these joints
would require to be airtight without benefit of solder.[14] Today ferrules
are used primarily to strengthen the ends of tubes such as the mouthpipe
or to reinforce permanent end-to-end joins. Together with stays, they
have from the earliest days afforded opportunities for decoration in
the prevailing taste; hence the older term *garnishes*. There are certain
traditional ornaments, such as a rope-like spiral, which are found on
these from the 16th century right up to the mid 19th. The embossed
or chased ball which appears about the middle of the bellpipe of most
natural trumpets even at the present day seems to have been inherited

from the pre-folding days and probably represents a rather specialised ferrule associated with an expanding tube.[15] From about the second half of the 16th century loose stays on the trombone began to give place to permanently fixed ones, either flat or tubular, and planted on small supplementary plates curved to fit the pipes. Sometimes both types are found together, and in such cases we must be on the look-out for replacements, older or newer. The tubular stay is the common form on all modern brass instruments though some makers are now turning again to flat strips of metal profiled according to recent trends in decoration, typography, etc. The quantity of tubing involved in modern valved instruments makes strong and ample staying essential, but even this will not stand up to actual abuse. The writer still sometimes thinks with a shudder of a trumpet of his which a weary film extra once unwisely used as a shooting-stick during a long wait on the set. The most vulnerable parts of brass instruments, as no doubt many readers have noticed, are the outermost bows of the main tubing, so these are frequently protected by *guards*, pieces of thicker metal moulded to the appropriate curve and soldered on. Occasionally the guard even carries a projecting fin and here, too, the maker has indulged his taste in ornament, sometimes producing veritable brazen cocks' combs. On the whole, the bell appears to be less frequently damaged than the tubing, possibly by reason of its very size. One does not so easily forget the most conspicuous feature of one's instrument even in casual daily handling. The rim of the bell does, nevertheless, call for mechanical strengthening of some sort and several methods have been devised. In early days, a suitably coned or curved ring of thin metal an inch or so wide was fitted outside the open end and its edge turned over that of the bell proper, little or no solder being used. This is termed the *bellband* or *garland* (Fr. *guirlande*; Ger. *Schallrand*). From about the middle of last century the method of attachment has generally been reversed, the edge of the bell being rolled *outwards* over the band. With either method it is common to find a wire, usually of iron, incorporated inside the rolled edge. The majority of modern instruments, with the frequent exception of the Orchestral Horn, are made without a garland, but the bell itself is 'spun' over a ring of wire. This, when well done, provides an excellent firm 'bead' to the bell rim, but it has been known for the wire to work loose and become a source of great annoyance. Moreover, once it has been damaged the wired rim is difficult to repair. In the 1930s trumpets and trombones with a plain bell unreinforced, except by some thickening of the actual metal near the edge, were assiduously pushed by certain makers, and some acoustic virtues were claimed for them, but they do not appear to have gained any lasting foothold. It is hardly surprising that the garland with its fairly wide surface has also come in for much decoration. Its generally thin substance makes it suitable for repoussé work, and here again traditional designs are recognised, notably embossed cherubs, or a repeated shell pattern; sometimes cast metal ornaments have been used. On the garland, too, is the obvious place for the maker's name, trade mark, mottoes etc., and on many older examples the date of manufacture. No doubt many musical historians would be glad if the old custom of dating had been more generally retained.

E. *Ancillary Fittings*

It is almost inevitable in the playing of any wind instrument that there will be some accumulation of moisture, and with narrow and convoluted tubes it can readily become an embarrassment to the player. This fact, incidentally, is the subject of another popular misconception. Contrary to a widely held lay belief, saliva forms only a small fraction of the liquid which gathers. It is really condensed water vapour from the player's breath—in fact, distilled water. Nevertheless, it is a nuisance to the musician to have frequently to unship a section of his instrument and empty it out, while to the onlooker this is often either funny or disgusting. A more elegant way is provided by the *water key* which is simply a small drainage tube or nipple kept tightly closed by a padded key with a strong spring like that on a woodwind instrument. The drain is placed at the point to which the moisture naturally gravitates during performance, in the trumpet usually on the bow of the mouthpipe, and in the trombone on the slide bow. Water keys are usually built into modern instruments as supplied by the makers, but they can also be obtained as accessories to be fixed to older ones.

We have already on p. 49 made reference to the constantly shifting centre of gravity of the slide trombone, and some players find this, especially in the lower positions, something of a strain on the supporting hand. The trouble is an intrinsic one which by its very nature cannot be entirely cured. By careful attention to average balance it can, however, be greatly eased, and to this end makers often build in a balance weight at the bell bow. Separate weights can also be obtained which clip on and can be adjusted to the individual player's liking.

Finally we should mention *music lyres* or *card holders*. These are spring clips on stems which can be attached to some convenient point on the instrument to carry small music cards which military or brass band musicians may read when on the march. The actual position of the lyre will vary somewhat according to the player's sight and probably the detachable sort which fixes on to the instrument by means of a metal band, termed a *ligature*, tightened by screws is the best. Permanent attachments for the lyre stem are, however, often provided.

NOTES

[1] This is, or should be, a matter of concern not only to the player himself but to his dentist. See 'Dental Aspects of Orchestral Wind Instrument Playing with Special Reference to the "Embouchure"' by Maurice M. Porter, L.D.S. Eng., *British Dental Journal*, Vol. XCIII, No. 3, pp. 66–73, August 1952.

[2] In 1941 the late W. F. H. Blandford told the writer that he then knew of a mouthpiece-maker in the United States who regularly made brass mouthpieces to order for individual clients, and that for this purpose he always prepared preliminary casts of their teeth. I am not aware of anything so advanced as this in Great Britain.

[3] It seems possible that this idea may have been suggested by some fancied analogy with the 'nicking' of certain organ pipes.

[4] The modern Cornet, short for *Cornet à pistons*, is now best known as the treble soloist of the Brass Band. It developed, by the addition of valves, c. 1825, to a small horn, usually about four feet long, known in France as the *cornet* and elsewhere as the *post horn*. For a period, such instruments found a place in French and Belgian military bands as the *cornet simple* or *cornet ordinaire*. Originally these instruments had a deep funnel mouthpiece, but before their demise this had become rather shallower and more of the trumpet pattern. It is this later form which survives on the modern valve instruments. (Compare with the trumpet and French Horn mouthpieces illustrated in the text.) Unlike its 'natural' form which was almost completely conical from end to end, the modern cornet incorporates a quantity of cylindrical tubing largely necessitated by the valve mechanism, and, owing to its over-all shortness, this amounts to nearly half the entire instrument when all three valves are in use together. From time to time ingenious though complicated valve systems (e.g. Webster's) have been devised which to some extent preserve the conicity, but these have not found such favour as to be in common use today. The tone of the cornet, while warm and appealing when well played, lacks the heroic quality of the true trumpet.

[5] The French have always been more rational than other nations in their use of the cornet. Their composers have often deliberately employed it in the orchestra in place of the trumpet when its suaver tone has appeared desirable, and sometimes separate and contrasted parts have been written in the same composition. In British orchestral circles the cornet is still subject to some prejudice as a result of having at one period been unfairly used as a substitute for the trumpet in essentially *trumpet* parts. The matter is well presented by Cecil Forsyth in his *Orchestration*, Macmillan & Co., London, second edition, 1935, p. 107.

[6] The mouthpieces found with old wind instruments are all too often not contemporary and can be very misleading. Their provenance should always be investigated with great care.

[7] The vagaries of pitch standards in Europe between the 14th and 20th centuries are well discussed and summarised by Alexander Wood in *The Physics of Music*, London, Methuen & Co., third edition, 1945, pp. 46 *et seq.* See also Chapter 6, p. 126 note 11.

[8] Praetorius informs us that crooks were a comparatively recent invention at the time he was writing. This may account for some uncertainty in the older German nomenclature where we find the terms *Stimmbogen*, *Krummbügel*, *Aufsatzbogen*, *Aufsteckbogen*, and *Einsatzbogen* all employed without any very clear distinction as to type or purpose.

[9] In 19th-century France particularly, the problem was attacked in a different manner with various attempts to produce 'Omnitonic' horns which should incorporate in their permanent structure all the tubing necessary for the different pitches in common use. These very ingenious affairs are fully discussed by Morley-Pegge in his book on the French Horn in this series, to which readers are referred.

[10] E. J. Dent, *Alessandro Scarlatti*, London, Edward Arnold, 1905: new impression 1960, p. 109. This is the earliest reference to muted *orchestral* trumpets at present known to the writer. The passage in the Opera is interesting for several reasons. Directions in the score call for 'Due Trombe nell' Orchestra alla Sordina'—'Two Trumpets in the Orchestra to the Mute'—and these are answered by two 'Trombe Marine'. The latter, as Professor Dent has very cogently argued, can hardly have been the stringed Tromba Marina or Nonnengeige, in England called 'Mock Trumpet', which was almost obsolete by 1707, and in any case little known at any period in Italy. In *Mitridate Eupatore* the Trombe Marine appear to have been 'stage' trumpets played on board a property ship on the scene, an early example of the device so effectively used by Verdi 164 years later in Act II of *Aida*. Scarlatti's two pairs of trumpets each had, we note, their associated drum, which seems to be throw-back to the more formal customs of the pre-orchestral period.

As early as 1649 we find a muted *solo* trumpet specified in a work of Marcus Ucellinus—*Sonate ovver Canzoni da Farsi a Violino solo et B.c.*, published in Venice by Alessandro Vincenti. A copy is in the Breslau Municipal Library.

[11] This would seem to be wasteful of the player's energy. The idea is contrary to modern acoustic thought—except among certain saxophone players who say that they like to feel the body of the instrument actually vibrate in the hand while playing it. Such vibration of the body tube might well exert a secondary influence on the contained air column and affect tone colour by reinforcing or suppressing certain partials.

[12] H. C. de Lafontaine, *The King's Musick*, London, Novello & Co., 1909, p. 373.

[13] An excellent detailed study of this feature in English trumpets of the Restoration period appears in the *Galpin Society Journal*, No. XV, March 1962, over the signature of E. Halfpenny. It is to be noted that in these the bell and mouthpipes are *not* parallel but cross each other at the 'ball' which is excavated to allow this.

[14] It occurs to the writer that grease might have been used to 'lute' the joints as modern players do in an emergency with chewing-gum, but he has no direct evidence to offer.

[15] See a Buisine reputedly by Sebastian Hainlein of Nürnberg illustrated by F. W. Galpin in *Old English Instruments of Music*, Methuen & Co., London, second edition, 1932, p. xii. Also Plate 10 B.

CHAPTER 5

Origins: The Trumpets of Primitive Peoples: The Trumpet in Antiquity

IN EMBARKING on a condensed history of any orchestral instrument used today the first question is where to begin, and almost inevitably the writer must make an arbitrary decision. In the case of woodwinds the difficulty is perhaps not too acute for, although the basic principles involved go back into the mists of pre-history, the point at which any instrument began to take on its modern form is usually pretty clear. In the case of the modern oboe, for example, not only the time of its emergence, but the men responsible are known almost with certainty. The situation is different in respect of the modern trumpet. Here we have an instrument which appears in two forms, one with advanced mechanism whose detailed history we know, the other a simple apparatus not fundamentally different from the earliest known examples. The trombone again is a different matter, for here we can trace and approximately date its emergence as an offshoot of the simple trumpet. Our starting point in trumpet history, therefore, should logically be made as far back as any evidence permits and this takes us into pre-historic times.

It is a generally accepted principle in Ethnological research that we may gain some idea of the life of pre-historic people by observing the behaviour of primitive races who still live in remote parts of the world in what we believe to be pre-historic conditions, as shown by the character of their artifacts, dwellings, and so on. Thus, for instance, we sometimes hear of the 'stone-age' people of central New Guinea. While it is no doubt basically sound, this principle must nevertheless be applied with considerable caution. We have no means of knowing for certain that the modern primitive and the pre-historic communities we wish to compare actually thought along the same lines, or indeed if they represent the same stage of mental development. Similarity in their artifacts may have been dictated by the availability of similar raw material, the result of mere geographical accident. The behaviour of a modern primitive community may not be a sure guide since it may possibly be conditioned by the very circumstances which make it amenable to observation. However normally the life of a community may appear to go on in the presence of such accustomed figures as the District Officer or the resident Missionary Doctor, it is probably not quite the same life as goes on in their absence. Further, in the particular matter of musical instruments, we must consider that today we find the continued use of quite unsophisticated 'home-made' folk instruments in the remoter parts of some European countries whose general level of culture is as high as any, and whose metropolitan centres provide up-to-date symphony orchestras of international repute. From these two or three examples alone it is evident that the musico-ethnologist must proceed with great care and weigh up many factors before pronouncing. There is today a large literature on special aspects of this very big subject but, apart from the monumental work of the late Professor Curt Sachs,[1] comparatively little that is comprehensive. It is mainly on Sachs that we shall draw in this chapter.

Primitives

In considering primitive trumpets the first thing we must note is that in the earlier stages no distinction was made between cylindrical and tapered tubes, and even as late as Roman times the difference was much less clearly appreciated than it is today. For this reason the word *trumpet* as used by ethnologists when writing of these periods has a *general* connotation only and, as we shall see presently, is more embracing than suits the strict musician. The distinction which we now value so much only makes itself felt at that stage of musical perception where tone colour and contrast become important, though it may well have been recognised to some extent long before either horns or trumpets were admitted into Art-music. We know, for instance, that the Romans reserved the *Lituus*, a cylindro-conical trumpet, for cavalry use, while the conical *Tuba* appears to have been used only by foot soldiers. This parallels our own use of cavalry trumpet and infantry bugle and suggests that distinctive tones were even then important in military signals.

In the foregoing paragraph a single line of thought has led us in one jump, we may observe, from the primitive to a highly developed Civilisation. We must return; and in doing so we may take warning that in all instrumental history, however circumscribed our immediate interest may be, we shall encounter such threads of continuity again and again.

The most primitive instruments that ethnologists regard as trumpets are not lip-energised at all, but are used as resonators to concentrate and distort the natural voice, either in magical rites or to frighten enemies in war; they are in fact *megaphones* of a sort. For such a purpose finely proportioned tubes, even if available, would have no special merit. On the contrary, the more hideous the howls, roars, or grunts of the witch-doctor or the warrior the more powerful their effect. Hence the employment of a wide variety of naturally occurring hollow bodies, horns, bones, shells, and plant stems. The use of lip-energised tubes as actual sound producers was, as it were, a 'second-stage' discovery though we cannot associate it with any specific period in human development.[2] We do know, however, that the megaphone and lip-reed principles are found side by side among a number of primitive races today. A particularly interesting illustration is provided by the *didgeridu* of the Australian aborigines which demonstrates both together.* In playing this instrument a basic note is sounded with the lips while the player elicits other harmonics by humming or roaring at the same time.[3] The didgeridu also illustrates the relative unimportance of tube proportions at this stage of progress, as well as the influence of available materials. Commonly the instrument is made from a tree branch from which the heart-wood has been eaten out by termites or other insects. Having found his hollow branch, the would-be player has to accept the bore (usually conical) presented to him by the insects. In certain parts of the country, however, large canes are the handy raw material and these, of course, furnish a cylindrical tube. Either type seems to suit the aborigine equally well.

From time to time the megaphone has also found its place in organised music. According to Sachs, in some Catholic cantons of Switzerland it is the custom to sound an Alp Horn at sunset while the evening prayer is intoned through a megaphone. Thus, in a present day rite we find preserved the true trumpet principle together with the earlier concept of the trumpet as a resonator. In some English country churches megaphones or 'Vamp-Horns' are known to have been used in the absence of instrumental support to the singing.

In this case unlike that of the witch-doctor or tribal rain-maker, distortion of the voice is obviously a disadvantage, and there is evidence that at one time a good deal of thought was given to the matter. For example, in the parish of East Leake in Northamptonshire, there is preserved a large vamp-horn of thin sheet iron which, though doubtless made according to rule-of-thumb experience, comes quite surprisingly

* See Appendix 3, p. 256.

near to exponential form. This, as we have seen in Chapter 1, is the type of horn which has the most even response over a wide range of frequencies.

About 1930 the dance band world was hit by a passing craze for the so-called 'sub-tone'. This was a rather pleasant sombre sound produced by playing a clarinet *sotto voce* in the low register with the instrument completely inside a conical megaphone with two holes in the side through which the player passed his hands. Here the natural sound of the clarinet was of course much distorted but the effect was by no means unpleasing though somewhat flabby and lacking in character.

We have already said that we do not know exactly when the lip-reed principle was first discovered, and we must admit that we do not know *how* either. We can *imagine* all sorts of possible circumstances which might have led to the discovery and farther we cannot go, though perhaps just one conjecture may be permitted here if only for the sake of the delightful picture it conjures up. To quote Canon Galpin[4]: 'It has been suggested that the method of raising the sound waves by the vibration of the lips was discovered by our forefathers' preprandial requirements or postprandial satisfaction. One of the earliest forms of lip-voiced instrument is the spiral shell, found as the *Čank* or conch-trumpet in Asia and as the *Biou* in Europe. Now, in order to get at the fish concealed within it, it was necessary to break off the tip of the shell and either to push it or blow it out. With the final blast that heralded the meal the vibration of the lips was discovered.' Is this idea too fanciful? Perhaps we may think so, but it is interesting to note that Sachs distinguishes between two forms of ancient conch-trumpet, an early one with the shell perforated at the apex, and a much later one, dating only from the *end* of the pre-Christian era, which has an opening in the side. It is evident, I think, that a hole so placed could have served a musical purpose only. It would have been of very little use in extracting the mollusc from its shell.

Historically, side-blown trumpets in general make their appearance later than the end-blown type. Sachs places these in the latest stratum of his Chronology, corresponding to Neolithic cultures, while he equates end-blown varieties with Paleolithic excavations. Side-blown trumpets of the Bronze Age are known from sites in Ireland and the type persists today among the South American Indians and certain African tribes who fashion them out of antelope horns or elephant tusks. As we have seen in Chapter 1, there is no acoustical difficulty in energising an air column at any point along its length, but it is clear that the transverse trumpet does not lend itself to development as does the end-blown type and all our modern instruments stem from the latter.

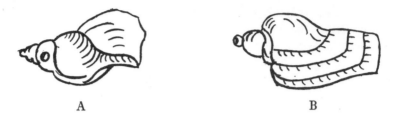

A   B

Fig. 23   Two conch Shell 'trumpets': A Primitive side-blown version, B Sophisticated end-blown instrument with an attached mouthpiece and incised ornament

Antiquity

Between prehistoric man and the earliest Civilisations with something of a recorded history we encounter the first great gap in our knowledge of musical instruments, though this, to be sure, represents a break in a cultural sense rather than any definite time interval. We must remember that the terms Paleolithic, Neolithic, Bronze Age, etc., signify phases in Man's technological development and not particular divisions of an absolute time scale. Nor did these phases necessarily give place to their successors at the same time in all parts of the world. Thus, the Stone Age drew to a close in the Middle East with the discovery of metals about 4000 years B.C. but in Britain Stone Age culture persisted for at least another two millennia. Further, we have some evidence to show that certain prehistoric peoples, though they may have lacked writing as a means of communication, had a way of life that was by no means primitive. Our difficulty lies in linking the prehistoric with the remote historic, and it was during this interregnum that a new concept emerged —that of music as art or for entertainment, and with it the seeds of a professional class of musicians. From this point on we can begin to divide instruments into two categories, folk or popular instruments, and those cultivated by professional players, though, of course, the two need not be mutually exclusive. Also, with written evidence to draw upon, we have to distinguish if we can between factual accounts, legends which may or may not be founded on fact, and frank mythology.

The history of the higher civilisations as it concerns us here appears to begin in Mesopotamia, the once-fertile plain between the Rivers

Tigris and Euphrates which is today divided between the States of Syria and Iraq. Here the earliest recorded rulers were the Sumerians, a people of uncertain race who seem to have entered the area from farther east between 5000 and 4000 years B.C. The writing of these people was Cuneiform and, since the problem of interpreting this script has been solved, Sumerian texts have yielded invaluable information on many subjects. After some 2000 years of occupation, more or less overlapping the period of the 'Old Kingdom' in Egypt, the Sumerians gave place to the Babylonians, a Semitic race. About 1750 B.C. the Kassites, a non-Semitic people, invaded, again from the east. These were succeeded in turn by Assyrians, again Babylonians (the Dynasty of King Nebuchadnezzar and period of the Babylonian exile of the Jews), and the Medes and Persians. Finally, from 331 B.C. the land fell under the domination of the Greeks as they extended their Empire eastwards and into Egypt. The following comparative table will help us to relate these phases with the generally more familiar history of Ancient Egypt and Greece. The figures indicate approximate dates B.C.

Mesopotamia		*Egypt*		*Greece*	
Sumerians	−2040	Old Kingdom	−2016	Early Crete	−2100
Babylonians	2040–1750	Middle		Middle	
		Kingdom	2016–1580	Crete	2100–1580
Kassites	1750–1160	New		Late Crete	1580–1400
		Kingdom	1580–1090		
Assyrians	1160–625	Nubians	1090–663	The Dorian Migration	
				during 11th century.	
Babylonians	625–538	Saites	663–382	The Classic Period	
				6th–4th centuries	
Medes and					
Persians	538–331				
Greeks	331–	Greeks	332–	Period of Alexander	
				336–323	

Excavations in Mesopotamia have yielded few actual musical instruments, and most of those we do have were found in the Royal cemetery at Ur, the birthplace of Abraham. On the other hand, illustrations of musical instruments and scenes on seals, sculptures, and mosaics from a period extending over three thousand years are fairly plentiful. Cuneiform texts contain a number of names of musical instruments, and the historians' particular problem has been to correlate the two in a satisfactory way.

From Mesopotamia comes the earliest account we have so far of the making of a musical horn or trumpet. It is found in a very ancient narrative (4000–3000 B.C.) of the labours of the Sumerian hero Gilgamesh, and it is most interesting to see that the Hero made his instrument from the hollow branch of a tree with a portion of larger bore attached at the end. Here we have again the basic construction and materials of the didgeridu, but with an added refinement that belongs to a rather more advanced culture than that of the Australian Aborigine.[5] We note also that, according to Canon Galpin, the Sumerian word used for the tube of this instrument also signified a 'reed'. Animal horns decorated with metals and precious stones are mentioned more than occasionally in Cuneiform scripts and these bear testimony to the technical and artistic abilities of the people. A detailed inventory of presents offered by King Tushratta to Amenophis IV of Egypt about 1400 B.C. lists forty such instruments, of which seventeen are particularly described as ox-horns and were presumably of the natural curved shape. Straight trumpets were also known to these people; they are recorded as sometimes made of gold, and as late as the Assyrian epoch they are depicted in the hands of soldiers, though it seems unlikely that the precious metal was used for military duty. No specifically cylindrical trumpets, either straight or curved, have been secured from Mesopotamian sites but some surviving illustrations suggest their existence.

Egypt

The average man with a mild interest in Antiquity is probably more aware today of the Art of Egypt than of that of any other ancient civilisation, and we can suggest several reasons for this. In the first place most of the major research in Egypt has been done during the last century and spectacular discoveries have been made within living memory. In contrast the great relics of Greece and Rome have 'always been there' since the dawn of our present West European civilisation. Next, the Egyptian remains are extraordinarily rich and, with modern transport, reasonably accessible. Due to two World Wars more people have travelled widely than ever before and, except politically, frontiers have largely lost their significance. Finally the advance of modern typography and colour printing has brought to all who may be interested material that a generation ago could only be found in scholars' books.

The methods and lines of reasoning employed by the archaeologist are inevitably influenced by many factors which will vary from one part of the world to another, and indeed from one investigation to the next. In respect of Ancient Egypt two such factors are of special importance to the musicologist. One is the climate, the other the psychology of the people. The extreme aridity of much of the country has favoured the preservation of organic materials, with the result that more or less complete musical instruments have been recovered in some quantity. As to psychology, for long periods the religious ideas of the Egyptians were dominated by the concept of a heaven in which the redeemed would live an idealised version of his earthly existence. The belief that representations of happy domestic scenes, feasting, singing, dancing, etc., could by magic influence assure the same felicity in the after-life gave birth to a wealth of tomb paintings and sculptures in which musical instruments figure often. Moreover, the tomb painters had a charming habit of filling in spaces in their compositions with simple written captions from which we know the authentic names of nearly all Egyptian instruments.

During the earlier periods of their history there seems to have been much contact between the great civilisations of Mesopotamia and of Egypt and in musical matters the relationship is particularly evident. Every instrument known to the Old Kingdom in Egypt was also possessed by the Sumerians at the same time and possibly earlier. At some time before about 2700 B.C., however, the link seems to have been broken.[6] The Kassite invasion from Central Asia ended the first Babylonian era, and that of the nomadic Hyksos destroyed the Egyptian Middle Kingdom. A period of darkness followed about which we have little information, but with the emergence of the New Kingdom, whose warlike rulers in their turn took the initiative and penetrated eastwards, fresh influences become evident. Rather surprisingly the characteristics of Egyptian music now appear as strongly Asiatic, as if the invaders had absorbed the culture and habits of the lands they conquered instead of imposing their own. It is from the New Kingdom that we have the first account of trumpets in Egypt and also the oldest known specimen of an all metal instrument with a cylindrical body tube. The celebrated trumpets from the tomb treasure of King Tut-ankh-amen which have already been described in our introduction belong to this type and there are paintings which show similar ones, but at this period a more completely conical form seems to have been commoner. These instruments are usually shown as played by soldiers but they are also known to have been used in the worship of Osiris. According to Eustathios, Homer's commentator, the invention of the trumpet was attributed to the god himself, and clay models of horns and trumpets are well known among votive objects of the Greek period in Egypt.

The length of known Egyptian trumpets averages only about two feet so their fundamental pitch approximates to our c′; an octave, say, above the modern duty bugle. Their average diameter suggests that they are unlikely to have produced more than the first, second, and third harmonics but, as we shall see in connection with Roman examples, the capabilities of an ancient instrument are not a reliable guide to its original use. It is quite probable that Egyptian military trumpets were only used rhythmically. Of their tone Plutarch remarks rather scornfully that it resembled the braying of an ass. This tends to suggest what we should today regard as overblowing, for, although very short tubes lip-energised do not produce a particularly rich sound, they need not be quite so disagreeable. The writer well remembers hearing one of the Tut-ankh-amen trumpets sounded by a skilled player in a B.B.C. broadcast in 1939 and the tone then suggested the 'tooting' of an English hunting horn at a lower pitch. The shorter of the two instruments then sounded approximately our b′, f♯′, and b″. Dr. Hans Hickmann, in his monograph on ancient Egyptian trumpets,[7] states that on this occasion a modern trumpet mouthpiece was applied to the instruments and that in these conditions the 4th, 5th, 6th, and 8th harmonics were obtainable. Dr. Hickmann himself experimented with facsimiles and says that in their natural state these produced two notes about a ninth apart— rather a curious acoustic anomaly we may think. See Plate 9 C.

Israel

The circumstances which face the enquirer into the musical activities of the Jewish people are very different from those affecting Egyptian or Sumerian research. Although the Jewish ritual *Shophar* is made and used today as it was in Old Testament times, this is the only ancient Hebrew instrument which we can now actually examine. As Mosaic teaching was opposed to depicting men or objects of any kind, scholars are deprived of the help of contemporary painting or sculpture, and philological sources are almost all that are available. The bulk of our information, then, is drawn from the Bible and the Talmud.

The ancient history of the Jews can be conveniently divided into the *Nomadic Period* which lasted till about 1000 B.C., and the *Period of the Kings* extending up to the dawn of Christianity. In the Pentateuch we find comparatively little mention of music, though, as Sachs has been at pains to point out, this does not mean that it was unusual or disdained. On the contrary, the references we have show that music was a common and universal expression of the people both in joy and in sorrow. At that period they differed only from some of their contemporaries in not recognising a specific musician class.

The shophar, being by all criteria a *horn*, is not itself of primary interest to us in this book, but we may note that it produces only two harmonics, the octave of the fundamental and the twelfth (see p. 6). Thus the player can command only two notes a fifth apart. In the ritual

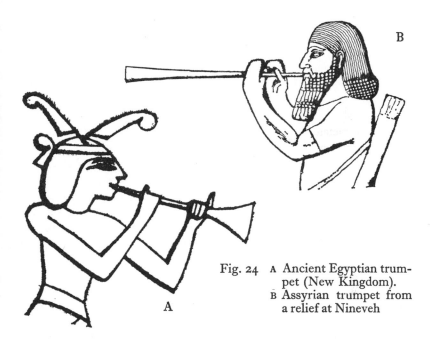

Fig. 24 A Ancient Egyptian trumpet (New Kingdom).
B Assyrian trumpet from a relief at Nineveh

of the Synagogue these two notes are used in four rhythmic combinations which are prescribed and discussed in the Talmudian Tractates *Rosh-hashana* III and IV. These rhythmic measures are known to have been codified in the first or second century B.C., but they are probably much earlier in origin.

From Scriptural sources we learn that trumpets, *Hatzotzeroth*, were also known to the nomadic Jews. Verses 1–10 of the tenth chapter of the Book of Numbers are particularly important in this connection, for they contain the Divine command to Moses: 'Make thee two trumpets of silver; of a whole piece shalt thou make them; that thou mayest use them for the calling of the assembly, and for the journeying of the camps.' Not only do these verses show unmistakably the purpose of the instruments, but they give us a measure of the technical skill of the Israelitish metal workers. The Tractate *Rosh-hashana* III is also specially valuable in that it sets out the particular functions of *shopharim* and *hatzotzeroth* and their relations to each other in traditional Jewish ritual. The Hebrew trumpets were evidently similar to those of the Egyptians. According to Flavius Josephus they appeared as straight tubes 'a little less than a cubit long' (i.e. something under 22 inches, perhaps rather shorter than the Egyptian average) and ending in a bell. Although, as we have said, the Jews did not depict their trumpets, a Roman sculptor has done so, for one figures on the Triumphal Arch of Titus together with other holy objects looted from the Temple at the conquest of Jerusalem. This sculpture corresponds to many Egyptian representations.

In the 11th century B.C. a complete reorganisation of Jewish life took place and the old Patriarchal system was replaced by a Monarchical government. The establishment of a Kingdom with a court modelled on those of neighbouring States opened the hitherto close Israelitish community to outside influences, and under Solomon there was a great influx of foreign ideas, especially from Egypt and from Phoenicia. At this time the whole picture of Jewish music changed; to what extent may be judged from a passage in the Tractate *Shabbat 56 b.* which says that when King Solomon took Pharaoh's daughter to wife she brought with her 'a thousand kinds' of musical instruments.

For the building of the first Temple, Solomon employed a veritable army of woodworkers from Tyre in Phoenicia, as well as the renowned master of metals, Hiram Abif, and these men undoubtedly introduced some instruments that were new to the Jews, notably a double reed-pipe which later the Romans called the 'Phoenician Pipe'. It must be admitted, however, that the records of this phase of Jewish history add little to our knowledge of the trumpet specifically, except to show how it quickly became an important element in pomp and ceremonial. Even before this, at the court of King David a class of professional instrumentalists had begun to develop, and he himself founded an official body of musicians to serve the Temple that was to be built. On the day of consecration under King Solomon no less than 120 priests sounded trumpets at the east end of the Altar (II Chronicles v. 12–14).

Greece and Rome

In such a condensed survey as this we may reasonably consider Greece and Rome together since in their times Southern Europe in general formed one musical area enjoying over-all the same heritage and influences. Basic instrumental types were the same throughout the area even if their names varied according to language or local usage.

The arts in which the Greeks excelled were those of Sculpture and Architecture, and, although naturally they derived technical principles from earlier civilisations, their genius was such as to create a classical canon which directed the progress of western art for 2,000 years and even influenced the Buddhist Orient. With such achievements in the visual arts it seems a little strange that music in Ancient Greece did not undergo a parallel development, but such appears to be the case. Certainly the Greeks worked out the mathematics of music to a very advanced degree and their philosophers discussed its psychological effects, but the *practice* of music seems in the first place to have been imported. The Phrygian and Lydian modes which became part of Greek musical organisation are interval sequences strongly reminiscent of some common in Asia Minor; and concerning instruments the geographer Strabo remarks: 'One writer says "striking the Asiatic cithara"; another calls auloi "Berecyntian" and "Phrygian"; and some instruments have been called by barbarian names.' Admittedly, when the Greek musical system with its scales and notation had been codified its terminology was clearly derived from instrumental allusions,[8] but the instruments themselves remained simple and indeed almost primitive by comparison with other appurtenances of Greek life. The words 'kitharody' and 'aulody', meaning the accompaniment of song on the kithara or the aulos, are common in Greek texts and indicate that among the Hellenes instrumental music was generally regarded as subordinate to, and taking its inspiration from, the spoken word. Plato, though he probably represented ultra-conservative opinion, went so far as to condemn pure instrumental performance as pointless 'show off' and to regard it as in the worst of taste. The literature of Ancient Greece abounds in references to music, as do her sculptures and especially her vase paintings. Here we repeatedly find representations of musical scenes and instruments, somewhat formalised it is true, but none the less informative for that. On the whole strings predominate among these illustrations, as we might perhaps expect since the invention of string music was traditionally attributed to Apollo. The *lyre* in particular symbolised for the Greeks the so-called Apollonian side of their ethos, harmony, moderation, and mental balance. Pipes on the other hand stood for the Dionysian aspect, ecstasy, and even inebriation. This, too, is readily understood, for the most prominent Greek wind instrument was the *aulos*, a reed-pipe of somewhat oriental appearance whose shrill voice could be as stimulating as any Highland bagpipe. In spite of a very persistent misconception, the aulos was no 'soft complaining flute'. This was the instrument that excited the warlike passions of Greek Heroes and encouraged the young men to prodigies on the athletic field.[9]

As far as we can now tell, trumpets seem to have held rather a minor position in Greek life, only one form being recorded. This, which they called *salpynx*, was a straight instrument no doubt closely related to similar Ancient Egyptian and Jewish types, and indeed, Sachs points out that philologically the s + vowel formation at the beginning of the name indicates a pre-Hellenic origin. To judge by the single surviving example, now preserved in the Museum of Fine Arts, Boston, Mass., and ascribed to the 5th century B.C., the Greek salpinx was rather longer than the more ancient instruments. The Boston specimen, which is made up of thirteen sections of ivory fitted together and furnished with bronze strengthening rings and a bronze bell, is just on 62 inches long. Its lowest available note would therefore approximate to our F or G. Lip adaptation was obtained not by any formal type of mouthpiece, although the external appearance suggests one, but by a slight coning out of the end of the tube (see p. 21, Stille Zink). As to the tone of the salpynx, Aeschylus in the *Eumenides* writes of it as *diatoros*—'yelling'.

In contrast to the Greek, when we turn to Roman sources we find abundant evidence of no less than four different types of brasses— or perhaps we should more properly call them 'bronzes'. Both the Greeks and the Romans attributed the invention of trumpets to the Etruscans whom they recognised as the great bronze workers of the Mediterranean area in pre-Celtic times, and bronze was the common material of these instruments. Like the trumpets of earlier civilisations, the four Roman types, *Tuba*, *Lituus*, *Cornu*, and *Buccina*, were all military instruments, but among them we find a much sharper definition of allotted duties than we have hitherto encountered. Horace, in his 'First Ode to Maecenas' writes '*Mutos castra iuvant et lituo tubae Permixtus sonitus*,' making a clear distinction between lituus and tuba, and in a commentary on the passage Torcellini clinches the matter thus: '*sunt qui lituum a tubae distinguunt, ex eo quod ille equitum sunt, haec vero peditum*'.[10]

The infantry tuba was the Roman equivalent of the salpynx and clearly shared the same parentage, although it seems generally to have been somewhat shorter than that instrument, if we may assume the dimensions of the Boston example to have been characteristic. A fine and typical specimen in the Etruscan Museum in Rome is just 46 inches long and the tube expands regularly from 0·4 inches at the mouthpiece end to 1·1 inches at the root of a moderately flaring bell. Its fundamental would therefore have been rather sharper than our four-foot c, and on an instrument of these relative proportions this note would probably have been playable. (See Plate 9 D.)

The cavalry Lituus, hooked like a capital J, is of particular interest as it represents the cylindro-conical or true trumpet in a form which demonstrates its ultimate origin. Quite clearly this instrument derived from the combination of a reed stem with a cow's horn as a bell, and just such a primitive construction is still to be found in Ethiopia and parts of Thailand. The bronze workers translated this into metal in its simplest terms and so created an instrument of great elegance. It seems probable that the Romans acquired the lituus through Etruscan or perhaps Greek sources, though we have at present no evidence that the Greeks themselves used such an instrument, and one of the finest surviving examples, now in the Vatican Museum, was unearthed at Cerveteri, at one time an important city of Etruria. This beautiful trumpet, of which there are facsimiles in several of the world's leading music collections, is just over 63 inches long and its pitch is about equal to our G. We have, it is true, certain rather indefinite evidence of litui of smaller size than the Vatican specimen, but this may be taken, I think, as typical of the instrument in its finest development. It is certainly the sort of instrument of which Acro was thinking when he observed that, though longer than the tuba, the lituus was 'acutus' in sound while the former was 'gravis'. Acro's comment is important, since it clearly suggests that the first sound of the slender lituus was the octave harmonic, while the rather larger-scaled tuba yielded its fundamental.

The third lip-voiced Roman instrument was the cornu, a large horn, gently tapered for the greater part of its length and with a moderate funnel-shaped bell. Its over-all length was some 11 feet, and with its adoption the Roman makers encountered the perpetual problem of all deep-toned wind instruments, the convenient disposal of a long tube.[11] In this case they solved it by coiling the tube in an open gyre about $3\frac{1}{2}$ feet across. A wooden rod, often highly ornamented with turning, was attached diametrically across the coil, and this the player rested on his shoulder. The cornu is frequently depicted in Roman sculpture and decoration and from these, as well as literary sources, we learn that its particular place was in high-ranking military activities, in the presence of the Commander-in-Chief where special fanfares were called for, in Triumphs and pageantry, and at Gladiatorial games. A number of cornua have survived in good enough condition to allow of reproduction, and on a facsimile a player with a modern mouthpiece has been able to produce a complete harmonic series from the 1st to about the 16th. This, however, as we have already pointed out, is no proof that Roman players used anything like so extensive a scale. Indeed it seems unlikely that they were even aware of the harmonic possibilities of a lip-voiced tube beyond the first two or three natural sounds. We know that it was the habit of Roman trumpeters to blow their instruments with great force and with the cheeks inflated. Sometimes they even supported their cheeks with the *capistrum*, a leathern head-band similar to the *phorbeia* used by Greek players of the double aulos. In such conditions the lips can, of course, do little to select upper partials or to control tone quality. In Roman literature there is much evidence on the latter point. The tuba has been termed 'horribilis', 'raucus', and 'rudis'; the sound of the lituus called 'stridor'—a shriek; and even the note of the long cornu was described by Horace as 'mimax murmur'—a threatening rumble. As we should expect with the techniques of highly skilled metal-workers available, the mouthpieces of Roman instruments are much more specialised than any which remain to us from earlier civilisations, and they clearly reveal a concern with heavy lip pressure. Unlike the modern rather flat everted ones designed to support the lips when under *tension*, the rims of most Roman mouthpieces appear as rounded cushions. A magnificent specimen from a cornu of *c.* A.D. 62 in the British Museum has an over-all diameter of $1\frac{1}{4}$ inches; the cup, which is nearly hemispherical, is just $\frac{1}{2}$ inch deep; but the rim, in the form of a rounded beading, is formed almost entirely on the *inside* of the cup. It is difficult to say if such mouthpieces were meant to be detachable or were permanently fixed to the body of the instrument. Being heavy castings they have often survived when the thinner metal of the body has perished, and when found together corrosion products have usually obscured the join. We may note, however, that they fitted *over* the end of the body tube.

Lastly, we come to the instrument known to Rome as the *Buccina*, and here we meet with some ambiguity. Originally the name signified the simple bugle-horn used to mark the four watches of the night in camp and to sound the reveille, but certain late classical writers extended the term to include the long cornu. This has caused some confusion

among later scholars interpreting Latin texts, and as a result we sometimes find illustrations of the long coiled horn labelled 'Buccina' and
its players 'Buccinatores' without any qualification or alternative title.
We must therefore be on the alert when consulting some of the 19th-
century musical history books.

INCHES.

Fig. 25   Section of cast bronze Roman mouthpiece,
c. A.D. 62—probably from a Cornu. (*Based on a specimen
in the British Museum.*)

The prototype of the buccina was the natural ox-horn with the tip
cut off and used either with or without a metal mouthpiece as it is by
country people today in many parts of the world. Virgil, in the *Aeneid*,
mentions the buccina specifically as the shepherds' instrument, and
later writers[12] attribute it to 'barbarian' peoples. In the Roman army
it took the form of an elegant tapered tube with no bell, and of a size
and curvature that clearly reveals its origin. The writer has been privi-
leged to experiment with one or two specimens in the British Museum,
and these, when the cracks due to perished solder are stopped up, are
quite easy to blow and by no means unmusical in sound. Here, though,
we must again note that we do not know what manner of blowing the
Romans used. Certainly their opponents blew similar horns with the
utmost violence, for we read in the second book of Polybius' *History*:
'The tumult of the army of the Celts terrified the Romans, for there was
amongst them an infinite number of horns and trumpets which . . .
made a clamour so terrible and loud that every surrounding echo was
awakened. . . .'

H

NOTES

¹ Curt Sachs, undoubtedly the greatest musico-ethnologist of this century, devoted a lifetime of study and travel to his subject. His *magnum opus Geist und Werden der Musikinstrumente* published in Berlin in 1929 became a classic in his own lifetime. Unfortunately it has not yet been translated into English. This work awaits the advent of a gifted linguist who is also an ethnologist and a profound philosopher.

² In his chapter on the Chronology of Early Instruments in *The History of Musical Instruments*, New York, 1940, and London, 1942, J. M. Dent and Sons, Sachs cites no trumpets from paleolithic excavations. He does, however, record both trumpets in a general sense and shells used as such from *neolithic* sites. There is clear evidence that the principle of the whistle-flute was known to prehistoric Man well before that of the lip-reed. Such flutes without side-holes have been found among paleolithic remains, and much more developed ones, with two or three holes, from the neolithic. An advanced example which has been fully investigated and which shows considerable musical possibilities is the 'Malham' pipe attributed with some certainty to the Iron Age in Great Britain, say between 200 B.C. and A.D. 200. See *The Galpin Society Journal*, No. V, 1952, pp. 28–38.

³ Dr. Trevor A. Jones, Department of Music, University of Western Australia, personal communication to the writer. See also: R. Morley-Pegge, *The French Horn*, pp. 147–8, on the subject of Horn Chords; E. G. Richardson, *The Acoustics of Orchestral Instruments*, p. 81.

⁴ F. W. Galpin, *A Textbook of European Musical Instruments*, London, Williams and Norgate, 1937, p. 214.

⁵ F. W. Galpin, *The Music of the Sumerians, Babylonians, and Assyrians*, Cambridge, The University Press, 1937.

⁶ Curt Sachs, *op. cit.*, p. 86.

⁷ Hans Hickman, 'La trompette dans l'Egypt ancienne', Cairo, *l'Institut français d'archéologie orientale*, 1946.

⁸ Curt Sachs, *op. cit.*, p. 129.

⁹ The use of a leathern mouthband, *phorbeia*, to support the cheeks as well as to locate the two reeds in playing the Greek double aulos has been cited as evidence of the great wind pressure used. On the other hand, there are many classical illustrations of the double pipes played *without* such support and occasionally we find poets praising the *sweet* tone of the aulos. Sachs points out that by a curious freak the leather mouthband still survives in Java where a double reed-pipe was known and pictured before the year A.D. 1000.

¹⁰ See Article 'Trumpet' in *Grove's Dictionary of Music and Musicians*, fifth edition, London, Macmillan & Co. Ltd., 1954.

¹¹ See also Chapter 3, p. 50.

¹² Ref. also Note 10, above.

CHAPTER 6

Natural Trumpets: Medieval to Modern

WE NOW ARRIVE at a period when further development of the trumpet became purely a West European manifestation. Between the fall of the Roman Empire and the 16th century almost all our information is derived from contemporary works of Art which often call for great care in interpretation. The illuminators of manuscripts, painters, and carvers of the Middle Ages depicted generously the musical instruments that they knew, but the limitations of their techniques leave us ignorant of many important details. Usually the most we can glean with any certainty is the general form of an instrument, how it was held, and perhaps its relative size. The great technical advances of Renaissance Art made more accurate representation possible, but they also opened to the artist a new and personal freedom of expression. At this time, therefore, we often find the essential forms of instruments displayed primarily as elements of pictorial composition with little regard for musical verity, and sometimes even endowed with purely imaginary ornament having nothing to do with functional requirements.[1] At the same time the growing preoccupation of the Renaissance mind with Classical Art and Literature occasionally led painters to place together the ancient, as they conceived it, and the contemporary. As an example we may cite Filippino Lippi's allegory 'The Worship of the Golden Calf' in the National Gallery, London, where he balances on opposite sides of the composition a 15th-century folded trumpet with a Roman cornu. (Plate 11 B.)

The musical legacy of Greece and Rome to Medieval Europe was in reality less than is sometimes believed—notwithstanding the Emperor Nero's apocryphal reputation as a violinist.[2] Most musical instruments in their basic forms entered Europe from the East, by way of Byzantium, from the North East along the Baltic coast, or through the Islamic Empire of North Africa. Arabian civilisations are much older than is often realised—for example Sheba, contemporary with the reign of Solomon in Israel, was an Arab state—so the line of communication with Western Europe via Islam may have existed earlier than is generally supposed.

It is evident that the principle of the lip-voiced tube as exemplified in the horns of hunters, watchmen, etc. could have been discovered in Europe quite independently of foreign influences, and indeed it probably was, and many times over, for it is hardly credible that so ubiquitous an object as the sounding horn should owe its existence to one single genesis. Bronze copies, too, could have been produced by any metal workers who had reached a certain stage of proficiency, though here we may perhaps trace a Roman element, at least in military instruments. The life of indigenous peoples must have been affected by the presence of Roman garrisons among them for several centuries, and the wave of barbarism which swept over the Continent after the withdrawal of the 'Pax Romana' surely cannot have obliterated all traces of their influence. There is some proof of this in an illustration of an undoubted Roman lituus in the famous Bible of Charles the Bald, Codex Latinus I of the Bibliothèque Nationale in Paris; and straight trumpets, evidently degenerated tubae, figure in certain Irish miniatures of the 8th century. In addition drawings in the Utrecht Psalter, a Carolingian manuscript of the mid-9th century which is of the greatest importance to students of musical instruments, show players on a type of *horn* which closely resembles surviving Roman buccinae. We cannot tell from the drawings if they actually represent natural or man-made horns; the thickness of wall indicated suggests the former, but the great length of the instruments and the banding on one of them point to an artificial construction. Similar very long horns are depicted in many medieval manuscripts, most frequently in the hands of angelic figures. Two notable examples in English collections are the Bodleian MSS. 352, an Apocalypse of the early 11th century preserved at Oxford, and another of the early 14th century catalogued as B.10.2 in the library of Trinity College, Cambridge.[3]

Now, examples such as we have just quoted, though they certainly tend to prove some survival of Roman influences in early medieval times, do not entitle us to assume that the lituus was the direct parent of the true trumpet in Western Europe. The horn, as we have already seen, was certainly carried into the West by invaders, but could also have been independently discovered there. The true trumpet, on the other hand, seems to have been twice introduced from abroad, and we have no evidence of any connection between its Roman manifestation as the lituus and those trumpets which began an independent existence in medieval Europe and ultimately became the instrument we recognise today.[4] The re-introduction of the trumpet (and from now on we use the name in its specialised connotation) is frequently attributed to the Crusaders, many of whom, however pure and devout their first motives, certainly returned from the Levant or Islamic Spain with enhanced fortunes and inflated ideas of personal grandeur. The trumpets and drums which they found in the East as the prerogatives of nobility and royalty they are supposed to have brought back with them and grafted into the growing organisation of European chivalry. Such an attribution would, of course, date the reappearance of the trumpet somewhere between 1096 and the end of the 13th century, but its illustration in an 11th-century wall-painting at Formia in southern Italy suggests that the instrument was at least tolerably familiar in that part of the world a good deal earlier. As F. W. Galpin pointed out over fifty years ago, commercial traffic between Islam and Christian Europe was in being long before the first of the Holy Wars, and the returning Crusaders probably did no more than popularise an instrument that was already partially known.

Be the matter of origins as it may, the progress of the trumpet in the Middle Ages is well enough documented from both pictorial and literary sources for us to follow it with some certainty. Almost as soon as we hear of the instrument at all we find it in two forms, a short version known as the *Claro*, and a longer called *Buzine, Buisine, Bocine*, or some variant, the word itself evidently deriving erroneously from the Latin *buccina*.[5] The claro, not more than two or three feet long at most, was, we learn, esteemed for its clear ringing tones—the name may imply as much—and its principal use was as a signal instrument. Early in the 12th century William of Malmesbury speaks of the 'loud melody of the Clarasii' (i.e. Claro-players) and a charter of the 13th century quoted by Galpin states that a public assembly should be summoned by the common herald 'with the tuba or claro, as the custom is'. Notice here again a back-reference to the Roman infantry trumpet. *Trumpet*, specifically, does not seem to have come into general use quite so early, and when it does there appears to be some ambiguity. The word is clearly a diminutive of *Trump* or *Trompe* which was used very early to denote a curved *horn* but the etymology of the latter name is itself dubious.[6] According to Galpin again, the early 14th-century poet Guillaume de Machault wrote of both the *Trompe* and the *Trompe petite*, and in his 'La Prise d'Alexandre' mentioned together '*Trompes, buzines, et Trompettes*', in this case implying a clear distinction between them.

Regarding the capabilities of the two forms of the early trumpet, it is evident that the relatively short claro can have had a compass of only four or at most five notes as is the case with the comparable 32-inch 'Tandem Horn' of Coaching days. The buisine, with a characteristic length of four to six feet, was clearly a superior instrument and fitted to be the progenitor of more advanced types, since, subject only to considerations of 'scale' (see 'Acoustics' pp. 6 and 7), the longer a tube is made the greater the number of harmonics to which it will resonate. In the opinion of the late Adam Carse, whose views command very considerable respect, it was an appreciation of this fact which quickly placed the long trumpet in its dominant position.[7] This idea is not, however, entirely borne out by pictorial evidence, and as an alternative we might guess that the buisine, with its more imposing appearance, would commend itself the more to lovers of pomp and circumstance. To cite just one example, there is in the National Gallery in London a magnificent 15th-century 'Christ Glorified' by Fra Angelico which shows many contemporary musical instruments in the hands of the Heavenly Host. Of these, six are buisines of at least six feet in length, and their appearance is indeed imposing. The angelic trumpeters are shown blowing their buisines with the cheeks *inflated* which suggests that, within the artist's range of experience at least, the possible compass of the instrument was still not fully exploited. In support of this conclusion we must also recognise that between the 13th and 16th centuries European instrumentation in general retained many signs of its Eastern origin, notably a basic division into mutually exclusive *loud* and *soft* groups, the one confined to outdoor and ceremonial performance, the other appropriate for use with the voice and reserved for artistic music, usually indoors. During several centuries the trumpet was kept entirely to the *loud* category, and the trumpeter probably remained for some time a 'one note man', as he is today in many Eastern outdoor bands. To the greater glory of the Saviour, Fra Angelico evidently brought together all the musical resources of which he knew, but it is interesting to note that in this composition he did not attempt to separate the *loud* and *soft* groups and balance them pictorially as many less inspired Renaissance painters often did. (Plate 10 A.)

In spite of the seeming persistence of a somewhat primitive blowing technique, it is clear that, once established, the long trumpet advanced very quickly. As in the case of the Roman cornu, the inconvenience of very long instruments again became evident, and, although the straight buisine was still being made well after 1450, as attested by at least one surviving dated specimen, efforts to improve matters by folding the tube had begun as early as the year 1300.[8] By successive stages the instrument was bent first into a broad flattened S shape, then more closely, and finally into the overlapped form which became more or less stabilised during the 16th century, and which is still today the basic arrangement of the main tube even in the most highly mechanised trumpets. (See also Chapter 2, pp. 38 and 39.) From time to time other

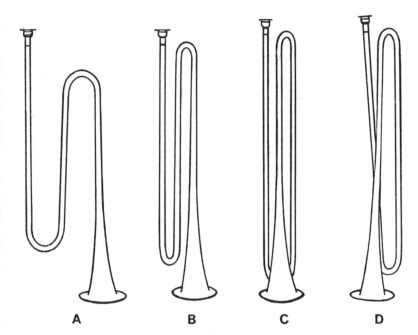

A   B   C   D

Fig. 26   Stages in the folding of a trumpet:
A First phase: wide zigzag in one plane. 13th–14th centuries
B Second phase: narrow zigzag
C Third phase: narrow zigzag in two planes. Late 15th–16th centuries
D Variant of C, with mouth and bell pipes crossed. Seen in German illustrations of the 16th century and employed in a less extreme form by English masters of the 17th and early 18th centuries

forms of shortened trumpet have appeared (even as late as c. 1850), some of them coiled in a hoop, others actually 'knotted', but it is clear that, on the whole, the simple arrangement of three parallel straight sections has proved the most satisfactory. The earlier folded trumpets were not provided with any sort of staying between the turns of the tube so, although more convenient to handle, they remained somewhat unstable structures. A detail from a picture of a joust held by King Richard II, part of the Lambeth Palace Library MSS. No. 6 (Plate 11 A), shows both the short and the folded long trumpet together, and we notice that the player on the latter holds his instrument both by the mouthpipe and near the bell. This example in particular is quoted here because of the evident realistic intention of the painter. Other illuminators of the time have been more successful with the proportions of the instrument itself, but in their concern for pictorial formality have given us less useful information. By the time that overlapped folding had become general the trumpet could, of course, be safely held with one hand only, a point to which we shall return in another connection later. The matter of staying folded instruments and some of the considerations involved have been discussed more fully in Chapter 4, pp. 76 and 77.

With the dawn of the 16th century our knowledge begins to depend less on the interpretation of literary references and pictures.[9] These still remain valuable check sources, of course, but from this period we have the first of the great general treatises on music and musical instruments, Virdung's *Musica Getutscht* (1511) and Agricola's *Musica Instrumentalis deudsch* (1528), as well as a few actual instruments in a fair state of preservation. The rather earlier *De Inventione et Usu Musicae* of Tinctoris (1487?) tells us nothing of the trumpet but it does prove the existence of a practical *trombone* at that date. By about 1500, also, terminology seems to have become fairly consistent and in the meantime a curious etymological transfer had taken place. The basic name *claro*—plural *clarones*—having appeared in such forms as *claron*, *claronceau*, and finally *clarion*, became detached from the original short straight instrument and was applied exclusively to the folded long type. We cannot, of course, date this change-over precisely, but the general distinction between *trumpet* and *clarion* was certainly recognised in the English Army at Crécy in 1346 when it is recorded that the King's entourage included two clarions and five trumpeters. Again, we know that 'one claryoner' and two trumpeters were attached to the Fleet under the Earl of Arundel in 1377. Comparison of these historical records with Machault's poetical *Trompes, buzines, et Trompettes* suggests, I think, that the word 'trumpet' began to replace 'claro' early in the 14th century when derivatives of the latter settled down to their special meaning. Two hundred years later the matter was clearly crystallised, for in 1529 Horman stated categorically, 'A Trompette is straight, but a Clarion is wounde in and out with a hope' (i.e. hoop). When Virdung published his treatise in 1511 he illustrated three different folded trumpets which he called respectively *Thurmer Horn*, *Felt Trumet*, and *Clareta*. The first of these, in spite of the 'horn', was a true trumpet of the flattened zigzag type, and, as the name suggests, was an instrument used particularly by the tower watchmen often employed in medieval cities to keep a lookout for fire, civic tumult, etc. At this time the simple unstayed S trumpet was clearly obsolescent, and it is a little difficult to account for its being specifically allotted to watchmen. Certainly, tower duties would not seem to demand so robust an instrument as would field exercises, but probably the real answer is that the military trumpeters who were already tending to an unofficial organisation (p. 225) held mere municipal servants in poor regard and were content to let them enjoy an old-fashioned instrument if they could. The Felt Trumet was simply a clarion of strong construction (though still unstayed) and with a relatively wide bore, while the Clareta was of similar length but with a narrower tube more fitted for the sounding of higher harmonics—the beginnings of the Art instrument in contrast to the Military. Perhaps the Clareta, too, was of thinner metal, for nearly a century later Altenburg[10] tells us that a large-bore trumpet has a more penetrating and powerful tone, and requires a firmer attack than a small-bore one; and again that a thick-walled trumpet has an unpleasing tone in the high register and is therefore unsuitable to a concert player though durable and useful in military duties. Seventeen years after Virdung the first of four editions of Martin Agricola's book appeared, in which we find the same three trumpets illustrated by copies of the same three woodcuts. Most of Agricola's text is expressed in doggerel verse and a great part of his matter is lifted bodily from Virdung. Unfortunately his printer was rather less successful with his cribbing, for he managed to transpose the captions to the Thurmer Horn and the Clareta, though his intention is quite clear. The appearance together of two trumpets of similar length, but in other dimensions clearly designed to favour one or other end of the harmonic series, is of the greatest importance to the musical scholar, for it indicates a dawning concern to extend the range of the instrument, and points the way to melodic use.

The great *Syntagma* of Michael Praetorius published in 1618 is a mine of information on many aspects of music in his time, and from his pages we learn a great deal about the next phase of trumpet history. In the first place it becomes evident that during the century after

Virdung the distinction between Felt Trumet and Clareta disappeared, and one type of folded trumpet took on the duties of both. This Praetorius identifies quite simply as 'Trommet'. By Praetorius' time, too, the potentialities of the fourth octave had been realised and advanced trumpet parts began to be shared between several players who took charge of different registers. In other words, it was now the player rather than the instrument who submitted to specialisation. This was necessary since few could command with certainty the entire possible range of the instrument, and the closely placed higher harmonics were increasingly demanded by composers for the sake of their scale-wise disposition. A system therefore developed whereby the compass of the trumpet was divided into recognised registers known as *Principale*, covering 3rd to 9th harmonics, and *Clarino*, 8th to 20th or even higher. Early in the 1700s the fundamental and octave sounds fell out of favour owing to the coarseness of their tone compared with the cultivated higher harmonics, though they had been regularly used in the two previous centuries. When the system reached its fullest flowering, subdivisions such as Clarino I and Clarino II were inserted and sometimes even a fourth called *Tromba*, which spanned the junction between Principale and Clarino II. It seems probable that the four-part arrangement came about among trumpet bands in particular from an analogy with four-part vocal writing. Fig. 27 shows the disposition of the four parts for a trumpet pitched in C. Note that the Principale was a medium register part and not, as we might suppose, the leading melody part with the most complete scale.

Fig. 27   Average relative distribution of trumpet
parts, 17th and 18th centuries

It was this specialisation among players that ultimately made possible the brilliant high trumpet parts of Bach and Handel, and the former exploited it as no other composer has ever done, though he seldom particularised either 'Clarino' or 'Principale' in his scores. The range he allotted to his different players probably depended on his knowledge of their individual capacities at any particular time, and we note that he usually labelled all trumpet parts as simply 'Tromba'. After the death of Handel the art of clarino playing languished and by the end of the century died out, to become only a subject for misunderstanding and disagreement among musical amateurs till early in the present century.

The technique of clarino playing was at no time easy to acquire, as witness Speer writing in 1687, and Altenburg, himself the son of a clarino player, in 1795. It called for a naturally suitable lip, good teeth, physical strength, and the most assiduous practice, and there seem always to have been few players who achieved it in perfection. The important thing to emphasise here is that no special instrument was employed by these musicians; the ordinary trumpet of their day served them with no more modification than the application of a personally selected mouthpiece to support the lips in the tense embouchure which had now become essential. A considerable number of these mouthpieces survives in museum collections and nearly all show common character-istics from the acoustic point of view, though the rims, usually broad, vary even more than among modern ones (see Chapter 1, pp. 17 and 18, and Chapter 4, pp. 65-70.)

From the pages of Praetorius and Speer, together with surviving specimens, we learn also that what we might call the 'standard' trumpet of the 17th century was pitched in D, with a sounding length of rather more than 7 feet,[11] though a similar instrument in C was likewise known at an early date. These instruments could be tuned down to C and B♭ respectively by the addition of a separate crook of the kind described on p. 71. Shorter trumpets in E♭ and F were also recognised in the 1600s but came into more general use in the time of Haydn and Mozart when it was the common practice to furnish the F instrument with a *semitone* crook or shank to lower it to E♮. By about 1800 the orchestral trumpet had settled down to an accepted pitch of F and this remained the standard until well after the beginning of the present century. During the greater part of the 19th century F trumpets were regularly supplied with a set of crooks which gave the keys of E, E♭, D, and C and by combination B♭ and A. Altenburg and other 18th-century writers tell of a trumpet in G used specifically in England and known generally as the 'English Trumpet', but it is difficult to find any evidence to confirm this, and a study of scores up to Beethoven's time suggests that composers did not like writing for trumpets pitched higher than F. Actual specimens of early high-pitched trumpets are exceedingly rare.[12] Some 18th-century writers also designated trumpets as 'French' and 'German', and from the contexts it is evident that the difference was then simply one of pitch. The same distinction made in the 16th century, however, seems to have gone deeper, though exactly what it implied we do not know. We gather from letters of the celebrated Nürnberg maker Jörg Neuschel (c. 1540) that *Welsches oder französische Trummetten* were troublesome to make and tune together and that he charged for them up to twice the price of the *deutsche*. In one place he refers to the former as *grossen* and in another we learn that a customer enquired about '*französische Trommetten* such as the Imperial Trumpeters use'. Was the 'French Trumpet' then possibly a robust wide-bore Clarion, perhaps more ornamented than usual, and suited to Imperial dignity? We cannot tell today, but we do know that Neuschel sent them out complete with cords and banners, and accompanied by two pairs of kettle-drums dressed to match.[13]

Most of the old trumpets now to be seen in public and private collections bear the names of German makers, and their custom of adding the date to the name has been of great help to scholars. Nürnberg was the main centre from which most of the rest of Europe was supplied during the 16th, 17th, and 18th centuries, and there the makers' craft seems to have been a family one whose mysteries were passed on from father to son under a system of apprenticeship. A list of the most celebrated makers will be found in Appendix 1, but we may just notice here that, according to Altenburg (1795), trumpets made by Johann Wilhelm Haas nearly a century earlier were still regarded as the best. A few French and Italian names are also recorded from this period and in England, from about 1650 on, some superb trumpets with very distinctive characteristics were made. Recently the most notable survivors of these have been fully described in the *Journal of The Galpin Society* by Eric Halfpenny, and interested readers are strongly recommended to see these authoritative articles.[14] We have already in this chapter laid emphasis on the care that must be taken in interpreting Medieval and early Renaissance illustrations of musical instruments. Even greater care is necessary when we come to enquire how they were played. By now a considerable mass of such evidence has been accumulated and evaluated by scholars and, from the relevant part of this, it appears certain that the early European trumpeters commonly used a loose-lipped embouchure with the cheeks more or less inflated. In consequence they were denied any considerable excursion into the upper part of the harmonic series, and this state of affairs seems to have persisted at least until the latter part of the 15th century. This fact, however, must not lead us to assume that many players did not feel the need to enlarge the scope of the trumpet long before this time, either by extending its compass or by filling in the natural gaps in the middle octaves. Progress upwards, we know, could only come after the adoption of a *tense* embouchure with controlled wind pressures, a technique foreshadowed, or perhaps already implied, in the woodcuts in Virdung and the so-called 'Leckingfelde Proverbs' of *c.* 1500.[15] Filling-in was rather a different matter, and there are good reasons to suppose that it was practised much earlier. The evidence has been well argued by Sachs in one of the most important of his short papers, and to quote from his introduction, 'The collaboration of a trumpet in part-music of the Middle Ages and the Renaissance is certain, yet its inability to play a normal melodic voice part is equally certain. How can this puzzle be solved?'[16] The answer can only be that the instrument used was not the plain natural trumpet of the period, or if it was, its acoustic properties were somehow modified by the player. Let us consider this possibility first.

The 'Stopt' or Stopping Trumpet

From Praetorius till well on in the 19th century we encounter at intervals either pictures or specimens of a true trumpet coiled in the manner usually associated with hunting horns but much more tightly. What was the special purpose of these? Praetorius captioned his picture *Jägertrummet* (Hunting-Trumpet), and it may be that such coiling was indeed adopted for convenience in the hunting field, but if so it seems strange that these instruments nearly always appear provided with a detached crook—surely an *inconvenience*. A fine specimen made by Pfeifer of Leipzig and dated 1697 figures as No. 1819 in the Heyer Collection catalogue,[17] and a similar instrument, also crooked as in Praetorius, is shown in E. G. Haussmann's well-known portrait of Gottfried Reiche (d. 1734) who was Bach's leading trumpet in Leipzig. Many years after Reiche we find several writers, among them Altenburg, making rather vague references to 'Italianische oder gewunden Trompeten' which may possibly be the same type of instrument again, but none of them allude to any special *raison d'être*. The clue may be found among a considerable number of rather curious instruments made during the period 1709–1850, notably in France, where they were called 'Trompette Demilune'. These were simply ordinary folded F

trumpets but with the whole structure curved 'on the flat', so that the
bell came within reach of the free hand and could be 'stopped' with the
fingers while playing. The majority of them were provided with a U
tuning slide near the middle and the usual set of terminal crooks for
E, E♭, D, and C, though some were made on the 'body crook' principle
also (Plate 12 c). Because the technique of hand-stopping, usually
attributed to Hampel of Dresden *c.* 1750, gave rise to an entirely new
concept of horn playing it is often thought of as applicable to that
instrument alone. This is not so, as we have seen in the Acoustics
chapter; but certainly the device is less useful and effective with tubes of
trumpet proportions. The most that users of the Trompette Demilune
could count on was to modify certain natural notes by a semitone, or
perhaps a tone, and the difference in quality between open and stopped
sounds (much more marked than on the horn) was a serious drawback.
Moreover the additional notes gained were still insufficient to make the
second and third octaves fully chromatic. It has been stated in a number
of reference works that one Fantini, a Tuscan Court trumpeter who
published a rather fantastic 'Modo per imparar a sonare di tromba'
about 1600, used a coiled trumpet on which he could sound a complete
chromatic scale by means of hand-stopping. It is now known that
although Fantini did experiment with the technique, and on a coiled
instrument, his chromatic scale was a myth based on Fétis' misunderstanding of a passage in Mersenne[18], and Mersenne himself belonged
to the one country in Europe where the art of clarino playing was least
cultivated, France.

Again, we may ask why Reiche should be painted holding in one
hand the manuscript of one of his 'Abblasen', a typical 'Thurmer'
fanfare which his municipal employment obliged him to provide, and
in the other so specialised an instrument as a Jägertrummet. Do they
perhaps symbolise the two sides of the man?—for Reiche was first and
foremost a clarinist, as the mouthpiece shown in the picture surely tells
us. From comparative measurements the late W. F. H. Blandford
calculated that the instrument shown must have been pitched in D (at a
standard rather flatter than our A = 435) and fitted with a C crook. This,
of course, corresponds with the pitch of the general-purpose trumpet of
the *Stadtpfeifer* class from whom Bach's Leipzig wind players were
drawn.[19] Some of these men, though not under Court patronage,
nevertheless enjoyed sufficient reputation and prosperity to warrant the
possession of a personal solo instrument, and this, no doubt, is what we
see in Reiche's portrait. He may have chosen the coiled form for its

reputedly less strident quality, or for its amenability to hand-stopping—
we just do not know; but we may observe that a good deal of the music
of the time imperatively demanded the correction of dissonant harmonics.
In a *larghetto cantabile* section from a Suite of 'Table-Music' the Viennese
Court composer von Reutter (1757) required his solo trumpet to ascend

in minims chromatically from to leaving

out only the bb", a virtuoso feat which could only have sounded intoler-
able without such correction.[20] Taking these various points into consideration I think we must conclude that although the close-coiled
trumpet of the Baroque period could be hand-stopped, the technique was
probably used more to correct relative intonation than to supply entirely
missing notes, and in any case it could not be carried as far as early
Renaissance polyphonic music required.

The Slide Trumpet, and the Mystery of 'da tirarsi'

In the foregoing section we have looked at the only method we know
of filling in the middle octaves of the classic natural trumpet and have
found it insufficient for some quite well-recognised requirements.[21] Yet
undoubtedly a suitable instrument did at one time exist, and the only
question is what form did it take. The required evidence has in fact been
available, if unrecognised, for many years, but it is only within the last
fifteen that details have been convincingly pieced together. The first
clue dates back to the time of Bach, and it is therefore convenient to
embark on our discussion at that point. In doing so we must remember
that after the death of the Master his choral works attracted little
attention for nearly a hundred years, and it was not until 1829 that an
historic performance of the B Minor Mass under Mendelssohn re-
opened the ears of musical Europe. The revival of a style of music
which had so long been disregarded posed many problems of interpretation and performance, and led to many misconceptions which
have only been cleared up in the present century by such devoted
scholars as the late Professor Sanford Terry. In particular was the
significance of Bach's trumpet writing misunderstood, and for years the
most pernicious nonsense was talked about 'the secret of the old
trumpeters which died with them'. It was not until musicologists,
acousticians, and trumpeters began to work together that the true nature
of clarino playing was elucidated and the realisation came that here was
no 'lost art' which was beyond recovery, given favourable conditions

(see note 20, p. 183). An interesting object of recent research has been to reproduce the 18th-century D trumpet with a minimum of mechanism added to relieve the present-day player of the old clarinist's intonation problem. We shall refer to this more fully later on (p. 123).

Although Bach and his older contemporaries could count upon the fourth octave of the trumpet for melodic use they were faced by the same dilemma as their predecessors if they wished, for example, to back up the soprano line of a Chorale with the weight and brilliance of that instrument. It is here that the detailed analyses of Bach's scoring made by Terry and others become particularly revealing.[22] Terry points out that Bach did not always rigidly avoid certain notes normally outside the trumpet's scale. For the 11th harmonic of the C trumpet (which is neither the one nor the other) he sometimes wrote f♮', and sometimes f♯", presumably leaving the player to temper the natural sound as the tonality

of the piece demanded. Rarely, also, he wrote 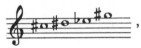 ,

which a skilled trumpeter might perhaps derive by 'faking' from the 8th, 9th, and 12th harmonics; but he did so with such careful avoidance of stress that some inaccuracy in playing might be overlooked, and their presence in a score clearly need not imply any abnormal instrument.

On the other hand, it is evident that Bach regarded

in the third octave as quite beyond the ability of the natural trumpet. When he did write these notes for a trumpet, the part is nearly always marked *Tromba-da-tirarsi*, in German *Zugtrompete*, i.e. Slide-trumpet, (or sometimes *Corno-da-tirarsi*, the precise implication of which we shall return to later).

At the present day there seems to be no doubt that this Tromba-da-tirarsi, once regarded as a mystery instrument, was no more than a typical folded trumpet with the shank of the mouthpiece prolonged to form a tube some 22 inches long which telescoped freely but accurately within the normal mouthpipe; and one such specimen used to belong to the Berlin Hochschule Collection[23] (Fig. 28). This trumpet, dated 1651, was made by Hans Veit of Naumburg, Saxony, and according to Sachs formerly belonged to the Stadtpfeifer body of that town. It was set in the E♭ of its period and, with its slide long enough to lower the pitch by any interval up to a minor third, was capable of meeting all the demands of Bach's trumpet parts. The manifest importance of such an instrument, and the availability of only one properly authenticated specimen, led Canon Galpin to make an interesting experiment. He fitted an inner slide to the mouthpipe of a fine Haas trumpet of 1650, one of the gems of his own collection, and with it was able to duplicate the behaviour of the Naumburg example. The results of the experiment are fully discussed by Terry[24] and it will suffice here to note that, the basic pitch of Galpin's trumpet being D, when the slide was drawn 5 inches it fell to C♯, at 10½ inches to C♮, and at 17 inches to B♮, in all

Fig. 28 Zugtrompete slide fully extended. *After* Sanford Terry—based on the Hans Veit example of 1651

a minor third. It is a great pity that no other undoubted specimen similar to the Naumburg instrument has so far come to light, for, until Sachs was able to produce important additional evidence in 1950, many respected musical scholars, including Adam Carse, have been disinclined to admit that the *single-slide* trumpet (as distinct from those incorporating a U slide) was ever a type in general use.[25] This scepticism regarding the single-slide trumpet appears to have two bases. One is that known 16th- and 17th-century writers do not mention the Zugtrompete although several late 18th-century authorities do.[26] Altenburg in particular says, 'The Zugtrompete, generally used for playing the chorales from church towers' (note the association with Stadtpfeifer and thence with Bach's players) 'resembles the alto trombone, since, during the act of blowing, its slide action conveniently produces the lacking harmonics.' This has often been taken as a categorical statement that the Zugtrompete *was* the alto trombone, and so Moritz Hauptmann regarded it when preparing Vol. I of the great *Bachgesellschaft Edition* of 1851. Mahillon too inclined to this view in 1880, but surely the term 'resembles', as used by Altenburg, might apply to a mechanical principle just as much as to a structural detail. Further, we note that in 1769, in a report on candidates for Stadtpfeifer employment in Leipzig, Johann Friedrich Doles made a clear distinction between the Zugtrompete and the *Discant Trombone*. The only other instrument which might conceivably satisfy Altenburg's description 'resembles the alto'.

I

The second basis is a more practical one. A single slide requires the mouthpiece attached to the inner tube to be held firmly to the lips with one hand while the other supports the body tubing and slides it backwards and forwards as required. The 17-inch extension necessary to lower a D trumpet to B is as much as an average man can conveniently make, especially when supporting the weight of the instrument, and the leverage at full extension is very considerable[27] (see also Appendix 2, p. 253). These points are beyond dispute, but can they be urged against the familiar use of the instrument? Surely not, for have we not a wealth of pictures from the *quattrocento* onwards showing trumpets held just in this manner and position? The famous Angel Altarpiece painted by Hans Memling (*c.* 1480) for the church of Majera, and now in the Antwerp Museum, is probably the best known of these because of its popularity in reproduction on calendars, greetings cards, etc., and it is specially important in that it shows two folded trumpets in company with a single straight one. The study from about 1908 on of many such pictures, together with the actual Naumburg instrument, convinced Curt Sachs of the existence of the Zugtrompete at least 250 years before Bach. In 1920 he drew attention to a 15th-century painting by Antonio Vivarini and Giovanni d'Allemagna, then in the Kaiser Friedrich Museum, Berlin. This is a crowded 'Adoration of The Magi' and in the retinue of the Kings stand two trumpeters, their instruments shouldered bell upwards and held with one hand, while the other hand holds the mouthpiece as if to prevent it falling out. The stems of both these mouthpieces as revealed are some 10 inches long and like that belonging to the Naumburg trumpet. Finally, shortly before 1950, Sachs' attention was drawn to the wood-carvings of Michael Pacher, completed in 1481 at St. Wolfgang on Lake Aber, Upper Austria, and here he found the most significant evidence of all. The central subject of Pacher's altarpiece is the Coronation of the Virgin, and, above this, symmetrically disposed, are two angels each playing a Zugtrompete and holding it by mouthpiece and body as described above. Here, at last, was not a mere flat painting, but figures carved in the round by a Master, from which relative dimensions could be determined. Most important of all, the angel on the right has his instrument in the closed or *first* position, but that on the left has the slide drawn out to what we might call the *third* position. Sachs' calculations and arguments anent these figures are clearly set out in *The Musical Quarterly* for January 1950 and he concludes that such trumpets, with only three shifts of the slide, could yield a scale uninterruptedly chromatic from the fourth open sound upwards, less only *one note*. They could certainly bear their part in early instrumental polyphonic music, and no doubt represent the type of folded trumpet often seen in early vignettes as forming a trio with two shawms of different sizes. (Plate 14, C & D.)

In the face of all this evidence I feel that we can no longer doubt that Bach's Tromba-da-tirarsi was a form of the Zugtrompete which had been known, at least in Germany, since the early Renaissance; but this still does not clear up one aspect of the mystery—what did he mean by *Corno-da-tirarsi* which in Cantata No. 46 he nominates as an alternative, and in Nos. 67 and 162 specifies without qualification? Be it noted that the parts he labelled with either name differ neither in compass nor in character. There are two points we must take into account. In the first place, the Horn as an orchestral voice was something of a novelty at the time Bach began to use it, and although terminal crooks had been *introduced* rather before this date, they certainly were not yet in general use among the majority of players.[28] We must therefore assume, lacking specific information, that any horn available to Bach was the simple instrument tapered from mouthpiece to bell and consequently incompatible with any form of telescopic arrangement. We know also that during the 18th century horn players did by degrees adopt, first cylindrical 'couplers', and later 'body-crooks' (*Inventionsbogen*), which inevitably interrupted the pure taper of the older horn, and the advantages they gave were bought at the expense of some slight change in tone quality which had to be accepted, but there is no evidence at all of any basically modified horn in Bach's time. 'Corno-da-tirarsi', then, remains still unexplained unless we accept the rather unconvincing theory that the special tone quality Bach demanded under that title was obtained from the known slide-trumpet by some players' trick—perhaps a change of mouthpiece, muting, or even both together. Neither suggestion is really satisfactory, for reasons fully discussed by Morley-Pegge.[29]

The English Slide-trumpet

Whatever conclusions we may have reached regarding the 18th-century Zugtrompete, there was a later form of the slide-trumpet which calls for no detective work, and which may be seen in the majority of public and private collections. This is the *English Slide-trumpet*, usually said to have been invented by the player John Hyde in 1804.[30] It was basically the natural trumpet of its period except that the bend joining the middlepipe and the bellpipe was made in the form of a U slide which could be pushed out towards the player by means of a rod with a touch-piece lying under the second and third fingers of the right hand and automatically closed again by a spring. The length of the slide was such that it could be used not only to correct the 11th and 13th harmonics, but it could also lower all open notes by a semitone and some by a whole tone (Fig. 29 A). Though never really understood or appreciated on the Continent, this was the instrument of the great English trumpet virtuosi of the 19th century, and in the hands of such men as the famous Harpers, father and son,[31] it remained in use till after 1890 when younger players had long embraced the valve trumpet. The esteem once accorded to the English slide is proved by the fact that many surviving examples are obvious additions to older simple trumpets which their owners cherished and were loath to abandon. From various instruction books we learn that the usual instrument was pitched in (6-foot) F, and provided with crooks for E, E♭, D, and C. These could be combined in various ways to put the instrument also into D♭, low B, B♭, A, A♭, and G, but as each increase in the sounding length naturally called for a corresponding increase in the movement of the slide the whole-tone 'shift' was limited to the higher keys. In the younger Harper's tutor, published in 1875, he says that whole tones were not practicable in keys lower than D. The instrument was customarily played with the bellpipe underneath, or as we might now think 'upside down', and therefore, for the sake of convenience, the two or three tuning bits which completed the outfit were often slightly offset. On the earlier examples the return of the slide was effected by the tension of a clock spring attached to it by a length of catgut, and two such springs enclosed in brass drums were usually provided, one active, the other in reserve. Later, elastic, and sometimes even a spiral spring enclosed in a tube, replaced the clock springs and often players had older instruments altered and the drums removed. In 1890 W. Wyatt introduced a model with a doubled slide which reduced the length of the shift by half, but for the sake of appearance he also added some dummy tubing at the fore end and thereby much increased the weight of the instrument. A short, four times folded, version with a single slide was also sometimes seen but it appears to have made little impression. Since in general size it resembled the 'short' duty trumpet of the British Army, it may have been designed primarily for military use. The writer once possessed an example which had an established military provenance and was reputed to have been used up to the turn of the present century. Both these types came, in fact, too late to compete with the improved valves of their time.[32]

In France, *c.* 1840, a rather different form of slide-trumpet had appeared (Fig. 29 B). According to Merri Franquin[33] this was introduced by Dauverné[34] as an improvement on the English model. A slide calculated to lower the basic pitch by anything up to a minor third was employed, and the necessarily greater length of this required that it should follow the trombone pattern and be placed *forward*. No provision was made for automatic closing and, in some examples at least, the slide could be locked in any position by the turn of a knurled thumbscrew bearing on a rod. Thus, when free, this slide could be employed for the same purposes as the English model, but when the lock was used it represented an alternative to the shorter crooks with the benefit of quicker changing. The instrument does not seem to have found much favour or to have lasted long, but a number of attempts were made to add the advantages of this type of slide to early valved trumpets.

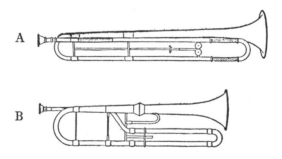

Fig. 29   A English slide-trumpet (basic instrument
shown without crooks or traditional
ornament)
B French slide-trumpet

Finally we should notice here the 'Orthochromatic' trumpet—a name that today suggests photography rather than music. This was produced by the London firm of Boosey and Co. about 1890 on the suggestion of George Case. In its normal state the instrument looked just like a State trumpet except for some additional cross stays. In fact the middle- and mouthpipes were connected by a U slide which could be pushed forward enough to lower the basic pitch by two whole tones, and when fully extended projected beyond the bell by some 9 inches. According to Boosey's catalogue of 1892 the slide was merely intended to replace detached crooks, and there is no suggestion that it should be treated like the free slide of a trombone. The Orthochromatic seems to have had a short life, for ten years later it had disappeared from the maker's literature altogether.

The Keyed Trumpet

It may be thought that we have already stressed quite enough the desire of the old trumpeters to chromaticise their instruments but, as the primary motivation of all the experiments that led up to the modern trumpet, we can hardly avoid referring to it again. When considering elementary acoustics we saw that the harmonic series peculiar to any given tube can be changed only by altering the length of that tube, and we have looked at a group of trumpets where that was achieved by means of a telescopic supplement. The converse principle has also been used, and between about 1800 and 1840 a form of trumpet in which the body tube was effectively *shortened* by means of side-holes had a limited vogue, mainly in military bands. Of course the 'shortening-hole' system, as Carse called it, has been employed in flutes and reed pipes since remotest antiquity, and by its application to natural animal horns the *Cornett* or *Zink* family of lip-energised instruments came into being towards the beginning of the 11th century. The earliest information we have concerning side-holes in brass instruments, however (with the exception of one atypical case which we shall consider separately), dates back only to about 1760 when Kölbel produced his *Amor-Schall*. Although accounts of this instrument are somewhat vague, it appears to have been a horn with two holes near the bell, both closed by keys, which raised the basic pitch by a semi-tone and a whole tone respectively. On the bell was a sort of perforated lid which, we may suppose, was intended to reduce the tonal difference between the bell notes and those sounded with the holes open, a defect that has often shown itself in the keyed brasses.

Although in Altenburg's book (1795) there are certain references which make it clear that he had at that time some knowledge of keyed trumpets, and although the manuscript of Haydn's Trumpet Concerto, for which the only feasible instrument at the time must have been a keyed trumpet, is dated 1796, it is not until 1801 that we hear anything more of the application of keys to the trumpet specifically. In that year Anton Weidinger, a trumpeter of Vienna, is said to have publicly introduced a keyed instrument which was made by one Riedl, a name well known in the musical trade in that city. This date, like some others mentioned in this chapter, is generally accepted and has been repeatedly quoted in reference works; it is probably as near the truth as we are now likely to get, but we should note that some respected authorities are inclined to regard it as only approximate. It has also been stated that Weidinger actually played the Haydn Concerto in the year of its composition, but if this is so the dates are not helpful. Perhaps a preliminary model of his trumpet was actually in Weidinger's hands five years before its general introduction, and perhaps Haydn may even have been aware of this. The idea is very attractive, but in 1945 the late W. F. H. Blandford told the writer that, having weighed up the available evidence (and he was in constant touch with the Gesellschaft der Musik-freunde in Wien who possess the manuscript of the Haydn concerto and other documents) he could only regard it as a pleasant conjecture. On the other hand, Klaus Blum appears to be convinced that this was indeed the situation, as he writes in his introductory notes to the Deutsche Grammophon 'Archive' recording of 1959.[35]*

Weidinger's trumpet was constructed on a very simple plan. An ordinary trumpet of the four-fold type was pierced with five or six holes placed at intervals calculated to raise the pitch by semitone steps when successively opened, the first being some 6 inches above the bell. All were covered by closed keys arranged conveniently for the fingers of the left hand, the instrument being held 'flatwise'. The mechanical principle of such keys was, of course, not new, since from at least the 16th century they had been used, in either closed or open-standing form, on woodwind instruments to control holes too large or too remote for the unaided fingers. By modern acoustical standards the Weidinger pattern trumpet had a number of defects the most obvious of which is the small size of the holes in relation to the bore (Plate 13 E). The implications of this in terms of physics have been discussed generally on pages 23 and 24, and here we need only say that the keyed notes must inevitably have been poor compared with the bell notes.

Fig. 30 is derived from a fingering chart published in London about 1835, towards the end of the life of the keyed trumpet,[36] and from it we learn two other things. First, the keys appear to have been designed for use singly and never in combination, thus ignoring the possibility of improving keyed notes by 'venting' the part of the air column below an open hole. The second point is that, like other trumpets of their time, the keyed instruments were commonly supplied with a set of supple-mentary crooks. G or A♭ was the favoured basic pitch and the supple-ments usually produced F, E♭, D, and C. Now, as the positions

* See Appendix 3, p. 256.

of the holes could not vary although the total sounding length increased as each lower crook was applied, it follows that sometimes one key and sometimes another would furnish the nearest approximation to the theoretical tube length for any given note. As a result the fingering varied somewhat with the crook selected, and it is evident that the placing of some of the holes was a compromise. Perhaps we may also see a

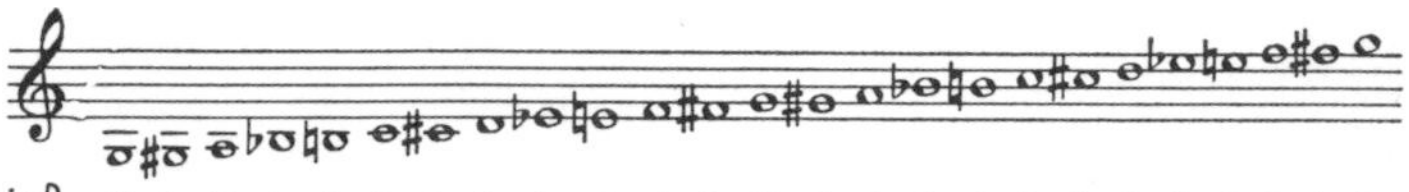

Trumpet in D		0	1	3	4	5	0	1	2	4	0	1	2	0	1	2	0	1	0	3	0	3	0	5	4	0
"	" Eb	0	1	3	3	5	0	1	2	4	0	1	2	0	1	5	0	1	0	3	0	3	0	5	4	0
"	" F	0	1	2	3	4	0	1	2	3	0	1	2	0	1	4	0	1	0	3	0	3	0	5	4	0
"	" G	0	1	2	3	4	0	1	4	2	0	1	2	0	1	4	0	1	0	3	0	3	0	5	4	0
"	" C	0	2	3	4	5	0	1	3	3	0	1	2	0	1	2	0	5	0	3	0	3	0	5	4	0

Keys are numbered counting from the bell.

Fig. 30 Fingering chart for a keyed trumpet,
published in London *c.* 1835

compromise in the choice of G as the basic pitch at a time when the favourite orchestral trumpet stood in F. In the chart the most logical fingering appears in the F line (with the whole-tone crook applied), the variations being distributed on either side between the uncrooked instrument and the deeper crooks. Although the story of the keyed trumpet seems rather a sad one, beginning as it does with partial success and ending in eclipse, on the Continent by the early valve trumpets and in Britain by the English Slide in the hands of virtuoso players,[37] there is no doubt that the instrument was at one time regarded as 'a likely lad' and worth a good deal of work. Specimens are now rather rare, but we can say that not only was the Weidinger pattern trumpet built as a soprano, but also as a bass an octave lower.[38] Also, about 1840 at least, an English maker, Sandbach of London, thought it worth reviving with an adaptation of the rather different key arrangement which had proved so successful in the Key or 'Royal Kent' bugle.[39]

It is one of the pleasures of musical research that even today a hitherto quite unsuspected piece of evidence occasionally comes to light and requires fitting into the general picture. Sometimes indeed the picture may require fundamental re-thinking, and the scholar must be prepared to do this. One such was the discovery in 1959 of a magnificent silver trumpet by the celebrated English maker William Shaw, which, complete with its case, accessory crooks, and tuning bits, had lain unrecog-

nised in the vaults of St. James's Palace, in all probability since a year
or two after its manufacture. Fortunately the Surveyor of the Queen's
Works of Art brought this instrument to the notice of Eric Halfpenny
who has examined it in detail and has published an excellent study of
it.[40] The particular interest of this trumpet, which bears the inscription
'William Shaw, London, 1787' and the Arms of King George III, is
twofold. Firstly, there is good reason to believe that the instrument was
specially supplied for the King's private band and was therefore
specifically an orchestral rather than a State or Herald trumpet; and,
secondly, it represents the earliest *dated* application of the side-hole
principle to a trumpet yet recorded. In general appearance this instrument resembles closely other English-made trumpets of its period, its
unique feature being the provision in the middlepipe of four rather
small holes (4-mm. diameter in a tube of 10-mm. bore). Three of these
are opened or closed at will by perforated rotating sleeves, and the fourth
by a conventional spring-closed key. The size and spacing of the holes
makes it clear that they have no affinity with any key system, such as
Weidinger's, based on semitone 'cut-offs' and there can be little doubt
that they were intended to encourage specific antinodes. The instrument is provided with three different sizes of crooks and Halfpenny's
experiments have shown that there is a hole appropriate to each, which
when opened raises the harmonic series by a fifth. Thus, the un-crooked
instrument standing in E♭, the first hole enables the B♭ *alto* series to
be sounded. With the D crook on, hole II gives the A series; the C
crook and vent III gives the G series; and the low B♭ crook and vent
IV furnishes the F. In his article Halfpenny has considered the musical
implications of the device, and he points out that its transposition of a
fifth adds very little to the diatonic possibilities of the third octave
of the trumpet, which, with the second, represents the compass mainly
employed by composers in Shaw's day. It does, however, give a quick
shift to the dominant tonality without the need to change the crook,
and this key relationship was, of course, the basis of the conventional
harmony of the Classical period. Halfpenny also says that the vented
series, on a quick trial, seem inferior in quality to the open ones. Perhaps by application a skilled trumpeter could overcome this defect,
but it may also account for the general neglect of Shaw's instrument.

In this book we have already referred more than once to the problems
which the high trumpet parts of the later Baroque present to the modern
professional whose daily musical life is vastly different from that of his
predecessors of Bach's or Handel's day. It has been repeatedly proved

by demonstration that there is nothing in these parts that many present-day players could not perform, and on the 18th-century instrument, given similar working conditions; but the versatility now expected of orchestral trumpeters in general rules out the rigorous specialisation necessary. In modern times, therefore, the difficulty was first attacked by making use of valve trumpets basically half the length of the old natural instrument whereby the sounds remain at the same pitch but are produced as lower members of several different harmonic series. In this way the player's technique remains that to which he is normally accustomed. Highly artistic performances are given with such trumpets every day but, however satisfactory these may be from the point of view of phrasing or interpretation, the purist still finds something wanting in them. There is, beyond question, some tonal difference between the third octave of a short D trumpet and the fourth of the old long one; not so very noticeable perhaps in the large-scale performances often given today, but obvious when we try to reproduce the internal balance of the small combinations for which Bach conceived his masterpieces. Short high trumpets, even with the most discreet blowing, do lack the warmth and blending qualities of the long instrument in its top register, a fact that is readily explained if we compare tonal spectra (see p. 14). The conclusion is inescapable—if we desire to reproduce exactly the sound that Bach and his players heard we must employ trumpets as long as theirs and cultivate the fourth octave as they did. This being so, the most recent and interesting experiments have been directed towards reproducing the old instrument in a form that may retain its very special qualities, but with such modern additions as will make it a practical proposition for the present-day professional trumpeter. It must, of course, be clearly understood that with a trumpet designed on these lines the player still cannot avoid making a special study of the fourth octave, but he can be relieved of the tremendous labour that had formerly to be devoted to learning how to control and 'humour' the defective harmonics.

About 1934, as the culmination of a great deal of comparative research among ancient instruments, Werner Menke of Leipzig devised a new trumpet in which he strove to incorporate all the features that appeared most helpful in *clarino* playing. Experimental work leading to actual production was done by the highly esteemed firm of Alexander Bros. of Mainz, and the instrument was introduced to the musical world in a book-sized essay by Menke.[41] For the sake of the orchestral players whom the sponsor hoped might adopt his instrument he avoided entirely the dissonant harmonics by basing his working scale on three different harmonic series supplied by two independent valves. The sharp bends inherent in the valves no doubt offset to some extent the other good features of the Menke trumpet, and, on the whole, it does not seem to have had any great success even in Germany. The writer has had no personal experience of this instrument, but he has heard from players who have tested it that, for some reason, it seems harder to blow than its simple and painstaking design would lead one to expect.

Although the Menke instrument was strictly speaking a valved trumpet, we have considered it at this point because of the special objectives which engendered it, and because these lead us in turn directly to the latest and most interesting of all the specialised modern trumpets. This is an instrument introduced as recently as 1961 by the maker Helmut Finke and the player Walter Holy of the Capella Coloniensis, and based on the researches of Otto Steinkopf to which we have already referred in an acoustical context on p. 24. The primary considerations were the same as in Menke's case, viz. that the trumpet should possess the tonal properties implied in the 18th-century *clarino* writing, and that the special study called for should be made as reasonable as possible for the modern orchestral player, particularly in respect of the dissonant harmonics. From the start it was accepted that the new instrument must be based on the full length of the 18th-century natural trumpet, and indeed that it should, as far as possible, be a reconstruction of the latter. A comparatively narrow bore was therefore chosen as favouring the higher harmonics, and the spiral coiling shown in Reiche's portrait was adopted since there is a good deal of evidence that the old clarinists regarded this as the most free-blowing form.[42] This construction has, in fact, a secondary advantage which we shall notice later. The equivocal harmonics were disposed of by boring a fair-sized hole some distance above the bell, which has the effect when opened of creating a second harmonic series a fourth above that proper to the full tube length. By this means the 11th and 13th of the first series are replaced by the 8th and 10th of the new one, both good notes. Fig. 31 (overleaf) shows how this affects an instrument pitched in the clarinists' favourite key of D.

We have already referred to Steinkopf's discovery of certain old trumpets in which pin-holes placed exactly at certain nodal points prevented the formation of the harmonics to which these particular nodes appertained. Following ideas suggested to him by these instruments, Steinkopf adapted the principle to his new trumpet though he applied it in a somewhat different manner. He placed two tiny holes

not exactly at nodal points, but where they would encourage the formation of *antinodes* slightly out of their normal position and so bring the
corresponding harmonics into just intonation. Thus, on the Finke

Fig. 31   Scale of Steinkopf-Finke Trumpet in D;
A Third hole closed. B Third hole open

trumpet in D, for example, the dubious 13th which lies somewhere

between   and   can be used as a good

and similar adjustments can be made elsewhere in the
scale. It should, of course, be noted that, as the placing of the holes is
critical and depends mathematically on the total length of the tube,
detachable crooks cannot be used to change the basic pitch. Accordingly,
the fully equipped player will probably require two or even three instruments, say in C, D, and F, but as they are entirely without the necessarily
expensive mechanism— in very truth a keyed-trumpet without even the
keys—it seems that the cost need not be excessive. As a consequence
of the coiled shape the three holes lie comfortably under the thumb and
fingers of the right hand and are easily governed. The tone is full of
character, warm and clear, yet dynamically adaptable to chamber playing.*

One final observation. It seems a pity that some confusion has already
arisen regarding the nomenclature of the Steinkopf-Finke instrument,
at least in Britain. On its first appearance it was announced as a
'Clarino Trumpet', i.e. a trumpet designed for *clarino playing*. In the
English advertising matter, however, the unfortunate phrase 'the clarino
(the soprano trumpet)', in itself inaccurate, was used. As a result, only
three years later, the instrument is often called the clarino, *tout court*,
and with a small c, so reviving the exploded fallacy that 'clarino' is the

* See Appendix 3, p. 256.

name of a particular instrument and not merely of a *register* within the theoretical compass of any trumpet. The fact that some clarino specialists seem to have used a relatively small-bore instrument is nothing to the point. In these matters we really should be meticulous; musical research is already sufficiently bedevilled with bad terminology, and we cannot nowadays afford to introduce any more.[43]

NOTES

[1] The degree of realism shown varies a great deal and for different reasons; sometimes purely ornamental use becomes extravagant to the point of absurdity. An excellent analysis of the subject has been made by E. Winternitz and published with selected illustrations in Vol. I of the *I.M.S. Congress Report*, New York, 1961. Modern painters also have not been guiltless in this matter. Burne-Jones, for example, in 'The Golden Stair' has brought together two buisines of reasonable proportions (one however lacking the mouthpiece) with other pipes that could have hardly existed outside his imagination. One may argue that in allegorical painting the needs of practical acoustics do not count, but one cannot help feeling sometimes that probability might have been preserved without loss of pictorial value.

[2] It seems hardly credible that 'Nero fiddled while Rome was burning' could ever have been taken literally, but it does illustrate the byways into which the musical researcher can be beguiled. Although we learn from Suetonius' *The Twelve Caesars* that Nero had at least some skill on the lyre, water-organ, flute, and bagpipe, and esteemed himself as a singer, we have absolutely no evidence that bowed strings were known in Ancient Rome. The derivation of the word 'fiddle' is disputed by etymologists. Probably, in the cant reference to Nero it originally bore its secondary meaning 'to trifle' or waste time. This, in turn, reflects the medieval idea that bowed instruments, since they were played especially by jongleurs and wandering entertainers, were but a slight matter. In Langland's *Vision of Piers Plowman* we find *fithelyn at festes* associated with *japen* (to make jests) and *jagelyn* (juggling). Of course, by Renaissance times bowed strings had come up in the world and were well on the way to the supreme position they now enjoy.

[3] Reproduced by Galpin in *Old English Instruments of Music*, London, Methuen and Co. Ltd., third edition (Revised) 1932, p. 182 and Plate XXXVI. I am informed by experts at the Natural History Museum, S. Kensington, that no cattle bearing horns of such size as those in the illustrations quoted were known in Europe in medieval times. The Massai cattle of Ruanda at the present day, however, carry horns of immense spread, single specimens measuring up to six feet in length. The cattle are traditionally bred for this characteristic and are greatly valued. (Personal communication to the writer from Dr. William Church of Cambridge who has spent a lifetime as a medical missionary in Ruanda.) Have we here perhaps further evidence of European trade with Islam in the Middle Ages? The people who breed these cattle are a Nilotic race and have no negroid affinities.

[4] After the disappearance of the actual Roman *Lituus* the name seems to have passed via Low Latin into fairly common use in Medieval Europe. See *Grove's Dictionary of Music and Musicians*, fifth edition, London, Macmillan & Co. Ltd., 1954, Vol. V, p. 343. Hereafter the word becomes infrequent but survives until the late Baroque. In a 'Partita a Viola d'amore, 2 Hautbois, Lituus, e

Basso' by the early 18th-century composer Joseph Brendtner, internal evidence shows that the lituus must have been a natural brass instrument (Trumpet or Horn) pitched in F and using the 4th to 13th harmonics.

Bach's Cantata No. 118 contains parts for two 'Litui' employing the same range of harmonics, but here the prescribed pitch is B♭.

More definite information is afforded by an inventory of instruments in the Bohemian Monastery of Ossegy, dated 1706, which refers to 'Litui vulgo Waldhorner ex Tono G'; and finally we have a positive statement from Kurzinger who says in his *Getreuer Unterricht* (Augsburg 1763) that *Lituus* can mean 'either a Trompette or a Waldhorn'.

⁵ Medieval etymology is very confused. Today we have enough evidence to be sure that the Classical *buccina* was never anything but a tapered instrument, but in later Latin the word might possibly, and quite understandably, be used for any instrument applied to the lips.

⁶ This is another case where etymologists refuse to commit themselves. The Italian form *tromba* which is in general use today appears to have its origin in Low Latin. It has been suggested that 'Tromba' is a corrupt derivative of 'Strombus', the Classical Latin name for a form of spiral shell of the sort used for primitive trumpets, but the idea seems desperately far-fetched.

⁷ Adam Carse, *Musical Wind Instruments*, London, Macmillan & Co. Ltd., 1939, p. 227.

⁸ Galpin, *op. cit.*, pp. 201 and 203.

⁹ The reader who would sample the wealth of these sources is referred to a masterly study by M. Valentin Denis, *De Muziekinstrumenten in de Nederlanden en in Italie naar hun Afbeelding in de 15°-eeuwsche Kunst*, Antwerp; N.V. Standaard-Boekhandel & Utrecht; W. de Haan N.V., 1944. As well as 20 plates this work contains 230 line drawings. Ian F. Finlay has also published a valuable study 'Musical Instruments in 17th Century Dutch Paintings' in which he lists some 150 references. *Galpin Society Journal*, Vol. VI, London, July 1953.

¹⁰ J. E. Altenburg, *Versuch an einer Anleitung—der Trompeter und Paukerkunst*, Halle, 1795. Reprint, Dresden, 1911, p. 10.

¹¹ In questions of nominal pitch relative to tube length we must always be rather cautious, quite apart from purely acoustic considerations. For example, during the Baroque period, particularly in Germany, organs were commonly tuned to 'chorton' or 'cornett-ton', a whole tone or a minor third respectively above the 'hoher cammerton' which—whatever its absolute value—was the customary pitch for concerted music. This introduces transposition questions which can be quite confusing to the unwary.

¹² Adam Carse, *op. cit.*, p. 230.

¹³ A. C. Baines, 'Two Cassel Inventories', *Galpin Society Journal*, Vol. IV, London, June 1951, p. 34.

¹⁴ Eric Halfpenny, 'William Bull and the English Baroque Trumpet' *op. cit.* Vol. XV, March 1962, pp. 18 *et seq.*; and 'Two Oxford Trumpets', *op. cit.* Vol. XVI, May 1963, pp. 49–62.

¹⁵ Verses taken from a manuscript of the time of Henry VII in the British Museum (18. D. 11) where they are described as 'The Proverbis in the Garet at the New Lodge in the Parke of Lekingfelde'. The verse in question runs:

Immoderate wyndes in a Clarion causith it for to rage;
Soft wynde and moderate makith the sounde to assuage.
Therfore he whiche in that instrumente wolde have swete modulacion,
Bustius wyndes must leve and use moderacion.

¹⁶ Curt Sachs, 'Chromatic Trumpets in the Renaissance', *The Musical Quarterly*, Vol. XXXVI, No. 1, January 1950, p. 63.

[17] Destroyed during the War. A good copy, however, exists in the Instrumental Museum of the Karl-Marx Universität, Leipzig.

[18] Fantini, *Modo per imparar a sonare di Tromba*, Frankfurt, 1638. Facsimile, Milan, 1934. Werner Menke, *History of the Trumpet of Bach and Handel*, English translation by Gerald Abraham, London, William Reeves Ltd., 1934, pp. 51–53. H. L. Eichborn, *Die Alte Clarinblasen*, Leipzig, Breitkopf, 1894.

[19] Charles Sanford Terry, *Bach's Orchestra*, London, Oxford University Press, 1932, pp. 8, 14, 21, 36 and 40.

[20] Quoted with comments by W. F. H. Blandford in *The Monthly Musical Record*, Vol. LXV, No. 767, London, June 1935, p. 99.

[21] Curt Sachs, *op. cit.* p. 62. '. . . a few fanfare-like overblown notes would not suffice, even if we surmise the polyphonic technique of an improved English discant of parallel thirds and sixths above the melody. An F trumpet—becomes diatonic only from f on, that is above the customary range of the highest polyphonic part'.

[22] Sanford Terry, *op. cit.* pp. 187–237.

[23] A second, dubious, specimen of unknown provenance belonged to the Grassi Collection in the University of Leipzig. It seems to have shared the fate of the Pfeifer instrument referred to in Note 17 above.

[24] Sanford Terry, *op. cit.* p. 32. We may perhaps grant the sceptics the justification of the following argument: 'Canon Galpin's experiment showed that a well-made natural trumpet could be turned into a tromba-da-tirarsi by means of a very simple supplementary tube. Only "artist-trumpeters" would, however, require this addition and therefore makers would not supply it as a routine matter. The law of supply and demand, after all, operated just as much in the Baroque period as today.'

[25] Adam Carse, *op. cit.* pp. 236–7. But; note that in his 'Gabinetto Armonico' of 1722 Bonanni tells us that at that time a 'tromba dritta spezzata'—a simple straight trumpet with a slide—was in use among the Italian country people, while Harrison and Rimmer in the admirably compressed text of their *European Musical Instruments*, London, Studio Vista, 1964, refer to the 'draw trumpet' as a matter of course.

[26] A. C. Baines, *op. cit.* We do not know who compiled the two inventories of the Cassel Hofkapelle instruments, but in both—dated respectively 1573 and 1613—*Zugen* (slides) are clearly distinguished from *Bogen* (crooks). In a similar list of new instruments at Schloss Marburg, Hesse, in 1601 we find the unequivocal entry 2 *Zugk Trometten*.

[27] The really important matter is how far the friction and inertia inherent in the device would limit its practical use. The writer has put the point to a number of players and musicologists and the consensus of their opinion is that it is perfectly practical in the light of what we know about Thurmer music in general. Modern players and composers have shown that the slide trombone, which has in a measure the same defects, is capable of an agility that was undreamed of in the 16th century.

[28] R. Morley-Pegge, *The French Horn*, London, Ernest Benn Ltd., 1960, pp. 20 and 21.

[29] *Ibid.*, pp. 143 *et seq.*

[30] A specimen formerly in the Galpin collection bears the inscription 'Woodham, Inventor and Maker', but we cannot rely too much on this for many 19th-century makers styled themselves 'inventor' with very dubious justification.

[31] Thomas Harper (1787–1853) and his son Thomas J. Harper, Sergeant-Trumpeter to H.M. The Queen, were the two most famous exponents of the English slide-trumpet. Successively they held all the most important trumpet

appointments in Britain, Harper the younger still adhering to the slide instrument after the general acceptance of valves. Their reputation was tremendous, a particular *tour de force* being the performance of all the most exacting Handel parts in the correct register, employing the slide only to correct the dissonant harmonics. Both published useful instruction books.

³² See R. Morley-Pegge, 'The Regent's Bugle', *Galpin Society Journal*, Vol. IX, 1956, p. 91.

³³ Merri Franquin, article 'La Trompette' in *Encyclopédie de la Musique*, Lavignac and de la Laurencie, Paris 1927.

³⁴ F. C. A. Dauverné, first trumpet at the Paris Opera *c.* 1830 and later Professor at the Conservatoire. Published a *Méthode pour la Trompette* in 1857.

³⁵ W. F. H. Blandford in personal communication to the writer. See also letters from Carse, Blandford, Karl Geiringer and others to *The Musical Times*, London, December 1939 and January and February 1940. Recently in the pages of *Brass Quarterly* Mary Rasmussen has drawn attention to a Concerto for 'Chromatic Trumpet' which ante-dates Haydn's composition by over twenty years. This piece, composed by a more or less obscure trumpeter named Albrechtsberger, is dated 1771 and came into the hands of the Esterhazy family in 1812. (Photo-copy in Library of Congress.) The technical demands of the work are not exacting, and in fact a simple slide-trumpet would suffice for them. There is nothing that imperatively demands a *keyed* instrument. Since the manuscript did not find its way into the Esterhazy Archive till after Haydn's period of service there it seems unlikely that he would have learnt of it while he was *Kapellmeister*; but it is known that later, in his Vienna days, he was well acquainted with Albrechtsberger.

This raises an interesting speculation as to whether Haydn may not have first heard of *a* chromatic trumpet (type unspecified) through Albrechtsberger, and have passed the information on to Weidinger. Did he perhaps compose his own Concerto rather to encourage Weidinger's experiments than at that artist's behest, as is usually supposed? We shall probably never know, but certainly the accepted dates are compatible with this idea.

³⁶ Reprinted by Carse in *Musical Wind Instruments*, p. 336.

³⁷ The elder Harper is known to have spoken in most disparaging terms of the 'new-fangled' valves adopted by Continental players.

³⁸ There is an excellent example in the collection of the Royal Military School of Music, Kneller Hall, Twickenham, Middlesex. (Plate 13 B.)

³⁹ Devised in 1810 by one Halliday, Bandmaster in the Cavan Militia. Originally provided with five side-holes covered by *closed* keys the instruments furnished a chromatic scale from c′ upwards. Additional keys added later supplied the low b♮ and improved the general intonation, and in this form the instrument was named Royal Kent Bugle in honour of the Duke of Kent. It seems possible that two keys added to a bugle by Courtois neveu of Paris rather earlier than Halliday's invention were intended to extend its compass to that of the contemporary military *trumpet*, but these could not afford a *chromatic* scale.

⁴⁰ Eric Halfpenny, 'William Shaw's "Harmonic Trumpet"', *Galpin Society Journal*, Vol. XIII, London, 1960.

⁴¹ Werner Menke, *History of the Trumpet of Bach and Handel*, translated in parallel text from the German by Gerald Abraham. London, William Reeves, 1934.

⁴² H. L. Eichborn, *Das alte Clarinblasen auf Trompeten*, Leipzig, Breitkopf and Härtel, 1894.

⁴³ The appearance of the Steinkopf-Finke trumpet raised once again the ghost of the 'lost art of the *clarinbläser*' and gave birth to a spate of ill-informed and

misleading articles in both the lay and the musical Press, especially in Germany. The volumes of published correspondence regarding the 'Bach' trumpets of Kosleck and Walter Morrow (see Chapter 8, p. 179) should surely have been a warning to present-day musical journalists, but the warning was disregarded. For a slightly acid but valuable summing-up the reader is referred to an editorial published in *Brass Quarterly*, Vol. V, No. 1, under the title of 'Bach-Trumpet Madness'.

CHAPTER 7

The Slide Trombone: Medieval to Modern

IN NOVEMBER 1906 the Rev. Francis W. Galpin read before the
Musical Association (London) a paper which was to assume great
importance in European musicology.[1] In it he reviewed all the then
accepted Trombone lore as well as a considerable number of fresh
references, many antedating Virdung, and although not all subsequent
scholars have felt able to accept his conclusions *in toto* few have added
anything of major significance to them. Throughout his life Galpin
revealed a special affection for the English aspect of ancient music and
its instruments, so it is not surprising that he used the old English
name *Sackbut* in the title of his paper and devoted a good deal of time
to examining the various supposed derivations of the word. To follow
Galpin's arguments in detail, though fascinating, would take more
space than we can afford here, and we must be content to record that
he finally became convinced that the most probable derivation is from
the Spanish *Sacabuche*,[2] a form known in the 14th century—probably
as a nickname—and of which a literal English equivalent would be
'draw-pipe'. In 1940 Curt Sachs[3] favoured a suggested derivation
from the Old French 'saquier', to pull, and 'boter', to push, combined
as *Saqueboute*. This term was already employed in the 14th century
to designate a sort of enormous boat-hook used by foot soldiers to
unhorse cavalry in battle but we must note that at the end of the same
century the musical instrument was rendered as *Saquebute*, which
may not be quite the same word. The writer of the 'Trombone' article
in the 5th Edition of *Grove* is probably wisest in admitting that the
etymology is still dubious.[4] The vagaries of spelling, among them
saykebud, *shakebutte*, and *shagbolt*, found in our earliest records suggest
that the name remained unfamiliar in England for some time, and we
know from the accounts of the expenses of the Privy Purse that when the
instrument first appeared in England, in the 15th century, foreign
players were employed.[5] By 1501, however, one of King Henry VII's
'shakbusshes' rejoiced in the good plain English name of John Browne,

and from this time on an English 'school' of sackbut players grew up which was later the envy of Continental princes.

Trombone, as used today in English-, French-, and Italian-speaking countries, is easily explained, it being simply *Tromba* plus the common Italian augmentative suffix *one*, i.e. 'big trumpet'. An older Italian form, *Tromba spezzata* (Fr. *Trompette brisée* or *T. rompue*), is still to be found occasionally, and in one respect it might be regarded as a better term since its literal meaning, 'divided trumpet', is descriptive and unequivocal. As we shall shortly see, *Trombone* transferred from Italian to English usage can sometimes be misinterpreted. The German name *Posaune* has also an interesting derivation. As the instrument itself developed out of the long straight trumpet *Buisine*, so the name underwent a parallel metamorphosis. In Middle High German the equivalent of *Buisine* was *Bûzine*. In the course of time the second vowel, subject to what philologists call 'assimilation', changed to a *û* also, so that by the end of the Middle Ages the German form had become *Busûne*, then *Buzaun*, and finally after the 16th century *Posaune* which has remained constant ever since. The transformation of words in the course of usage is an absorbing subject, and unawareness of it has occasionally led to curious misunderstandings. One such oddity is sometimes to be found in German art and literature whereby the Archangel is represented as calling Mankind to Judgement with a Trombone and not a Trumpet as generally understood in other European countries (e.g., Luther's translation of the wonderful line in Chapter 15 of 1st Corinthians '. . . . es wirde die *Posaune* schallen'). To English speakers in particular this appears strange at first sight, but, on reflection, may not the tone of the Trombone indeed seem fitter for the Dread Summons?

Turning now to the trombone itself, the oldest reliable illustration we know of a lip-voiced instrument having a free U-shaped slide dates back to the early mid 15th century, probably less than 100 years after the first recorded occurrence of *Sacabuche* in Spanish literature, and these two pieces of evidence together give us the nearest approach yet made to a time-fix on its origin. The records of the Great Council of Constance (1414–18) tell us that before the investiture of Frederick Hohenzollern as Elector of Brandenburg the 'Posaunen' and 'Pfeiffen' paraded the streets of the City. By that date, however, the *Bûsine–Buzaun* transformation in Middle High German was already under way and we must therefore interpret these accounts with some caution. The *Posaune* at that period in Switzerland *may* still have been the long straight trumpet traditionally used to summon public assemblies. The exact circumstances under which the true trombone emerged we do not know, but there is little doubt that the Buisine was the ultimate parent. When that instrument had gone through the stages of folding, first in one plane and then in two, the addition of the telescopic section was all that was required. This was a beautifully simple conception, though it depended for realisation on a deal of technical skill, and the unknown originator deserves the gratitude of every subsequent musician. Again, we do not know exactly *where* in Europe the genesis took place, but paintings and some rather obscure accounts of public festivals both suggest northern Italy or southern France.

In some older reference books the student may find earlier attributions than are now accepted, and, indeed, it has been stated positively (and repeated as recently as 1891 in Day's *Catalogue of Musical Instruments in the Royal Military Exhibition*) that the trombone was known to the Romans. Modern scholars reject this assertion, and perhaps a short digression here to examine just why may prove interesting.

The first 'Roman' attribution was based on a report, often repeated and varied in the process, that in 1738 excavators working at Pompeii or Herculaneum had unearthed certain large bronze instruments, one of which was presented to King George III. This particular specimen was recorded in the first edition of *Grove* as preserved at Windsor *c.* 1856, but all subsequent enquiries have failed to locate it. If, as Galpin pointed out, the initial date of 1738 is correct then the excavations in question must have taken place at Herculaneum, but the massive reports 'Antichità di Ercolano' published by the Neapolitan Government from 1757 onwards make no mention of the instrument. On the other hand, the *Encyclopædia Londonensis* (1795–1819) is specific on the point. It seems therefore that some ancient instrument from a Neapolitan excavation was indeed presented to George III, but probably not from the Herculaneum diggings of 1738 since that was actually the King's birth year. We note that according to the legend the Royal presentation instrument was not the only one discovered, and it is but reasonable to suppose that others would have found a place in the National Museum at Naples along with most of the rest of the treasures from Pompeii and Herculaneum. The Naples collection does in fact include bronze wind instruments but they are all of the Cornu type—large horns or, in the broad sense, trumpets which would naturally be described in Italian as *Trombe grande* or *Trombone*. This is no more than a sketch of the situation which Galpin investigated very fully, but it certainly indicates how confusion between the general and the particular meaning of one Italian word in the mid-18th century became the foundation of a whole edifice of fallacy.

A claim to classic antiquity for the slide principle itself was at one time based on a passage from Book II of the *Metamorphoses* of the 2nd-century writer Apuleius. Speaking of the rites of Isis and Serapis this author described in some detail the playing position and movements of certain musicians (*tibicines*). In 1629 Fortunatus Scacchi[6] writing of the ritual music of ancient times, seized on this passage, but in so doing read *tubicines* for *tibicines* and thus transformed his reed players into trumpeters. Having done this he then made the quite gratuitous assumption that the movements described by Apuleius must have been the drawing in and out of telescopic slides. Only seven years later Mersenne[7] drew upon Scacchi and thus another fallacy became current and was repeatedly quoted right up to the first edition of *Grove*. In spite, however, of the recognised value of much of Mersenne's treatise some scholars, notably Gevaert and Mahillon, remained unconvinced, and when preparing his 1906 paper Galpin went back to the original text and was able to demonstrate its true meaning.

At the present time we have no reason to suppose that the free-slide principle was employed musically by the Romans, though their metal workers were certainly capable of making tubes fitting accurately one over the other, as is shown by some further remains dug up at Pompeii.[8] In 1892, also at Pompeii, a fresco was uncovered which depicts a long and closely folded trumpet. At the time of its discovery some details of the picture were thought to indicate the existence of a slide, but this idea has not been generally accepted. The most that we can safely conclude from this single illustration is that in late Roman times a form of trumpet was known which was folded in a manner that did not appear again in Europe until the 14th century. The majority of surviving Roman instruments show gentle curves, and it would seem that the close folding shown in the Pompeiian fresco was not a common feature. Incidentally, coiling in full circle appears to have been equally uncommon in Roman instruments, though we have one example at least in a terra cotta miniature 'bugle', probably a votive offering, now exhibited in the British Museum.

To summarise, we have some indication that Roman technology extended both to the making of close-fitting tubes and to some method of forming U-bends, but we have no evidence of a musical instrument of that age which incorporated both these features. It seems that the limited Roman idea of the use and purpose of lip-reed instruments made no demand for such an apparatus. The term *tuba ductilis* used by certain Latin writers Galpin has shown to refer to a method of manufacture—drawing out the metal with the hammer as against the common process of casting—and not to any specific instrumental type (see also p. 187).

We return then to the end of the Middle Ages—to the last quarter of the 15th century—when we hear of Hans Neuschel, the first recorded maker of the *Posaune*. Doppelmayr, whose account of the early artists and mathematicians of Nürnberg was published in 1730,[9] speaks of Neuschel's skill and reputation which gained him orders from Royal establishments several hundred miles from his home town. It is recorded that he made silver trombones for Pope Leo X and himself demonstrated the instrument in Rome, for which he was handsomely rewarded. Hans Neuschel died in 1533 and was succeeded in his craft by Hans the Younger and Jörg Neuschel, who made the second oldest dated *Posaune* now known to survive.[10] This magnificent instrument (Plate 8 B) now belongs to Anthony Baines and formerly adorned the collections of the late Canon Galpin and of the author. Although it has been subjected to a good deal of restoration over the centuries, this specimen is still in playing order and gives a good idea of the original dimensions of its tubing etc. The instrument is, in fact, in all major respects a trombone as used today, the only differences being in the loose stays already mentioned in our descriptive chapter (p. 76) and in the less marked 'flare' of the bell. The ivory mouthpiece, although obviously ancient, is possibly not contemporary.

Except for Doppelmayr's references, which, of course, form part of an historical survey written some 200 years after the event, we have little evidence concerning the trombone in the first half of the 16th century. Virdung (1511) and Agricola (1528 and 1545), it is true, both published versions of a rather crude woodcut, but neither give useful data, and the latter honestly admits that he really does not understand the instrument. Then from the middle of the century the picture changes entirely. With the surviving Jörg Neuschel specimen (1557) and others by the Nürnberg makers Anton Schnitzer (1579) and Cunrat Linczer (1587), as well as an example by Pierre Colbert of Rheims (1593), doubts are resolved and all the characteristics of the early trombone become clear.[11] From early in the 17th century onward quite a fair number of trombones survive, many of them dated and bearing their makers' names. The majority of them are now to be found in German musical collections, which is hardly surprising in view of the supremacy of the Nürnberg makers of their period. From the early 17th century, too, we begin to have really adequate written material and, while the major writers, Praetorius, Mersenne, and Speer, tell us little about the instrument itself that we cannot now learn from museum specimens, they wrote as musicians who heard or handled the trombone of their day and were aware of its place in contemporary art. Mersenne, indeed, mentions the seven positions of the slide. It is a great pity that we have no English musical historian of the time to set beside the German and French writers, for comparisons would be most interesting. In the Britain of the 16th and 17th centuries the sackbut was cultivated in so high a degree that British players were frequently sought after by Continental patrons. The Church, Court, and municipal archives of both England and Scotland abound in records of the trombone and its players, their fees, liveries, etc., and there are many references, too, in general literature. In passing we may note also a description of the early trombone by a Spanish(?) author. *El Melopeo* by Cerone, though written in Spanish, was published in Naples in 1613 (Galpin, op. cit.) and in it we find an account of the compass of the instrument and the use of crooks. This rather minor work, however, tells us nothing that is not more fully dealt with by Praetorius some five years later.

A composer of Praetorius' day (and probably fifty years before) would find a maker prepared to supply a set of trombones in four different sizes, and then, as now, the common or type instrument of the family was the tenor in B♭.

The group as Praetorius named them were as follows:

Alto   *Alt* or *discant Posaun* in F. (Possibly also in E♭?)
Tenor   *Gemeine Rechte Posaun* in B♭.
Bass   *Quart* or *Quint Posaun* in F and E♭ respectively.
Contrabass *Octav Posaun* in BB♭.

The historian tells us that in his day the Contrabass was rather uncommon and that two varieties were known; one was quite simply a double-size tenor sounding an octave lower; the other, not so large over all, achieved its low pitch by the combination of a proportionately larger bore with a crook inserted between the slide and the bellpipe. Praetorius' illustrations show all four instruments very clearly and we notice particularly that in the Bass and Contrabass members the bellpipe is coiled once or twice to reduce the total length. These instruments are also provided with a hinged handle of quite modern appearance to control the slide in the lower positions. In addition the *Quart* or *Quint* sizes shows a fixed transposing slide among the convolutions of the bell-pipe, and this is evidently shifted by a push-rod which projects forward towards the player's ear. The mechanism is very similar to the 'quick-change' slides fitted to some modern trumpets (p. 42). A fine example made by J. L. Ehe of Nürnberg just over a century after Praetorius is in the collection of the Gesellschaft der Musikfreunde in Wien, but this instrument must, I think, be regarded as rather old-fashioned for its date. It seems a little curious that Praetorius makes no reference to the double-slide method of shortening these unwieldy instruments (p. 51) for J. Neuschel's business papers include an enquiry from a client regarding one as early as *c.* 1540, and an actual example by Jobst Schnitzer dated 1612 still survives.

Marin Mersenne, the first of the important French musical historians, wrote two works, a Latin treatise *Harmonicorum* and a French work *Harmonie Universelle* (1636) in both of which he carefully describes the trombone which he calls *Tuba tractilis*. He adds little if anything to what we have already gathered from Praetorius, but his books are valuable to us as an indication of French usage in his time. He does not distinguish between the different sizes of trombone, but does inform us that in France it was customary to obtain a bass by adding to the tenor a crook or 'tortil' (in contemporary England a 'wreath'), which lowered the pitch by a fourth. This, it will be seen, anticipates in principle the German *Tenor-Bass Posaune* of today. Such a crook for the tenor instrument, though limited to a whole tone, was in fact depicted by Praetorius. Mersenne, further, deals with the seven positions of the slide and gives the diatonic scale for the first octave, noting particularly the apparent mystery of overlapping harmonic series yielding the same note with different shifts.

In 1687 Daniel Speer published the first edition of his treatise on the Art of Music[12] and from him we learn something of the trombone in the last quarter of the century. His account is rather more technical than those of the earlier writers we have mentioned, and shows perhaps a fuller appreciation of the capabilities of the lengthening-slide principle. Even so, he seems, like his predecessors, to regard the trombone as a diatonic instrument and he allows only four 'draws' of the slide, numbering them according to the intervals of a diatonic scale. Thus on a B♭ tenor instrument his 'erster Zug' yields the harmonic series on A and therefore corresponds to our 'second position', while the others follow as in this table:

'Draw' according to Speer	Modern 'Position'	Harmonic series
..	1st	B♭
Erster zug	2nd	A
Anderer zug	4th	G
Dritte zug	6th	F
Vierdte zug	7th	E

Some recognition of the chromatic nature of the trombone is shown when Speer points out that for semitones or notes sharpened or flattened the slide must be drawn in or out to intermediate positions, but the passage still seems to be rooted in a way of musical thinking ruled by the bonds of 'key'. It suggests a rather deliberate and dignified use of the slide and none of the agility we see today. This we shall touch on in another place when we look at the use to which the trombone has been put in the music of different ages.

The reader will no doubt have noticed that the family of trombones we have so far considered is short of one member. Taking the group to be centred round the B♭ tenor, we have lacked so far a treble or true *discant* a fourth above Praetorius' *Alt-Posaun*. This instrument did not appear till quite near the end of the 17th century, and formerly the alto had been used as the highest voice in the trombone choir. Indeed we have noticed that Praetorius himself used the terms *alt* and *discant* as alternatives. Shortly before 1700 German makers (and one Swede) began to produce these little trombones pitched an octave above the B♭ tenor, and these may in some respects have formed a link between 17th- and 18th-century practice. The earliest-known English composition in which some such treble instrument was imperative was Purcell's 'March and Canzona' written for the funeral of Queen Mary in 1695. In this four 'Flat Trumpets' were specified, and Cummings suggested that the name was connected with the fact that in Purcell's time music in the minor was regularly called 'flat' music. Canon Galpin, however, pointed out that no ordinary natural trumpet can furnish the flat third of the minor key and so concluded that Flat Trumpets must have been treble sackbuts—more especially since these instruments were sometimes known as 'Trumpets harmonious'. Since Galpin drew his conclusions the Talbot Manuscript of *c.* 1690 has been analysed by A. C. Baines in the pages of the *Galpin Society Journal*, and in it we find the following entry: 'Flat Trumpet. In a Flat Trumpet the mouthpiece stands oblique towards right. 2nd Crook placed near left Ear & by it you draw out the Inward yards, whereof one reaches to the Boss of the Pavilion, the other to the 1st Crook: its size with the yards shutt the

same with common Trumpet.' This description suggests very strongly
the much later English Slide Trumpet (p. 115). In the light of this
evidence we must now, I think, discard the idea that Purcell employed
trombones, whatever function these instruments may have fulfilled
on the Continent.

The opening of the 18th century, then, saw the family of trombones
complete, but it also ushered in an unexplained fall in their popularity
in England, France, and Italy. In Germany this was perhaps less
marked, but even so the supremacy of Nürnberg as a centre of brass
making and playing was in decline. The names of makers working in
other towns in Germany and beyond, begin to appear with some
frequency on collectors' specimens dating from the 1700s, and it is
clear that the craft was then becoming decentralised. This, of course,
would imply a loosening of the Guild and Apprentice system which
had formerly kept a close tie between playing and manufacture.

Late in the century Dr. Burney tells us that much difficulty was
experienced in finding players to complete the great band for the Handel
Celebrations of 1784. He writes—'the Sackbut or Double Trumpet
was sought; but so many years had elapsed since it had been used in
this kingdom that neither the instrument nor a performer on it could
easily be found. It was however discovered . . . that in His Majesty's
private Military Band there were six musicians who played the three
several species of sackbut—tenor, base and double base' (sic).[13] This
observation of Burney's is doubly interesting in that, besides reflecting
the contemporary status of the trombone, it contained, as we now
recognise, two pointers towards its future in the next century. The first
indicates that from being very largely confined to formal duties in the
Church or at Court[14] and civic functions, the trombone was then beginning to enter on a new phase as an important element in the 'new idea'
of military music, where it was to lose much of its sombre character
and finally achieve great brilliance. To quote Adam Carse: 'Until
near the close of the 18th century the trombone was hardly what we
would now call an orchestral instrument', and again, '. . . with the
exception of a few isolated cases, parts for trombones are not to be
found in opera scores till late in the 18th century'. The second pointer
lies in Burney's implication that in 1784 tenor, bass, and contrabass
were the only sizes of sackbut generally known; and Burney was well
in touch with musical practice on the Continent as well as in Britain.
In spite of the completion of the theoretical group c. 1700, it is clear that
soon after the mid-century the treble instrument had virtually dis-

appeared, and even the higher alto in F was being employed less and less frequently. The standard group which was to pass over to the 1800s consisted of Alto in E♭, Tenor in B♭, and Bass in E♭ or F.

To conclude our short survey of this very important period in trombone history let us turn again from usage to the instrument itself. The early 18th-century trombones were very little different from those of the late 1600s. The old loose flat stays still supported the bellpipe, but before long these had given place to permanently fixed tubular struts. And here a note to collectors of old instruments: many specimens as we now see them have been repeatedly repaired, even brought up to date by former owners, so it is not uncommon to find fixed tubular stays as replacements. In these cases we have only the colour of the metal and the character of the workmanship to guide us. Again, during the first two or three decades, the trombone bell retained its gently curving, vase-like form, although trumpets by the same makers already showed a marked terminal flare. By about 1740, however, the trombone, too, began to show this feature and, though we must make allowance for individual variation between different workers, we may say that the instrument had at this time assumed its modern form. Indeed, but for the absence of such details as the 'stocking' (p. 48), it is often difficult for the layman to tell a late 18th-century trombone from one made fifty years after. Of mouthpieces it is difficult to speak with certainty for lack of examples of undoubted provenance. The most we can say is that in general during the period under review the truly conical mouthpiece of the early sackbut seems to have given place to a deep curvilinear cup with a distinct 'throat', but even so we cannot afford to be dogmatic, for no doubt in the 18th century personal preference was just as influential as it is today. Finally, during this time, the employment of detached crooks gradually died out and by c. 1800 was virtually unknown.

The year 1800 we may conveniently, though quite arbitrarily, take as marking the beginning of the 'modern' period of the trombone. After its partial eclipse towards the end of the previous century the next two decades saw a great revival. Beginning with the efforts of such men of position as the Duke of York, who interested himself in the reorganisation of the Coldstream Guards band as far back as 1780, military commands in many parts of Europe began to set their musical houses in order, and therein the trombone very soon showed that it could produce a tone both weighty and brilliant. No doubt there was much that was vulgar and meretricious in this essentially outdoor music—due perhaps to a reversion to that desire for display which first made the parent Buisine prominent in Western Europe—and certainly critics were not wanting to mourn the departed refinement of the old sackbut.[15] The point they so often missed was that, in judicious hands, the old refinement was still there to be called forth when required, and the street-band crudity for which the trombone became for a time notorious was a fault in the player or conductor and not in the instrument. We have already alluded to this in another context (p. 71). Laying criticism aside, however, we must thank the military activities of the early 1800s for a lasting revival of the trombone, and the rising demand for instruments is reflected in the many new names that now begin to appear in the lists of makers in Germany, France, Belgium, Italy, and Austria. At this time, too, the trombone began to find a regular place in the opera house, where before it had only been used occasionally for effects of particular solemnity and grandeur. With the rising popularity of a more romantic Italian opera, brilliance in the middle and lower brass was called for and here the trombone in its new guise could serve magnificently. Only one short step farther brought the trombone into the normal complement of the symphony orchestra and by mid-century re-establishment was complete, though, to be sure, not all the members of the family had fared equally well.

The three trombones taken over by the opera and symphony composers of the early 19th century were, as we have already indicated, the E♭ alto, B♭ tenor, and F bass, and these remained nominally the standard trio for some fifty years. In actual practice the tenor soon became again, as in Praetorius' time, the dominant instrument. The wide compass of which the trombone is capable allowed the tenor in a great measure to replace both the alto and the bass, particularly in French orchestras where these two were hardly to be found at all. Perhaps such an economy of man-power was sometimes really necessary in respect of an instrument that was still at the period something of a novelty, but it certainly resulted in a loss of tonal variety. In a Tutor published c. 1830 the well-known Vienna player Nemetz calls the B♭ trombone Bass, Alto, or Tenor and specifies a different mouthpiece for each function. The bass in F he recognises separately under the old title of *Quartposaune*. In Germany the bass in E♭ or F continued in favour but was sometimes replaced by a special wide-bore B♭ tenor which masqueraded under the title of *Bassposaune in B♭*. Among the Germans, too, the alto remained in use longer than anywhere else in Europe, making its final surrender only in last quarter of the century. There also, although admittedly the evidence is slender, we find the last faint traces of the treble which elsewhere had been obsolete for some fifty years. In Britain the alto seems to have disappeared quite early, yielding place to a second tenor playing mainly in the upper part of its compass and so leading to the now usual group of two tenors and one bass which is found everywhere from the symphony orchestra to that essentially British institution the Brass Band. As to the contrabass, we know that in Britain, at least, it had a place in the first reformed military bands under Royal patronage (Burney, op. cit.), but it seems to have failed to keep its position in the general reorganisation that took place on the Continent. We may guess that its size and vulnerability under real Service conditions would soon put it at a disadvantage beside even the more primitive of the valved basses (p. 59). In this context it is perhaps a little puzzling that when Wilhelm Wieprecht, that remarkable civilian musician,[16] began his reform of the Prussian military music *c.* 1828, the only trombones he had in his first band were three *basses.*

The restoration of the contrabass trombone to a place, albeit a limited one, in the modern opera and symphony orchestra we owe to Wagner, whose continual demands for enhanced orchestral colouring up to his death in 1882 stimulated musical instrument-makers in many directions. The first contrabasses constructed to meet his requirements were, we must admit, not entirely satisfactory, but this should by no means detract from his credit as a musical force.

To round off, let us summarise briefly the position of the slide trombone at the beginning of the present century. In the full orchestra, the brass band, and the military band of normal size the usual complement was two tenors and a bass. The tenors were always in B♭ but the bass varied. In Britain it was most commonly the smaller bass in G which had become popular there in the mid-19th century. This instrument was also to be found in France in those orchestras which employed a true bass at all and did not still adhere to the traditional three-tenor group. Under German influence the bass remained the *Quartposaune* in F, but this was rapidly being rivalled by the so-called *Tenor-bass posaune*, a wide-bore B♭ tenor transposable down a fourth to F by means of a valve and supplementary tubing (p. 55). Today, with our much freer international communication these differences are becoming less and less marked, and probably the preference of individual players is now more significant than any ingrained national custom. Finally, the present-day interest in all ancient music has resulted in the reproduction and special study of all the old trombones and their techniques, so that we can today sometimes hear sackbut playing which the good Father Mersenne would have applauded instead of shuddering.*

NOTES

[1] F. W. Galpin, 'The Sackbut, its Evolution and History', *Proceedings of the Musical Association*, London, 1906, pp. 1–25. This paper as printed is a model in the fullness of its documentation and the wide coverage of the references cited.

[2] *Op. cit.* p. 2. and *European Musical Instruments*, London, Williams & Norgate Ltd., 1937, p. 240.

[3] Curt Sachs, *The History of Musical Instruments*, London, J. M. Dent & Sons Ltd., 1942, p. 326.

[4] Though they did not positively clear up the matter, Galpin's researches revealed how unreliable, even fanciful, some of the most respected 19th-century reference books are on this subject.

[5] F. W. Galpin, *Old English Instruments of Music*, London, Methuen & Co. Ltd., third edition revised, 1932, p. 208.

[6] Fortunatus Scacchi, *Sacrorum Elaeoschrismaton Myrothecium*, Rome, 1629.

[7] Marin Mersenne, *Harmonie Universelle*, Paris, Baudry, 1636.

[8] *Op. cit. 1*, p. 7, footnote 1.

[9] Doppelmayr, *Historische Nachricht von der Nürnbergischen Mathematicis und Künstlern*, Nürnberg, 1730.

[10] *Op. cit. 1*, p. 11 and footnotes. Galpin gives some most interesting details and translations from some of Neuschel's business letters, quotations, etc. which are still extant.

[11] The Schnitzer and Linczer instruments are preserved respectively at Verona and Hamburg. The French specimen, though later, is probably rarer than the others. It is in the Gemeente Museum at The Hague. An even earlier example by Erasmus Schnitzer (1551) has come to light in recent years in the collection of the Germanisches National Museum, Nürnberg.

[12] Daniel Speer, *Grund-richtiger Unterricht der Musikalischen Kunst*, Ulm, 1687 and 1697.

[13] Charles Burney, *Account of the Musical Performances in Westminster Abbey, etc.*, London, 1785. Introduction, p. 7. Russell and Elliot in *The Brass Band Movement*, London, J. M. Dent & Sons Ltd., 1936, quote a manuscript account by the secretary of the Manchester Musical Festival of 1828 concerning his Committee's resolution that 'the King . . . be applied to . . . to be Patron, and *to order his Trombones*'. It looks as if the Manchester committee were somewhat concerned for the prestige of their festival, and perhaps Burney really meant 'not a *good* player could be found'. It is on record that the famous Besses o' the Barn, based only five miles from Manchester, included one trombone when they were formed as a brass and reed band in 1818.

[14] In spite of its decline as a popular instrument the trombone seems always to have survived in the favourable atmosphere of Court. In England sackbuts, presumably retained Court musicians, played at the coronations of both George I and George II.

[15] Even in 1906 Galpin was to observe, 'How Mersenne would shudder at the ordinary trombone playing of the present day!' And again, 'would it not be possible to revive in this 20th century the true sackbut playing for which England was so famous in the sixteenth century?' Since that was written Galpin's

* See Appendix 3, p. 256.

question has been answered more than once and in the affirmative. The writer remembers an occasion in 1935 when he heard the brass section of the then B.B.C. Variety Orchestra huddled together in a corner of the studio during a programme break and playing just for themselves the Beethoven *Funeral Equale*. It was a truly glorious sound.

16 See Chapter 8, note 9, p. 183.

The Age of Mechanisation: Valves and Valve Systems

BECAUSE BOTH THE natural trumpet and the simple slide trombone have important functions at the present day, this chapter necessarily overlaps in time coverage the two previous ones. The period extends from the last two decades of the 18th century to modern times, and as much of the material we have to consider is based on written records, patent specifications, and actual specimens of instruments, we can, on the whole, speak with some precision. Nevertheless, even in this recent phase of trumpet history there are some areas of speculation.

In Chapters 1 and 2 we have seen something of the purpose and *modus operandi* of valves, and some possible motives for their invention have been suggested. We have seen, too, that it was among horn players that the need for such devices was first and most acutely felt. Trumpets and trombones acquired valves at a second stage, as it were, and after these had to some extent already proved their worth.

Simple enough in conception, the valve is in fact no more than a spring-controlled 'two-way tap' by which, at the touch of a finger, supplementary lengths can be added to or cut off from the main tube of a brass instrument; but the ingenuity and patience which has been devoted over the years to perfecting it make it one of the most interesting mechanisms known to music. Moreover, once the simple and reliable valve had become more or less a commonplace, the facilities it offered led to new fundamental thinking among instrument makers. Thus, in the last hundred years we find old instruments completely re-designed, as well as entirely new families created. These latter we hardly need to consider here, except to note in passing that the application of valves to large tubes of 'bugle-horn' proportions gave rise to the various brass basses, some of which, in spite of considerable tonal difference, at times threatened the existence of the deeper-voiced trombones. To the men, both known and unknown, who did this work our tribute of recognition is due.

A complete valve consists of two essential parts, an outer casing to which the various tubes of the instrument are attached, and a close-fitting inner body, pierced by alternative windways, which, according to its position, connect the external tubes in different ways. The following several diagrams will help to make this clear. At the present day two principal classes of valve are recognised; the piston type in which the inner body moves in a vertical direction, and the rotary type which is in fact just a refined adaptation of the age-old plug cock used to tap beer barrels or wine casks. The former is generally favoured in English-speaking countries and in France, while the latter usually betokens German influence. Both types as now made are equally efficient acoustically, and in the sizes required for trumpets or trombones are equally responsive. Large rotary valves are sometimes a little sluggish due to friction, but on the other hand equivalent piston valves often require a depth of travel which is awkward for the player's fingers. Both have their virtues and it is not unknown to find both together performing distinctive duties on the same instrument. Finally we must notice here a sort of double piston valve which, though losing ground generally, is still held in high esteem by Viennese horn players and others bred in their tradition. We shall describe this more fully in its proper chronological place.

Apart from the work of the Bohemian Kölbel who seems to have experimented (c. 1760) with two flap keys covering holes (see *Amor Schall*, p. 118) the first recorded idea for making brass instruments chromatic by any means other than the free slide goes to the credit of an Irishman, Charles Clagget, who in 1788 obtained an English patent for his 'Chromatic Trumpet and French Horn'.[1] Briefly, his notion was to fill in gaps in the harmonic series by uniting two instruments pitched a semitone apart and arranging for one mouthpiece to connect with either at will. This could of course be done readily with a simple modern valve but, even so, elementary acoustics show us that the scale furnished could not be chromatic below the fourth octave. However, from his description Clagget's device can hardly have been a valve as we understand it and a vital part of the mechanism seems to have been 'a piece of elastic, gum, or leather' which united the mouthpiece with a joint while another similar closed off whichever tube was at any time out of use. In 1793 Clagget published a pamphlet, now very rare, called *Musical Phenomena* in which he expatiated on the defects of natural instruments and attributed to his own invention a mysterious power of 'tempering' defective notes. Unfortunately Clagget's writings are both

L

diffuse and obscure and have so far defied really satisfactory interpretation. Morley-Pegge has gone into the matter more deeply than any other musicologist and his assessment of both the original material and other students' comments is particularly valuable as coming from a player-scholar.[2] There seems to be no doubt that most of Clagget's 'geese were swans' and that he over-valued his invention;[3] nevertheless his 'chromatic horn' was undoubtedly constructed and a few public performances given upon it. The important point for us here is the early date of Clagget's invention.

We come now to the invention of the valve proper, the parent of all those now in use, and here again Morley-Pegge's researches have not been bettered.[4] To quote him, 'Which of the two, the Saxon Heinrich Stölzel or the Silesian Friedrich Blühmel, who jointly took out a ten-year patent for valves in Berlin in 1818, was actually first in the field will now probably never be known, for even their contemporaries were unable to agree about it'. Of the two Stölzel is known to have been a horn player, first in the private band of the Prince of Pless, and later in the Royal Opera orchestra in Berlin. He also held the appointments of Royal Chamber Musician and instrument repairer to the King of Prussia. Blühmel was more obscure and the most we know of his general circumstances is that he was a musician in a mine company's works band. We first know of him as a signatory to the above-mentioned patent application, and thereafter hear little until after the patent had expired and the partners separated. In the meantime, he sought unsuccessfully to secure an exclusive patent on another valve which he had invented and, on failing to do so, asserted that he was in fact the originator of the 1818 idea. The Prussian Patent Office, however, remained unimpressed. It is beyond question that Stölzel was in Berlin early in 1815 with a valve horn which he claimed as his own idea, and which was readily taken up by the well-known instrument makers Griessling and Schlott. Summing up the evidence, much of it conflicting and highly partisan, Morley-Pegge concludes that in all probability Stölzel was the first to plan an actual valve, while Blühmel made the first more or less satisfactory one.

The valve which was the subject of the 1818 patent was, we may perhaps think, a curious and clumsy contraption, square in section and, to judge by the few examples now known, heavy and rather sluggish. On the other hand it had one excellent feature which its early rivals lacked—the windways in the body were unrestricted and the angles involved were not sharp. The Carlsruhe firm of W. Schuster undertook the making of these square valves and persevered with them for some ten years before they finally gave place to more elegant though acoustically inferior types. Fig. 32 B is a sectional plan of the passages, the 2nd valve being at rest in the *up* position and the 1st *depressed* to cut in the supplementary tubing. Plate 17 A shows a trumpet on this system in the collection of the Brussels Conservatoire.

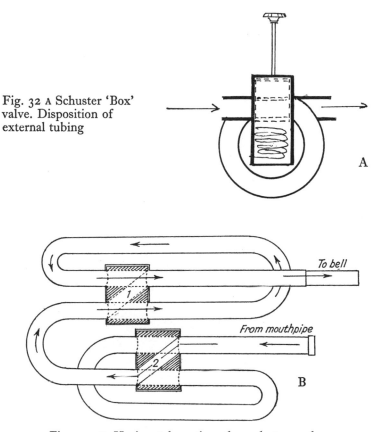

Fig. 32 A Schuster 'Box' valve. Disposition of external tubing

A

Fig. 32 B Horizontal section through two valves:
1. Depressed. 2. Up position
(B *After Morley-Pegge*)

The precise form of the horn valve submitted by Stölzel to Griessling and Schlott early in 1815 we do not know, but the likelihood is that it was a primitive version of the model that has become traditionally associated with his name, and was still being fitted to cheap French cornets as late as 1914. This 'Stölzel' valve was much more elegant than the Schuster type, being cylindrical and not much larger in diameter than the associated tubing. Its great fault lay in the fact that the bottom of the outer casing served as a windway and this necessitated a sharp right-angled turn and some constriction of the passages passing through the body of the piston. Fig. 33 will make this point clear. Players,

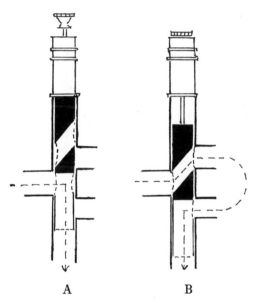

A   B

Fig. 33   Diagrammatic section of the Stölzel valve
          (spring not shown):
          A Piston up
          B Piston down. Though not to scale, the
            drawing shows the two defects of the
            system, i.e. sharp bends in the air column
            and constricted internal passage

especially the more conservative of those brought up on the technique of the hand horn, were not slow to comment on this defect, but in spite of this the Stölzel valve with minor improvements soon ousted the square type and began a long and useful life, albeit latterly on second-class instruments.

The next real invention, as distinct from mere structural improvements, was a British one. In 1824 English patent No. 5013 was granted to John Shaw of Glossop, Derbyshire, for 'transverse spring slides for trumpets, trombones, French horns, bugles, and every other instrument of the like nature'. Shaw, who seems at different periods of his life to have been both a farmer and a brass worker, was evidently a man of character and ingenuity, and we hear of him more than once in the pages of instrumental history. His first invention consisted in arranging part of the body tube of an instrument in the form of a long narrow U and at calculated intervals breaking into the parallel limbs with pairs of short tubular casings standing at right angles to the plane of the U. These pairs of casings were occupied by pairs of hollow pistons united at the top by a cross tube making a sort of tubular 'staple'. When retained in the *up* position by a spring these staples did not interfere in any way with the main windway, but when depressed by means of a touch-piece they made a short-circuit or 'shunt' across the U of the main tube, at the same time cutting off the loop beyond. Thus the 'spring slides' were in fact *ascending* valves which on being pressed *shortened* the main air column. Shaw also realised that by turning his spring slides upside down so that the shunt was *removed* when the touch-piece was pressed they could likewise serve as ordinary *descending* or lengthening valves. In the actual instruments depicted by Shaw in the patent specification the trumpet had three ascending valves each raising the pitch progressively by a semitone, and one, placed nearest the bell, which lowered it by a whole tone. For the trombone five ascending valves and one descending were envisaged. In common with the Stölzel valve, the spring slide clearly had the acoustic fault of sharp bends in the air column, but it did avoid constrictions. The great importance of Shaw's invention, however, lies in the fact that it incorporated three distinct new principles each of which was to be exploited later by some of the most famous instrument makers. These were *twin pistons*, *independent valves* (for by their nature the spring slides could only be used one at a time), and *ascending valves*. No example of a spring slide instrument is known to survive, but that manufacture was indeed begun seems certain. Russell and Elliot tell us that according to Enderby Jackson, a stalwart of the early Brass Band days who got his information from Shaw's own papers, the instruments were made in the workshop of a Sheffield brass repairer called Battee, and that George Metzler of London was appointed agent for their sale in 1825.[5] (Fig. 34, p. 151.)

With the third decade of the 19th century the student of brass instruments becomes aware of a gradual change in the pattern of progress. No longer do the needs of the horn player appear as the first consideration in the mind of the maker, and from now on inventions and improvements in valve mechanism become the common property of all the different brass families. This is therefore an appropriate point to interrupt our history for a moment and to try to picture the thinking of instrument makers and composers of the time. What benefits could valves confer on the trumpet and trombone in particular? The case of the trumpet is simple; by making it chromatic throughout its entire compass, instead of in the fourth octave only, valves restored to it the status of a melodic instrument which it had lost since the decline of clarino playing in the post-Handel era. Moreover, with the lower octaves chromatic, melody playing without constant crook changing came within the capacity of the average trumpeter instead of the specialist only, and in a register more generally useful to the composer. (The English slide trumpet, originated *c.* 1804, had already anticipated these points to some extent but, as this instrument was virtually unknown on the Continent, it has no bearing on the general argument.) In regard to the trombone, however, the matter is less clear-cut. Apart from dreams of a unified technique for all brasses, the revival of the trombone in the armies of Europe and the departure from its traditional 'sackbut' treatment in military music were probably the first influences to operate. In the circumstances surrounding musicians who at that time were becoming more and more regular soldiers instead of mere uniformed servants of Royal patrons, the trombone slide could certainly be something of an anxiety, and, indeed, some European countries, who would not today countenance a valve trombone in their symphony orchestras, retain that instrument for army use. Secondly, the sackbut, with its new voice, had by now found a fresh welcome in the opera house. There the vulnerability of the slide would seem to be no particular problem, but it could not compete with valves in sheer agility, and this characteristic for a time appealed mightily to the new generation of operatic composers. Such men as Rossini began to write *bravura* trombone parts which, even today, are not easy to realise fully except on the valved instrument. Modern slide trombonists overcome the purely technical difficulties with extraordinary success, but these specifically valve trombone parts written in the early 19th century have a characteristic quality which is almost impossible to define in words, though the musician recognises it at once.

Under such influences as we have just outlined inventions in the field of brass mechanics came thick and fast in the years after 1825. Some few of these embodied new ideas of lasting worth but many were no more than improvements or modifications of earlier work. Sometimes really excellent devices became popular for a time and then disappeared again, either because in the long run they proved inefficient mechanically, or because they cost too much to make and could be replaced

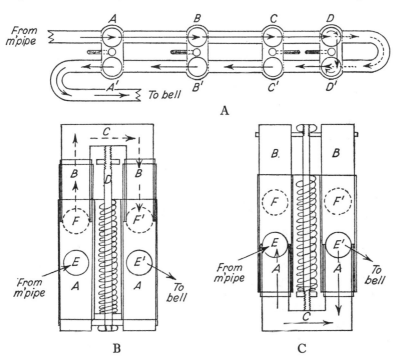

Fig. 34 A General lay-out of Shaw's spring slides as applied to the trumpet
B Details of spring slide used as an ascending valve
C Spring slide inverted as a descending valve
(*After Morley-Pegge*)

by others that were only little inferior musically. The instrument-makers again found themselves obliged to compromise. At this time, too, the element of competition between rival manufacturers began to be felt, and by the mid-century the trade, especially in France, was bedevilled by litigation over patents and priorities. Curiously enough, the French did not concern themselves very much with valves in the early stages, their approach to the detached crook problem being along 'omnitonique' lines (p. 73). When they did enter the field they quickly became very active and their influence has lasted till the present day.

In 1826 the Italian composer Spontini, who was then chief Kapell-meister to the King of Prussia, sent a number of two- and three-valved instruments to Paris.[6] Out of this consignment Dauverné, first trumpet at the Opéra, secured a trumpet furnished with Stölzel valves, which he pronounced defective both in tone and intonation.[7] In spite, however, of Dauverné's poor opinion, the distinguished horn player Meifred was attracted by the Stölzel invention and he set himself to improving its general construction. As a result, in company with the maker J.-C. Labbaye, he produced a two-valved horn which gained a silver medal at the Paris Industrial Exhibition of 1827. In the same year Dauprat, professor of the horn at the Paris Conservatoire, got one of the square-valved instruments direct from Schuster of Carlsruhe, but very soon gave up trying to use it. Meifred, on the other hand, found this instrument good, at least in respect of the clearer passages through the pistons, but he remained convinced of the over-all superiority of cylindrical valves and adhered to them for his own future work. He made a number of general improvements but his most important contribution was the provision of tuning slides in the supplementary tubes which are now regarded as essential on all brass instruments.[8]

While French makers, notably Labbaye and Halary, were busy with Stölzel's valve, in Germany Blühmel had come to the fore again with his *Drehbüchsen-ventil*, which we may suppose to be the valve for which he had already been refused a Prussian patent. In the absence of drawings or a detailed description it has been suggested that this may have been a rotary valve, but if it was, why was the patent with-held? Some years later Wieprecht[9] devised a very well-known mechanism which he called a *Stecherbüchsenventil* and this he admitted to be a development of Blühmel's model. From this it appears that the Dreh-büchsen-ventil could only have been a piston valve of sorts; Rode,[10] writing in 1860, says that it found much favour in Vienna, Pesth, and especially Prague, where in 1829 it had been much improved on lines suggested by Joseph Kail, professor of trumpet in the Conservatoire.

We have seen that in the course of just over a decade the formative work in valve mechanics was done in Germany, France, and then Ger-many again. Now for a matter of five years the main focus of our interest shifts to Austria. In 1830 the Vienna instrument maker Leopold Uhlmann secured a *k.k.Privilegium* for the twin-piston mechanism to which we have already alluded, and which was to become extremely successful throughout Central Europe and in Belgium under the title of *Wiener-Ventil*. In the latter country its popularity at one time became so great that French makers tended to identify it as 'système belge'. It appears that this device was not entirely original with Uhlmann, for a form of it is to be seen on a trumpet made by Michael Saurle of Munich and dated 1829, now in the Crosby Brown Collection of the Metropolitan Museum of Art, New York.[11] As will be seen from Fig. 36, p. 155, Uhlmann's version is much the better, for in it the pistons proper are completely enclosed and so protected from dust and grit which are the bugbear of all exposed slides. Because of the twin-piston feature (the only one in common) some workers have suggested that the Vienna-valve was no more than an adaptation of Shaw's spring slide. This, I think, is hardly tenable. In Shaw's instruments the paired pistons were placed in opposite limbs of a looped windway and the tube uniting them provided a 'shunt' across it. In the Vienna-valve the piston cases are placed side by side on a single tube; there is no tube connecting the pistons themselves, and they serve only to divert the main air column into a subsidiary loop and back again. Shaw's valves were *independent*, the Vienna type *dependent* and used in combination. As our diagrams show, the 'sharp corner' problem was still present in the Vienna-valve, but there somehow it seems to have been less objectionable. In 1835 Johann Strauss the elder and his orchestra visited Berlin. These outstanding musicians used trumpets and horns fitted with the Vienna-valve and it may well be that besides introducing it in the Prussian capital, their touring performances served as a testimonial much farther afield.

The next event of major significance in brass history was the grant in 1832 of a *k.k.Privilegium* to Joseph Riedl, also of Vienna, for his *Rad-Maschine*. This is the earliest-known official recognition of an undoubted rotary valve, and, though experimental models may have been in existence for a year or two, it certainly dates the commercial advent of the device. Curiously enough, the rotary valve never gained much favour with English, French, or Belgian horn players, though other countries adopted it almost at once. Distin of London,[12] Higham of Manchester, Courtois, the two Saxes, and Gautrot in Paris, and Mahillon of Brussels all made a few rotary instruments, but none seem to have attracted players much until the wholesale switch from the French to the German pattern of orchestral horn in the 1930s virtually abolished all choice.

The simplest in essentials of all valves, the rotary, consists of an

inner cylinder perforated or grooved on the periphery with two chan-
nels, and fitting accurately into an outer casing to which the main and
subsidiary tubes of the instrument are attached (Fig. 35). With this

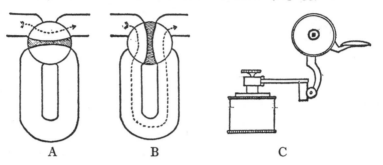

Fig. 35   Horizontal section of rotary valve:
        A Normal position
        B Touch depressed
        C External appearance. Typical crank
          action. The return spring is housed in
          the upper cylinder near the touch-piece

'rotor' in the normal position the air column passes almost straight
through the valve, but a quarter-turn diverts it through the supplementary loop. When generously constructed the windway is virtually
unrestricted, but sometimes in efforts to keep down the size of the valve
this point has been rather neglected. Its cross-section too is sometimes
rather distorted in the grooved type of rotor though this is of much less
acoustic significance than actual compression.

Although from our vantage point of a century and a quarter we now
see that the two Viennese patents mentioned were to have a lasting
effect on the development of valves, it is not to be supposed that a local
success, however brilliant, in one European capital would immediately
discourage all research elsewhere. Moreover, European commercial
history tells us that with the intense rivalry, not to say dislike, that
existed at the time between the Austrian Empire and other German-
speaking States, a Viennese invention was liable to find a cold reception
there.

In Berlin in 1835 Wieprecht, then well on his way to a dominant
position in Prussian military music, made the first big stride in improving piston valves. Together with the maker J. G. Moritz he devised a
new type which was soon to be generally known as the *Berliner-Pumpe*.
By making the piston itself relatively large in diameter, Wieprecht was

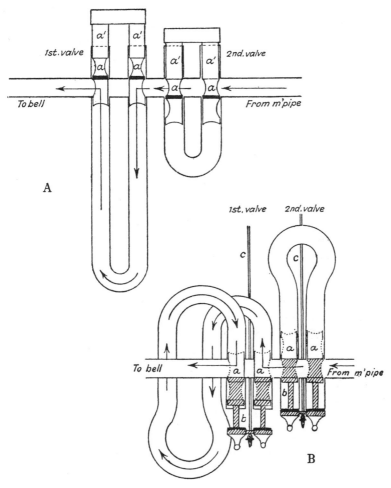

Fig. 36 A First type of Wiener-Ventil: *a* Piston,
a portion of piston exposed when the
valve is depressed (the first valve is shown
depressed)

B Uhlmann improved Wiener-Ventil: *a*
Piston. *b* Connecting-rod exposed when
the valve is depressed. The piston itself
remains entirely enclosed. *c* Actuating
spring-controlled push-rod operated
by the finger (the first valve is shown
depressed)

(*After Morley-Pegge*)

able to design curved internal passages which got rid of the sharp right-angles. At the same time by bringing all the external tubes to the casing in the same horizontal plane he minimised the vertical movement necessary in the piston and avoided using the bottom of the casing as a windway (Fig. 37). Under Wieprecht's powerful influence Berliner-

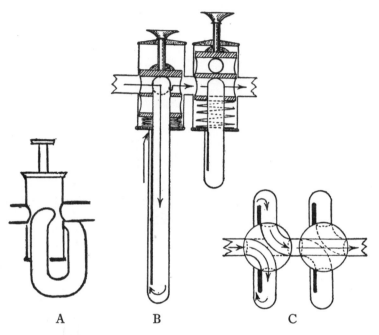

A   B   C

Fig. 37   A Berliner-Pumpe. General proportions
and arrangement of external tubing.
B & C Horizontal and vertical sections
(B & C *After Morley-Pegge*)

Pumpen were soon standardised in all Prussian bands. When the young Belgian Adolphe Sax started his business in Paris in 1843 he began at once making Berliner-Pumpen—without acknowledgement to the inventor, we suspect—and there is no doubt that these excellent valves contributed much to his early reputation.[13] In the hands of Henry Distin,[14] both as agent and as a member of the celebrated family Brass Quintet, the Sax instruments became widely known in Britain and were, when finances allowed, eagerly taken up by the early workmen's brass bands.

In chronological order the next innovation to enjoy some success was a British one. John Shaw, inventor of the spring slides, obtained another patent in 1838 covering what he called *swivel valves* for brass instruments, and the London maker J. A. Köhler immediately negotiated the right to exploit these for a term of years. This invention of Shaw's was in no way related to the spring slide. It consisted basically of a pair of flat metal plates placed face to face and held in contact by nuts on a central pivot so that one could rotate against the other. One plate, rigidly built into the instrument, was pierced with two holes leading to the mouthpipe and the main tube respectively, while the movable plate carried two knuckles of tubing of different lengths, each bridging two holes. In the normal position the shorter knuckle completed the windway through the instrument, but when the plate was turned through about 60° the longer one took its place and so lengthened the air column (Fig. 38). As originally designed the opposed plates were in the form of a wide capital I with large cusps, but the inventor himself pointed out in the patent specification that circular discs would have the advantage of never exposing the contact surfaces to dust and dirt. It was with circular plates that Köhler produced what he called *Patent Lever Valves*, evidently to the annoyance of Shaw who saw no reason to change his original title of 'swivel'. After sponsoring the original model for a year or two Köhler presented a much improved version in which the fixed plate was pierced with four holes and carried both the main windways and the supplementary tubing. The moving plate then carried two small connecting knuckles only. This arrangement Köhler called the *New Patent Lever Valve*. As with so many musical inventions some doubt has been cast on the originality of Shaw's idea, for Meifred records a disc valve devised by Halary of Paris in 1835 which seems to have been very similar.[15] Several authorities have stated that Halary patented this valve but recent researches into the French records have failed to reveal any protection granted (Morley-Pegge, op. cit.). On the other hand, the writer of the relevant section of Day's catalogue was inclined to attribute the original idea to Shaw and to assume that somehow Halary got knowledge of it before the British patent was granted.[16] At all events it is known that Halary did not proceed to the commercial manufacture of disc valves. Possibly he foresaw the one great weakness in the system which in the long run was to cause its downfall even in England. Considered quite objectively the Shaw-Köhler instruments had some excellent features. The windway was quite unconstricted throughout and the U bends were much less compressed than in many modern instruments, both of which

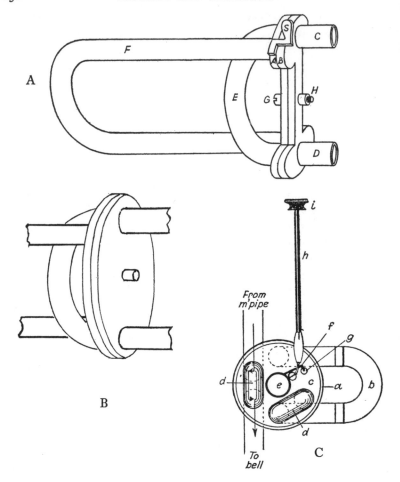

Fig. 38 A Shaw's patent swivel valve:
   A. Movable plate perforated with holes corresponding
   with each end of each tube. B. Corresponding fixed
   plate to which are soldered the main windways C and
   D. E. Bow ensuring continuity of windway when the
   finger-plate is not depressed. F. Supplementary
   tubing brought into the circuit in place of E when the
   finger-plate is depressed. G. Screw pivot fastening A
   to B. H. Nut to hold A and B in their correct positions.
   S. Finger-plate. The spring is a flat one attached by
   two screws to the far side of B. It is not visible on the
   drawing.

points made for good intonation and free blowing. A large number of Patent Lever instruments were supplied to the British army, and no less than eighteen were sold at one time to the Band of the Crystal Palace when that institution was opened in 1854. Eventually, however, the difficulty of keeping the pairs of opposed discs airtight when a little worn proved insuperable and the idea was discarded after a life of some twenty years. One wonders if the whole story of valved brass might not have been very different had Köhler been able to call on modern methods of hard metal plating and lapping mated surfaces.

The piston valve of the present day is basically that introduced in 1839 by François Périnet of Paris, an instrument-maker of whom surprisingly little is known in view of the importance of his work in several fields. Périnet also adopted the principle of building up curved passages inside the piston, but by placing them on the diagonal he was able to reduce its over-all diameter and therefore the attendant friction and inertia, which in the Wieprecht valve gave a tendency to sluggishness (Fig. 39). These advantages were secured at the cost of some departure from a truly circular section throughout the passages which had been a feature of the Berliner-Pumpe, but the cross-sectional area of the windway was well maintained and abrupt changes were avoided. We have already referred several times to the compromises that instrument-makers have always had to make between the ideal and the practical, and nowhere is this more evident than in the matter of piston valves. Some early makers of the Périnet valve, in their concern not to constrict the air column, went too far the other way and made some of the piston passages slightly larger in diameter than the main tubing. This of course

---

B Principle of circular plate version sold by Köhler as the Patent Lever Valve

C Köhler's modification called the New Patent Lever:
   a. Fixed back plate carrying the valve loop b; c. Movable plate carrying two short bows d, d; e. Spring-box containing coiled watch spring; f. 'Finger' fixed to the revolving outer part of the spring-box and engaging in a ring g on the movable plate; h. Push rod; i. Finger button
   (A & C *After Morley-Pegge*)

resulted in a sharp discrepancy between the ends of the passages and the corresponding circular holes in the outer casing. The net result was to replace one source of tonal trouble with another. In spite, however, of disappointments such as this, work on the Périnet valve continued, mostly in France, but with one notable contribution from England. About the middle of the century Dr. J. P. Oates, a medical

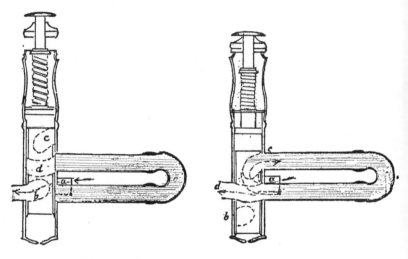

Fig. 39   Besson's improved Périnet valve

man and acoustician of Lichfield, designed what he termed an 'equitrilateral' valve in which he made the best geometrical use of the available cross-section of a piston by bringing the internal passages to the surface at the points of an equilateral triangle (Fig. 40). Dr. Oates presented some instruments built on his principle at the Great Exhibition of 1851 where they were awarded a prize medal. The next year a further improvement was registered as the 'Eclipse' piston and this the Paris maker Courtois at once secured for use on his celebrated cornets which many held to be the finest of their time. Dr. Oates also invented about this time a piston with four straight passages which was taken up and used quite extensively by Sax.[17] It is a matter for regret that this fertile inventor did not protect any of his ideas on his own behalf; he seems to have disposed of his rights quite casually to professional manufacturers who were therefore able to patent them in their own names. By about 1850 it had become clear that the Périnet type of valve was to hold the field, and in the next decade the most valuable work was done on it by

Gustav Besson. After two preliminary attempts (1851 and 1854) Besson patented in 1855 a system of valves in which the same dimensions of bore were maintained through all the windways and in all possible combinations of the pistons. This was a tremendous advance on all previous devices and on the expiry of the patent it was readily adopted by instrument-makers in general.

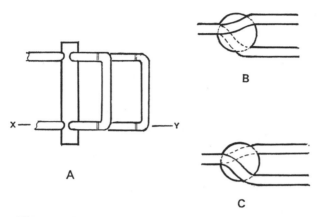

Fig. 40   Oates' Equi-trilateral valves: A Disposition of the external tubing. B Horizontal section on line x–y. Piston up. C Ditto. Piston down. (Diameter of casing exaggerated for clarity in B and C)

The minor patents granted all over the world in respect of valve mechanisms between 1850 and the present day are legion. Very many of them deal with points peculiar to the products of individual makers; very few have been concerned with fundamentals since the definitive forms of the piston and the rotary valve emerged. No account would, however, be complete without reference to three schemes which, though commercially unsuccessful, were both ingenious and truly novel. In 1834 Meifred together with a Paris mechanic named Deshays patented a system of 'valvules'. These were essentially twin wedge-shaped shutters or diaphragms working inside the windway itself and designed to divert the air column smoothly in and out of a supplementary loop as required. Rather sadly Meifred himself had to admit that the difficulty of manufacture and cost would probably render his idea non-commercial. The same idea seems, however, to have been used with some success by Nathan Adams of Massachusetts in 1825.

The second of these devices, the *finger slide*, did have a short

M

commercial life. It was patented in England in 1862 by one Samson and, rendered practical by Charles Goodison, technical adviser to Rudall, Rose, Carte and Co., was produced by that firm. Rather like the Wiener-Ventil, the finger-slide was a valve that worked entirely within the windway, though the push rod and spring were enclosed in a casing similar in appearance to a conventional piston valve. This casing lay parallel to the main tubing and the operating lever projected through a slot in its side. The makers secured a prize medal for their finger-slides at the International Exhibition of 1862 and applied them to most classes of brass instruments; but at a relatively higher price they could not compete with the Périnet valves of the time and the system soon languished.

The last of these ideas was never produced commercially, though it would appear to be nearer to theoretical perfection than any of the others. It consisted of an intricate arrangement of telescopic U slides which could be extended and withdrawn the required distances by appropriate pressure on finger buttons. Thus the main air column would always remain intact instead of being disturbed from time to time (however briefly) by switching. The scheme was patented in 1869 by E. Ford, but no manufacturer took it up because of the complexity and delicacy of the mechanism required.

Mechanics

It is clear that, within the two main categories, different makes of valve have superseded each other chiefly on acoustic considerations, i.e. by reason of progressive improvement in the windways; but there are a few details of pure mechanics which have also been influential. The disc valve, for instance, though acoustically excellent, proved difficult to keep airtight after a short time. Again, the Berliner-Pumpe, equally good as to windways, was apt to be unsatisfactory in fast-fingered passages by reason of the natural inertia of so large a body and even Périnet valves were not entirely free of this fault as proved by the creation in 1864 of Henry Distin's *light valve* (p. 194).

The least satisfactory feature of many rotary valves is the connection between the rotor and the player's finger. Where the lay-out of an instrument admits of a simple lever with a touch-piece attached directly to the rotor spindle nothing could be more efficient, but most frequently the valves have unavoidably to be placed at some distance from the hand, and then the old mechanical problem of converting linear to rotary motion crops up. Both lever and button type touches have been used, connected to cranks on the rotor spindles by rods with hinge

or ball-and-socket joints; and in one American action[18] the motion
of a push-rod is communicated direct to the rotor by a loop of fine cord
passing round and anchored to a pulley (Fig. 41). All these arrangements

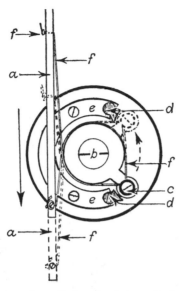

Fig. 41 American String Action: *a* Spring-controlled pushrod of which the finger plate is an
integral part; *b* Screw holding rotor in place;
c Reciprocating driver arm; *d* Cork buffers;
e Buffer holding plate; *f* Driving spring. Nylon fish-
ing line is commonly used. (*After Morley-Pegge*)

are good enough when well designed and made, but they usually involve
a multiplicity of small parts and are more tricky to adjust and maintain
than any piston valve. For the return power a watch spring enclosed
in a casing has always been popular, but plain helical springs have also
been used, as well as the 'mouse-trap' variety placed under a lever-type
touch-piece. The latter is particularly favoured on horns of the best
class at the present time.

The earlier mechanical troubles with pistons were mainly due to
the return springs themselves. Where the bottom of the casing served
as a windway the spring could not be placed below the piston, and
putting it above complicated the mechanism. Clearly, the spring
had to rest on some fixed anchorage in the casing so that it could be
compressed by a collar on the valve stem when the touch button was

pressed down. In the first Stölzel valves a long screw was passed right through the casing and through two slots in the piston. This served the double function of supporting the spring which surrounded the stem and preventing the piston from turning and so losing the alignment of the passages. Its great disadvantage was a noisy and rather uncertain action. In a rather later model the cross screw was discarded, and instead the spring bore on the bottom of a sort of sub-casing fractionally larger in diameter than the piston and resting in turn in a recess worked in the body of the main casing. This arrangement was a good deal quieter in action but it did not maintain automatically the alignment of the ports. A small 'nub' was therefore soldered to the piston near the top and this slid up and down in a groove milled in the casing proper. The same arrangement is still used in the most up-to-date valves (Fig. 42A and C). When the bottom of the casing ceased to

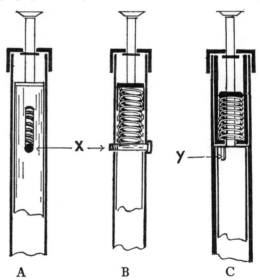

A   B   C

Fig. 42   Return spring mechanism of Stölzel valve:
    A Early type with transverse retaining screw
       shown at x.
    B Section of same at 90° to A.
    C Section of later English type with separate
       spring casing.
       Locating 'nub' shown at y.
    The clearance and thickness of walls have
       been exaggerated for clarity.

be used as a windway it became possible to place a simple open-coil spring directly beneath the piston and this arrangement is to be found nowadays in many first-class valves. The disadvantage of the early 'undertype' springs, especially in the wide shallow Berliner-Pumpen, was that they tended after a time to distort and grate against the inside of the casing. Various schemes were devised to obviate this annoyance, of which perhaps the most interesting was John Davis' patent of 1858 in which he proposed winding the spring in the form of a double cone so that no more than one or two turns need actually make contact with the casing. Probably the best of all methods of springing piston valves is that patented early in the present century by the London firm of Boosey and Co. Here the spring is again placed above the piston, but in this case it is a *closed* coil spring from which the piston is virtually suspended. Thus the spring is constantly under tension and can never buckle and rub on the casing. From time to time brass players have been troubled by the frank sticking of both rotary and piston valves. This should, of course, never happen with proper care, but the close tolerances required do admittedly make lubrication a bit uncertain. Recent metallurgy has however practically eliminated the trouble by providing special low-friction bronze alloys which are also used for 'stockingless' trombone slides.

Valve Systems

We have in this section so far considered the history and construction of the valve as an individual mechanism, but this is obviously not the whole story. We have seen (pp. 11 and 144) that a single ordinary valve can only make one change in the tonality of an instrument, and that the trumpet and trombone require at least three employed in different combination to afford a full chromatic scale. We have also noticed that for simple mathematical reasons, two or more valves used *additively* can never provide quite enough supplementary tube length to lower the basic pitch by accurate semitone stages. With the shorter instruments such as the cornet or the modern four-foot trumpet the defect is controllable by the player, but with longer air columns, some extra *compensation* is almost essential. Once the valve had become reasonably reliable in its primary function it was only a very few years before instrument-makers had the idea of using it to provide compensation as well. From the middle of last century onward, as much ingenuity was devoted to this matter as to improving the efficiency of valves themselves. Hence we have a considerable number of special *valve systems* devised by different makers or players, and all directed towards securing perfect intonation in all circumstances. Some of these have had only a transitory life, and some survivors have found their main application only in wide-bore bass instruments. All are extremely interesting and would make a special study by themselves, but here we can do no more than take a general look and must confine ourselves principally to those which have been applied to the trumpet and trombone.

Before examining some of the more important schemes there are two points that it may be well to repeat. One is that valves can be arranged so that when operated they either add extra length to the basic tubing or cut off a length from it. They can be *descending* valves which lower the fundamental pitch, or *ascending* valves which raise it (p. 149). The other point is that there is no reason why a valve may not be lengthened so that two or more sets of passages can pass through the piston or rotor, allowing one movement to switch several windways simultaneously. Sometimes both ascending and descending valves have been employed together, though this naturally imposes a fingering which many brass players today would regard as 'non-standard'. Some years ago, for example, horn players in France were very partial to an ascending third valve.

Valve systems in general fall into two main groups, (1) the *Independent* in which each valve is used separately, and (2) the *Dependent* or *Additive* where two or more valves are used in combination as required. The following brief summary of the most important or original is adapted with some amplification from Adam Carse.

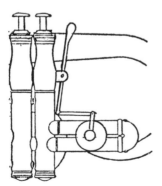

Fig. 43   Besson's 'barillet' of 1853 (not to scale)

1852 *Adolphe Sax* (Paris). A six-piston arrangement with ascending valves, and therefore not strictly a *compensating* system. We shall refer to a more modern version of this later.

1853 *Gustave Besson* (Paris). Each supplementary tube was provided with an extra length which could be added at will by means of a rotary cylinder (barillet) with a touch-piece close to that of the main piston (Fig. 43).

1856–57 *Gustave Besson.* The supplementary tubes all passed through a fourth valve placed horizontally and which when depressed substituted a longer set. This fourth valve was called a Régistre (Fig. 44).

1856 *de Rette* and *Courtois* (Paris). Two additional piston valves were provided which added extra tube length at will.

1858–59 *Besson* with *Girardin* produced a similar but better Régistre which they called a *Transpositeur*.

1873 *Léon Cousin* (Paris). A five-valve system in which the fourth and fifth lowered the fundamental pitch by a perfect fourth and a major third respectively. This arrangement of course avoided the old compromise of tuning the third valve flat (p. 12) but at the cost of a non-standard fingering. There was no compensation for valves used together but in fact this procedure was absolutely necessary for only one note in the ordinary compass of the instrument. Otherwise combined valves gave a downward extension outside the normal compass.

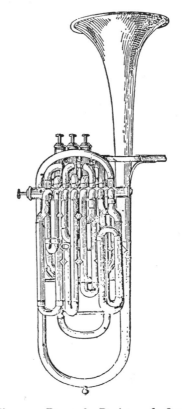

Fig. 44   Besson's *Registre* of 1857 applied to trombone

1874 *Thibouville-Lamy* (Paris). Two keys placed near the bell of an instrument allowed the main air column to be adjusted to the theoretical length required when the valves were used in combination.

1874 *Boosey and Co.* (London). Compensating valves designed by D. J. Blaikley, a distinguished acoustician and technical adviser to the firm. This is probably the best and most elegant system yet devised, for with no more than three pistons fingered in the normal manner theoretical tube lengths are brought into circuit automatically whenever the valves are combined. These compensating valves are fitted to the highest-class instruments produced by the present-day firm of Boosey and Hawkes. The annexed drawings show the air passages through a set of Blaikley valves in various circumstances (Fig. 45). In bass instruments of wide bore where a fourth valve is normally supplied to carry the compass down to the true fundamental, the Blaikley system is equally successful.

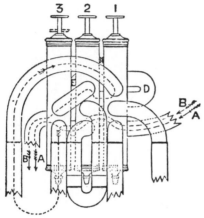

Fig. 45 D. J. Blaikley's compensating valves of 1874. On the left A indicates the windway with all valves up. B is the windway with the third valve down. On the right C shows the windway with all three valves down. This drawing is made from the opposite side so as to show D and E, the supplementary tubes of the first and second valves, and the various cross connections

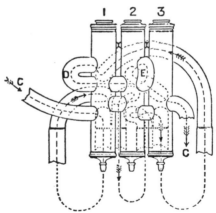

1881 *Sudre* (Paris). A device affording compensation by automatically pulling out the valve slides by mechanical means. It was soon discarded as being too delicate and liable to derangement.

1883 *Arban* (Paris). This celebrated cornet player devised a scheme in which, in addition to the usual three valves, a fourth, lowering the pitch by a tone and a half, was worked by the left middle finger.

The left index finger controlled a lever which pulled out the third valve slide against a return spring to give a major instead of a minor third. This device applied to the first and third valves, or sometimes to the first only, was reintroduced a few years ago by Boosey and Hawkes of London on some of their high-class cornets. In addition the slides of the first and second pistons were linked to the touch-piece of the fourth. The instrument gave in all twenty-one possible 'positions' allowing the production of numerous enharmonic intervals usually available on free-slide instruments only. The weight and complication of this instrument proved a considerable obstacle to its general adoption.

1884 *Daniel and Sudre* (Paris). Another method of automatically adding extra tube length when valves were combined.

1885–88 *Arban and Bouvet* (Paris). During these years Arban, in conjunction with Bouvet, a civil engineer with musical interests, produced a series of modifications and adaptations of the Arban (1883) and Daniel (1884) devices which (after passing through a six-valve independent phase) finally crystallised into a compensating system without any extra valves. The final Arban-Bouvet system enjoyed much success and was applied to brass instruments in general.

1886 *Mahillon* (Brussels). Victor Mahillon of the Brussels Conservatoire also devoted much thought to the compensation problem. His first design required a fourth valve to introduce extra tube length, but in his final model, by a cross connection between the first and third valves somewhat on the Blaikley principle, this became automatic (Fig. 46).

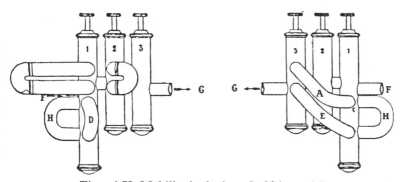

Fig. 46 V. Mahillon's device of 1886 providing automatic compensation when combining first and third valves. (*From the Patent Specification*)

c. 1910 *Couesnon et Cie* (Paris). *Système Petit* adopted for Trumpets and Cornets 'Monopole': valve slides adjustable while playing, through levers acting against bias of return springs.

1916 *Thibouville-Lamy* (Paris). In spite of the benefits offered by some of the above systems, they have not satisfied all players by any means. During the period of the First World War, Merri Franquin of the Paris Conservatoire concluded his researches (which he began as far back as 1888) with the design of a five-valve trumpet which finally satisfied his critical demands. This instrument could be played as a common three-valve trumpet, but two additional valves could also be brought into use. One, operated by the right thumb, *raised* the over-all pitch by a whole tone, while the other, allotted to the left thumb, lowered it by a major or a minor third according to how the slide was pre-set. Thus ascending and descending valves were combined, a thing uncommon on the trumpet. Fig. 47 is a drawing of the instrument which was constructed by

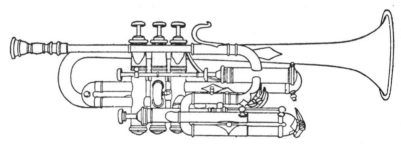

Fig. 47   Five-valve trumpet on the Merri Franquin system

the firm of J. Thibouville-Lamy. For detailed information on most of the above up to 1889, as well as on many minor matters, the reader should consult Pierre's *La Facture* (see note 23, p. 184).

It is to be noted that the principal valves in all the above systems were of the piston type, but we should not omit reference to one very ingenious device conceived by Gustav Besson as early as 1855 and which depended entirely on rotary action. Each of three rotary cylinders was provided with two touch-pieces turning it respectively clockwise and anti-clockwise. Thus each cylinder could switch in two alternative supplementary loops of different lengths. The following figure re-drawn from the patent specification will make the action plain. The arrangement gave many different combinations; the windways were beautifully clear (Fig. 48).

With so much past effort and ingenuity on record the reader may perhaps feel inclined to ask: What has become of it all? What is the present position? And why? The best answer is, I think, to be found in up-to-date makers' catalogues, for supply reflects demand. As regards the trumpet these show us that in English-speaking countries, and indeed, in most other parts of the world, the three simple descend-

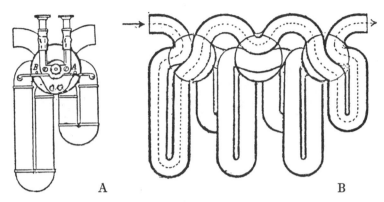

Fig. 48   G. Besson's two-way rotary valve of 1855:
A External appearance. B A cluster of three valves in
section showing the alternative windways

ing valves, whole tone, semitone, and minor third, are regarded as all that is generally necessary. Mechanically these are now highly efficient; they make possible a fingering system that is almost universal; and their acoustic deficiencies in combination are not too difficult to overcome. In France perhaps, among older players and their pupils, there may linger some attachment to special designs, for in their day such eminent Professors as Arban or Merri Franquin were in a position to make their own systems obligatory on their students. In general, however, it seems that modern students prefer to concentrate on learning to play a simple instrument in tune rather than burden their minds with a complexity of alternative fingerings. The point is emphasised if we compare the tablatures of the ordinary three-valve instrument with that of the Merri Franquin trumpet, for instance. (Fig. 49 overleaf.)

In the case of the trombone, the classical slide instrument, sometimes with the addition of a single transposing valve, is predominant, and modern players seem to find the subtlety of its intonation ample recompense for the inconvenience of long 'shifts'. As we have already observed, the valved instrument finds today a limited employment in military music and in some Continental opera houses, and it is here that, together with the normal types, we encounter a curiosity— nothing less than the resurrection of Sax's six-valve independent system of 1852 (Fig. 50). In this remarkable instrument the air column passes from the mouthpiece through all six pistons, round a long loop, back again through the pistons, and so to the bell. With all valves 'up' the

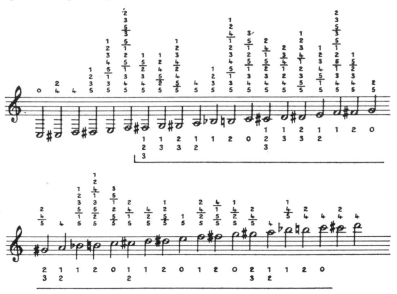

Fig. 49   The compass and fingering of a conventional three-valve trumpet are indicated below the stave. Alternatives offered by the Merri Franquin five-valve instrument are shown above

length of tubing involved equals that of an ordinary trombone with the slide fully extended to the seventh position. When any valve is depressed, however, it cuts off communication with all tubing beyond it, and substitutes a shorter loop of its own, thus raising the fundamental pitch. The lengths of the valve loops are in ratio to each other as are the 'shifts' of the ordinary trombone slide. Thus 'no valve' = 7th position; 6th valve = 6th position; 5th valve = 5th position, etc. On the face of it this system, if properly calculated, should give seven harmonic series correctly in tune with each other. Its main disadvantage lies in the complexity and weight of the instrument, for the total length of tub- ing required equals that of a normal trombone with the slide in the 7th position plus the lengths of the slide in each of the other positions—some 52 feet for a B♭ tenor!

It seems rather a pity that some recent makers, evidently impressed with the capabilities of the six-valve trombone, have attempted to extend them in rivalry to the slide Tenor-Bass. A seventh valve, this

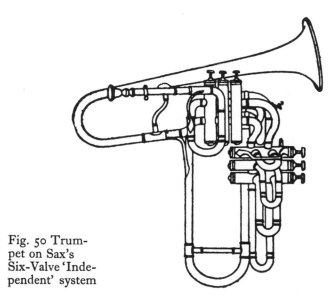

Fig. 50 Trumpet on Sax's Six-Valve 'Independent' system

time a *descending* one, has been added, and this brings in sufficient extra tubing to lower the basic pitch by a fourth. The whole idea runs contrary to the original independent-valve concept, and the additional length inevitably upsets the ratios of the six valve loops unless the player be given time to adjust each of them. Possibly an experienced player might, without touching the valve loops, make use of his seventh valve for certain specific purposes, but it can hardly be regarded as an instantaneous transposer as on the duplex slide trombone. Inspired by the use of these unusual trombones by specialists in the Brussels Opéra orchestra the late Sir Henry Wood had a set made by the Belgian firm of Lebrun and brought to England early in the present century. A thorough trial in the Queen's Hall Orchestra, however, did not reveal them to be the trombones of the future, at any rate for British players.

The inventiveness—and commercial energy—of Adolphe Sax was truly remarkable. At one period his influence was deeply felt in every branch of the wind instrument trade, and the concessions he obtained from the French Government gave him almost a concealed monopoly in the military field. Of course many of his ideas never progressed beyond the drawing board or provisional patent stages but others, the Saxhorns,[19] Saxotrombas, and above all the Saxophones went into active production and have had useful lives. It happens that only a few of Sax's products, such as the six-valve trombone just mentioned, fall strictly within the purview of our present study, but of these two are among the most remarkable instruments ever to appear. They are a trumpet and a trombone based on another application of the independent valve system. In these six valves used one at a time diverted the air column from a single mouthpipe into one or other of what were in essence seven almost complete trumpets or trombones. The mass of tubing was folded into one large bundle surmounted by seven separate bells and the appearance was grotesque indeed. One can hardly suppose that such monsters were seriously intended for either orchestral or military use, and their only place would seem to be in the 'show band', but other makers than Sax took up the idea. Fig. 51 shows an alto horn constructed on this principle by Henry Distin, *c.* 1878.

To conclude this section there is one final point which I think should be made lest the reader be left with a false impression. It is that all the ingenuity and labour of the 19th-century brass instrument makers— and we have no more than outlined them above—have not gone to waste. It is generally recognised today that short instruments, such as the trumpet now is, gain comparatively little benefit from compensating devices, but without these in some form or other the large lip-voiced instruments could never have attained their present honourable status as the foundation voices of the wind band.

The Valved 'Bach' Trumpet

The high lying trumpet parts of the early 18th-century composers have already been alluded to under several heads (pp. 70 and 122) and it has been explained why they present a special problem to the modern orchestral player. We have seen also how in recent years scholars and instrument makers have contrived to ease the worst difficulties of the fourth octave of the '7-foot' trumpet so that modern players may tackle these parts without recourse to the intense (and today quite uneconomic) specialisation required in Bach's time. There is, however, one most interesting stage in the story which we have not yet looked at, and as this was fostered directly by the growing acceptance of valves among orchestral players it is, I think, most appropriately considered in the present chapter. It is a strange tale, full of persistent error and mis-understanding, which was not properly cleared up until the late W. F. H. Blandford attacked it in three authoritative articles published in 1935.[20] Briefly the position was this. By the end of the 18th century

Fig. 51   Alto horn by Henry Distin, *c.* 1878

the art of the 'Clarinbläser' was virtually extinct in Continental Europe. In Britain the traditions of natural trumpet playing persisted for some time longer, thanks to the appearance, *c.* 1800, of the English slide trumpet which, except for its tempering device, was still the instrument that Handel knew. But even English players, brought up to a man in the Handel idiom, were hardly able to deal with Bach's more florid passages and frequent unprepared notes in the highest register. In Germany, in the middle of the 19th century, 'Clarinbläsen' seems to have been generally regarded as an inexplicable mystery, with the result that when, following Mendelssohn's lead, the great Bach revival came, all sorts of expedients were tried, from octave transpositions to frank 'farming out' of clarino parts among the woodwind. To quote Blandford: 'For forty years musicians had wandered in this wilderness, until an event of historical importance took place—one that was ultimately to lead to the performance of Bach's trumpet parts by means of specially designed instruments, and thereby to assist in laying the foundations for the present regard in which the composer's music is held. It was also to give rise to one of the most surprising and persistent errors of modern musical history.'

On October 19th, 1871, Julius Kosleck gave to the Musical Artists' Association of Berlin a demonstration of clarino playing on an ancient instrument he had discovered in a private collection in Heidelberg. This performance led to a considerable correspondence in the German musical press following a report from the critic Otto Lessmann[21] who wrote, *inter alia*, 'It [the instrument] stands in B♭, but can be converted into the old trumpet of Bach and Handel by the addition of a straight tube four feet in length. With the help of this extra tube Mr. Kosleck easily performed parts from our old church music that our modern players are mortally afraid to attempt.' Lessmann's report was soon translated and appeared in the Brussels *L'Echo musical* where it attracted a distinctly critical commentary from Victor Mahillon. This in turn drew an open letter from Lessmann in which he amplified somewhat his first remarks. Study of the correspondence shows that Lessmann was neither well informed nor particularly accurate, but his description of Kosleck's find is sufficient to identify it with some certainty as a medieval buisine. Who first added the extra tubing to it Lessmann does not reveal, though his account suggests strongly that it was Kosleck himself. Quoting Blandford again: 'The obvious explanation of the whole matter is that Kosleck, admittedly a great performer, wished to demonstrate his mastery of the lost art of the clarinist. Finding to his hand a buysine, dating probably from the fifteenth century, which lent itself exceptionally well to the production of the highest notes, he adapted it for use as a D trumpet. Presumably his performance would have been as successful if he had used a folded trumpet by one of the Nuremberg makers of the Bach period, and why he did not do so . . . can only be guessed at. It is not necessary to attribute to him any wilful deception. He may have been one of the many players who have no special antiquarian knowledge of their instruments, and his primary object was to demonstrate technique and not trumpets.' The real culprit was, of course, Lessmann, who stated in his original notice that the instrument of the Bach and Handel virtuosi was thought to have disappeared without trace, and that Kosleck's discovery was an actual surviving specimen. Mahillon appears to be the only contemporary sceptic who is on record, and many distinguished musicians who should have been more cautious accepted and quoted Lessmann's nonsense without question. Thus it is once again that fallacies arise and are perpetuated.

Naturally Lessmann's announcement created a great stir, and it is almost incredible that no one thought to follow the lead and experiment with some of the known Bach period instruments which were quite readily available in Germany, even if Kosleck himself had not done so. Almost it seems as if everyone had agreed that since Kosleck had demonstrated successfully with a *straight* trumpet, *ipso facto* all folded instruments must be ruled out of consideration. In the light of subsequent developments we may also guess perhaps that the unfamiliar appearance of a long straight trumpet suggested some peculiar and mysterious virtues. Some thirty years later, C. M. Widor put a very shrewd finger on the matter when he asked why, with abundant 18th-century instruments of different kinds known to survive in museums and private ownership, the trumpet of the clarino player alone should have completely vanished. Widor made no attempt to answer his own question, but coming from so distinguished a source it made some musicologists think again.

Between 1871 and 1884 Kosleck's name does not figure in the records in connection with anything unusual, but in September of the latter year he appeared as first trumpet at the celebrations to mark the unveiling of the Bach statue at Eisenach, though *not* as a clarinist. He used a 'Bach trumpet' designed by himself, which some say made its first public appearance on this occasion. It was modelled on the ancient buisine used in the 1871 demonstration, and possessed the same simple contours which led to its being described as having a 'post-horn bore and bell'. Unfortunately no exact record of its dimensions seems to exist, but it is known that it stood in A (alterable to B♭), being two-thirds the length of the old D trumpet, and it was fitted with two valves.

N

Thus it enabled parts for the D or C trumpet to be transposed as if for the A or B♭ cornet (which was, of course, the instrument which Kosleck taught in the Berlin Hochschule für Musik). In adopting this curious hybrid—*valve-buisine* we might call it—Kosleck completely abandoned the old clarino technique in which he had proved his mastery thirteen years earlier. In 1885, on Joachim's recommendation, Kosleck was engaged to play first trumpet in the Bicentenary performance of the B minor Mass at the Albert Hall. This was the first occasion on which the original trumpet and oboe d'amore parts were played unaltered in Britain. In support Kosleck had Morrow and Solomon, probably England's two finest trumpeters of their time, both using orchestral valve trumpets. Blandford, who was in the audience on the occasion, writes that Kosleck's instrument resembled 'a sort of valved coach-horn of unmistakably modern appearance'; but however strange it may have looked the sound was evidently magnificent and the player won unstinted praise for his brilliant execution and his pure, rounded, tone. The latter was probably to some extent concerned with the very unorthodox mouthpiece he employed, and which he was careful not to exhibit to his British colleagues. According to Eichborn (in correspondence with Blandford) this was virtually a horn mouthpiece of the sheet-metal type (p. 69) long disused in Britain, and the mouth-pipe of the trumpet was tapered to accommodate it. This feature would, of course, also affect the characteristic tone (pp. 22 and 39) and it is perhaps significant that the Heidelberg buisine of the 1871 demonstration was, by Lessmann's account, conical throughout when in its original state instead of cylindro-conical as was more common in these ancient instruments.

I have been unable to assess the extent (if any) to which the Kosleck instrument was taken up by German players after its sensational debut at Eisenach, but it is certain that in Britain the idea took root. After Kosleck's departure Walter Morrow designed a two-valved trumpet in A which he introduced at the Leeds festival of 1886. Unlike Kosleck, he adopted the bore and contours of the modern trumpet as he knew it, but he adhered to the straight main tube for the very good reason that he thought it well to avoid as many potential sources of uncertain notes as possible. Some knuckles and diagonal passages in the pistons were, of course, unavoidable, but I am informed by practical players that the instrument was freer in blowing than the average valve trumpet of its time. Blandford had the advantage of hearing Morrow both play on his own instrument and demonstrate clarino playing on a

natural trumpet by J. L. Ehe of Nürnberg (for Morrow too had studied
the technique), and he averred that the former was no mean substitute.
Unfortunately, no opportunity ever occurred of comparing it directly
with Kosleck's version. Morrow, incidentally, employed a normal
trumpet mouthpiece. His own instrument was made, or at least supplied,
by G. Silvani, later Silvani and Smith, who began business in London
in 1884. A similar trumpet made for John Solomon also bears Silvani's
name but is marked 'Made in Paris', so the actual manufacturer is in
some doubt, and in answer to enquiries Solomon himself could give no
help on this point. The Silvani and Smith instruments were surprisingly
light and easy in the hand. (Plate 16 A.)

When it was first introduced the true nature of Morrow's trumpet
was no better understood than was that of the Kosleck instrument. The
Musical Times, reporting on the Leeds festival of 1886, observed that
all three trumpets were 'of the old German model', meaning, of course,
Kosleck's, but this is almost certainly incorrect for Morrow's second
and third there were McGrath, a notable slide trumpeter, and Ellis
who was primarily a cornet player. However the misconception persisted
and even grew, till in 1892, after a magnificent performance of the B
minor Mass again in Leeds, the *Saturday Review* went so far as to state
that 'For the first time since the revival of the Mass, all three trumpet
parts were played on instruments copied from the trumpet of Bach and
Handel's day—an instrument the recovery of which is among the most
curious incidents in recent musical history'. But not, as Blandford was
to write many years later, half so curious as the fact that such a belief
was entertained in the country of the Harpers, the younger of whom
was alive and could have been consulted. Let us read the immediate
sequel in Blandford's own words. 'As no one else came forward to
correct the false belief, I wrote to the *Musical Times* to explain with
sufficient fulness, as I thought, why these trumpets had no claim to be
accepted as restorations of the instruments of the Bach-Handel period;
but the editor would not insert a letter so subversive of current opinion
until he had sent for Morrow (who himself told me) to ask whether it
should be ignored, or inserted and crushed by a reply. Morrow, however, cordially agreed with it. It duly appeared (November 1892) and
was never answered.' In spite, however, of this careful and detailed
explanation the musical journalists still cherished their pet delusion—
it was, perhaps, too picturesque to be discarded on the mere say-so
of one young man—and no later than the next March *The Times* critic
wrote of 'trumpets of the pattern used in Bach's day' when reporting

on a concert given by the Bach Choir. Again Morrow and Ellis appeared, this time with Blackwell of the Philharmonic and Opera orchestras in the second desk.

Although the above-mentioned instruments certainly brought Bach's clarino parts within the reach of a really good modern orchestral trumpeter, these still called for much special study. This was readily admitted by Morrow to Blandford, and by Solomon to the present writer, but the fact that such busy players could now accept Bach engagements without unduly jeopardising their ordinary work was very valuable. Ultimately it encouraged Werner Menke to believe that his two-valved instruments, modelled accurately this time on the old D and F trumpets (p. 122), would prove no more difficult to master, though unfortunately this hope has not so far been fully realised. In the meantime instrument-makers, now that their interest was really aroused, applied themselves more and more to easing the players' lot, and produced the various smaller valve trumpets that we have already listed in Chapter 2. The first of these emanated from the Brussels firm of C. Mahillon and Co. in 1892. This was a short trumpet, first made with two valves, and later with three, and pitched in D one octave above the classical D instrument. The 16th proper tone on the latter was therefore represented by the 8th on the new trumpet, and so on, with great gain in certainty of production. The makers claimed that with their specially designed mouthpiece the thrice marked d″, the highest note called for in Bach's Mass, could be secured with comparative ease. Mahillons also retained the straight form of Morrow's instrument, but apparently without appreciating his original intention, for they constructed the main tube with two quite avoidable right-angle bends where it entered and left the valve assembly. Although the Mahillon D-octave trumpet was unquestionably inferior to the Silvani and Smith model, both in volume and quality of tone, it soon became popular and by degrees most of the few players who had followed Morrow and adopted the A trumpet began to drop it again in favour of the shorter type. Other makers besides Mahillon then came rapidly into the field with octave trumpets and, using these, such men as found even the Morrow instrument too exacting in time or technique were able to do useful work. These players, however, soon found the straight trumpet inconvenient in the orchestra and the makers responded with a type folded in the conventional manner. As Mahillons had already sacrificed the minor advantage of the straight main tube in their original high D instrument, little tonal difference was perceptible. Since that time octave trumpets have been built in several different keys, the most important being probably that in F designed primarily for playing the famous part in the second Brandenburg Concerto. The names of Besson and Co., of London, and Alexander Bros. of Mainz, in particular, are associated with this instrument which, we believe, made its first appearance in Britain in 1922.[22] As early as 1885, for the performance of the Bach Magnificat, Teste of the Opéra obtained from Besson of Paris a three-valve trumpet in high G, an eleventh above the classical D instrument.[23] Even this was later outstripped by Mahillons with a B♭ trumpet, octave to the modern B♭ orchestral instrument, but the usefulness of this is strictly limited, being nowadays almost entirely confined to the performance of the second Brandenburg Concerto for which some players find it preferable to the older F instrument.

At the time of writing the favoured instrument for interpreting Bach and Handel parts is the octave trumpet in D or F, many players preferring the latter for all *obbligati*. Recent examples embody all the improvements afforded by modern technology and are as finely made as any other trumpets, as, for instance, the elegant little instruments produced by Scherzer of Augsburg which are much esteemed in Germany and Austria. The incisive—all too often acid—tone of the octave trumpet is no doubt useful in maintaining something approaching a proper balance in the 'big' Bach performances to which we have become accustomed in the present century. We are, however, repeatedly told by the older writers that a good clarino player was expected to produce an almost flute-like sound in the top register, which incidentally does not imply that the trumpet was not expected to dominate. No doubt, also, the main idea of modern 'Festival size' performances is to do honour to Bach, but one cannot help feeling that there may be wrong thinking somewhere, and that good renderings on the original scale would make quite as fine a tribute. Happily these can now be realised thanks to the advent of the Steinkopf-Finke trumpet (p. 123) which has been so beautifully demonstrated in Germany by Walter Holy and the originator, and by Philip Jones in Great Britain.

NOTES

[1] British patent No. 1664 of 1788. E. L. Gerber in his *Historische-biographisches Lexicon*, Leipzig, 1790–92, mentions one, J. A. Maresch, who by some means had contrived to unite two complete horns sounding a minor third apart.

[2] R. Morley-Pegge, *The French Horn*, London, Ernest Benn Ltd., 1960, pp. 26–30.

[3] See Busby's *Concert Room and Orchestra Anecdotes*, Vol. II, p. 175.

[4] R. Morley-Pegge, *op. cit.*, pp. 30 *et seq.*

[5] J. F. Russell and J. H. Elliott, in *The Brass Band Movement*, London, J. M. Dent and Sons, 1936.

[6] See G. Kastner, *Manuel général de musique militaire*, Paris, 1848.

[7] F. G. A. Dauverné, *Méthode pour la trompette*, Paris, 1857.

[8] J. Meifred, 'Notice sur la fabrication des instruments en cuivre', Paris, 1851. (From *l'Annuaire de la Société des Anciens Élèves des Écoles des Arts-et-Métiers*.) The earlier German makers had apparently not thought to provide tuning slides to the supplementary tubes. Morley-Pegge has suggested that this might be related to the German concept of the Horn as an instrument of fixed tonality, while the French from quite early days had used a variety of crooks with freedom. In any case, the removal of condensed moisture must have been very tiresome in the absence of withdrawable slides.

[9] Wilhelm Wieprecht (1802–1872), a civilian musician who settled in Berlin in 1824, was fortunate in forming influential friendships in Prussian military circles. His ideas on military music therefore received a fair hearing and he was eventually entrusted with the reorganisation of the bands of the Prussian Cavalry Guards. His reforms later penetrated the entire Prussian army and were felt throughout Continental Europe. See Kalkbrenner, *Wilhelm Weiprecht*, Berlin, 1882.

In 1845 Wieprecht wrote several letters to the *Berliner Musikalische Zeitung* in one of which he gave an account of the invention of valves. Adam Carse has discussed this letter at some length and compared it critically with earlier articles on the same subject from other German musical journals. See *Musical Wind Instruments*, pp. 65–67.

[10] T. Rode, in the *Neue Berliner Zeitung*, 1860.

[11] The International Patents Convention, by which a number of nations agreed to respect each other's patents, was not signed until 1883. Prior to that date there was nothing to prevent an invention, fully protected in the country of its origin, being freely copied once it had crossed the frontier. Before 1870 also, the various independent German-speaking States granted their own patents or privileges, but would not necessarily recognise one another's unless specific trade agreements were in force.

[12] Henry Distin (see also note 14) was the member of the family who devoted himself particularly to the musical instrument trade. The business began in 1845, and the following year H. Distin secured the British agency for the Sax instruments which he retained until 1853. In 1850 Distin appears to have begun the actual manufacture of brass instruments in London, and in 1851 his family started to introduce these to the public. This was probably the first cause of a breach with Sax who, in 1853, transferred his agency to Rudall, Rose and Co. The Distin business came under the control of Boosey and Co. in 1868.

[13] Adolphe Sax, son of a well-known Brussels instrument maker, set up on his own account in Paris in 1842. His 'intrusion' was much resented by the established Paris makers, but by perseverance and the excellence of his products Sax survived all attempts to oust him and soon secured powerful patrons, among them Hector Berlioz. Sax was a fine workman and most ingenious, but his tendency to claim as 'inventions' instruments that were at best no more than practical improvements on pre-existing ones infuriated his rivals. The result was a series of appeals to the Government to annul his patents, as well as many law-suits which did no more than damage both parties. In spite of his ambition and commercial energy Sax was not a good financier and was twice declared bankrupt. The fullest accounts are given by O. Comettant in his *Histoire d'un Inventeur*, Paris, 1860, and by de Pontécoulant in *Organographie*, Paris, 1861.

Excellent engravings of the first Sax instruments are to be found in Kastner's *Manuel général de musique militaire*, Paris, 1848. Probably the fairest assessment of the case on both sides is given in Constant Pierre's *Les Facteurs*, Paris, 1893.

Sax's use of the Berliner-Pumpen seems to have followed on the purchase by himself (or his father) of two instruments from Moritz of Berlin, Wieprecht's maker. In 1845 Wieprecht challenged Sax face to face on this matter, but concluded that recourse to law would be profitless.

[14] The Distin Family Quintet consisted of John, the father (b. 1798) and his four sons, George (d. 1848), Henry (b. 1819 and still living in 1896), William (d. 1884), and Theodore (1823–1893). Distin senior first attracted attention as a bandboy in the South Devon Militia, when he played on an English slide instrument the first trumpet part in the *Dettingen Te Deum* at the Exeter Music Festival of 1812. Two years later he joined the Grenadier Guards as a key-bugle player. There followed periods as trumpeter in George IV's private band under Kramer, and then as bandmaster to the Marquis of Bredalbane. By 1837 John Distin had abandoned Service life and with his sons, and his wife as pianist, had embarked on the remarkable series of concert tours which were to take them all over Europe and to America during the next eighteen years.

When visiting Paris in the spring of 1844 the Distins made themselves known to Sax, and as a result of this meeting adopted his newly designed instruments. There are conflicting stories about this, and for a balanced account of the whole affair the reader is referred to *The Music Review* of November 1945, in which Adam Carse set out both sides very clearly.

As a slide-trumpet player, John Distin in his prime was held by the critics to be second only to the elder Harper.

[15] J. Meifred, *op. cit.*

[16] C. Day, *Catalogue of Musical Instruments at the Royal Military Exhibition*, London, Eyre and Spottiswoode, 1898, p. 184.

[17] A somewhat acrimonious correspondence was carried on by Oates and Köhler in the columns of the *Expositor*, in which each criticised the other's designs. This terminated with the honours even when the Exhibition jury awarded a medal to each of the rivals.

[18] The American 'string action' appears to have been first marketed by the Schreiber Cornet Manufacturing Company of New York. Curiously enough it was covered by them in *British* patent No. 2468 of 1866.

[19] Although we must give Sax credit for a great deal of labour expended on perfecting the Saxhorns and making them into a homogeneous family, we cannot recognise in them anything in the nature of an original invention. Valves were applied to instruments of Bugle-horn proportions by many makers, both before and after Sax, though admittedly in a rather unsystematic way. At his encounter with Sax at Coblenz in 1845 Wieprecht was able to name an already known German instrument of similar character to each of the Saxhorns. In the Saxotrombas, with their more trumpet-like bore, there may have been more original thinking, but even here the existence of a genuine novelty is doubtful. Sax's habit of incorporating his own name in the titles he invented for his instruments was one more source of irritation to his rivals, though it may have been good commercial advertising. Sudre in France followed the lead later on, as did the Italians Albisi and Bimboni, and most notably Heckel in Germany.

[20] W. F. H. Blandford, 'The "Bach Trumpet" ', *Monthly Musical Record*, London, March–April, May, and June 1935.

[21] Otto Lessmann, a Berlin music critic, became the proprietor and editor of the *Allgemeine Musikzeitung*. His account of Kosleck's demonstration was

however published in the *Neue Berliner Musikzeitung* for October 25th, 1871, presumably before he acquired his own paper.

[22] The late Herbert Barr used such an instrument, specially made by Besson of London, at the Leeds Festival of 1922 accompanied by members of the London Symphony Orchestra.

[23] Constant Pierre, *La Facture Instrumentale à l'Exposition universelle de 1889*, Paris, Librairie de L'Art Indépendant, 1890, p. 116. From the accompanying illustration it appears that this instrument was built in straight form.

CHAPTER 9

Materials and Manufacture

THE MATERIALS which have been used to construct lip-energised musical instruments are many and various—truly Animal, Vegetable, and Mineral. With primitive peoples and folk cultures the choice of material has often been absolutely dictated by availability, and equally the natural form of the available material has influenced the shape of the instrument created. Thus, the configuration of animal horns and tusks has given rise to taper-bored instruments which are trumpets only in the broad ethnological sense and do not much concern us here, while the stem sections of reeds and grasses have guided Man ultimately to the construction of cylindrical flutes. In this book we are interested mainly in the trumpet and trombone as members of the modern orchestra, so we can limit our consideration to metal as a basic material, with just a passing reference to wood in Wagner's 'Holz-trompete'[1] and Talbot's 'Box Trumpet'[2] for the former was indeed conceived as an orchestral instrument. Other wooden horns and trumpets belong almost entirely to the realm of Folk instruments. Ivory, carefully turned and bored, and fitted together in sections, was the tube material of the one known specimen of the ancient Greek *Salpynx* (p. 94), a true trumpet; and glass, clay, and porcelain examples are known, though not as practical orchestral instruments.

A malleable yellow brass (Fr. *laiton*) of approximately 70 per cent. copper to 30 per cent. zinc is the usual material for the bodies of trumpets and trombones at the present day, with one of the 'white bronzes' for the mounts and sometimes for moving parts also. This, however has not always been so, for in the 18th and early 19th centuries it was not uncommon to find 'brass' instruments of all sorts made of copper, with the yellow brass reserved for the mountings. Key-bugles have always been made with copper bodies, and indeed I have seen only one example made entirely of brass. Army duty bugles also are still made of copper in Great Britain, though the equivalent instruments elsewhere are usually of brass. In Germany and in America a more golden coloured alloy, *gold-messing* or *gold-brass*, of about 80 per cent. copper and 20 per cent. zinc is now much used, especially for horns. It is rather heavier and more expensive than the paler brasses and looks very handsome when well polished, but whether it has any tonal advantage is perhaps doubtful. At the present day the finished colour of a brass instrument is little guide to the composition of its metal, for transparent lacquers are often applied which are in themselves tinted.

The white bronzes, of which there are a number of recognised varieties, usually lumped together under generic titles such as 'German Silver', *Neusilber*, or in France, *Maillechort*, a compound word derived from the names of two metallurgists who first prepared it.[3] These are all basically alloys of copper with nickel and zinc, and although they are somewhat difficult to work, they have occasionally been used for complete instruments, particularly horns. A few players have found these tonally better than brass, but this seems to be very much a personal matter. The whole question of the best material for sonority in wind instruments has occupied experts for many years and opinions are by no means unanimous. As long ago as the late 17th century Talbot, writing on the contemporary trumpet, said 'Best Mettal Bastard Brass mixed with solid brass; Worse Silver, and worst copper springy.' What he meant is not at all clear, especially as until the coming of 19th-century metallurgy the composition of the older brasses was very uncertain. Of course, we can today determine these by a process of destructive chemical analysis, but, as Menke pointed out, few possessors of cherished old instruments are willing to sacrifice even scrapings for such a purpose. Recently a non-destructive method of analysis making use of fast neutron bombardment has been successfully applied, but unfortunately the necessary facilities are available to very few musical researchers. In early days brass was obtained by placing a mixture of powered calamine (native zinc carbonate) and charcoal in a crucible, putting ingots of copper on top, and fusing the lot together. As the purity of the mineral could hardly be controlled the composition of the resultant alloy was necessarily inconsistent, batch to batch. Moreover, at high temperatures zinc is much more volatile than copper so that, until techniques had been devised for regulating accurately the heat and atmosphere in the melting pot the zinc was liable to 'burn off', more or less, leaving a poorer alloy than was desired. The object of placing the calamine below the copper in the crucible was to minimise this loss, but it was not very effective at best. It was also the custom for the older brass makers to add a proportion of scrap brass to each new melt, and this led to even greater uncertainty.[4]

Near the beginning of the present century the processes of metallurgy had become more precise, and more complex and consistent alloys began to be made. These bronzes with a relatively high tin and phosphorus content were adopted for valve bodies and trombone slides on account of their low friction characteristics when mated with normal brass. They are, however, somewhat intractable materials, and today they have been displaced again by normal 'hard-drawn' brass with the rubbing surfaces electro-plated with hard chromium. Of course it must be remembered that when we speak of instruments made of 'copper', or, for that matter, of silver which has sometimes been used for specially rich or ornate examples, neither of these metals are absolutely free of alloy. In a pure state both would be too soft for practical purposes. The sets of so-called Silver Band instruments which we often see are in fact merely plated, though again, in rich examples sterling silver is frequently used for mounting. For the same reason it seems hardly credible that the gold instruments occasionally mentioned in ancient writings can have been other than plated or gilt.

A celebrated *Dictionary of Arts and Sciences* published in London in 1754 by a 'Society of Gentlemen' states that brass as then known was not malleable when cold, and that this quality was supplied by the addition of a small proportion of lead. This is curious and does not conform with accounts by various Continental writers from the 16th century onward. At one period in Germany the trade of *Messing-schläger* or 'brass-beater' was well known. Most brasses used in instrument making today are malleable cold but quickly show the phenomenon of 'work-hardening' which is tiresome at certain stages of manufacture but is valuable in the finished product.[5]

The basic techniques of brass instrument making are no more than special adaptations of those traditionally used by the makers of domestic hollow ware, though in recent years much laborious hand work has been eliminated by special machinery, and certain entirely new processes have been introduced. In Roman times the general bronze workers may well have produced musical instruments as well as domestic vessels, for identical techniques of hammering, casting, and soldering[6] are revealed by both classes of goods. Incidentally, this reference to Roman metal technology brings us back once again to the old canard regarding the alleged Roman trombone. In certain Latin writings the term *tuba ductilis* occurs, and this has been taken to show that the Romans were acquainted with a *draw-trumpet*. When preparing his classic paper of 1906 (p. 130), however, F. W. Galpin examined his literary references from the point of view of a Latin scholar as well as that of a musicologist, and he was able to show that by *tuba ductilis* the writer really meant not an extensible trumpet, but one made of metal *drawn out* or thinned by the hammer—an interesting case of one branch of scholarship complementing another.

The actual methods of brass instrument construction are probably best considered under three heads, the tubing, the bell, and the valves, since different processes are involved in each. Until quite recently tubing, both cylindrical and tapered, was made by rolling annealed sheet metal round a polished steel mandrel, brazing together the accurately opposed edges, and then drawing the whole forcibly through a hole in a block of lead which squeezes the tube into intimate contact with the mandrel. This produces a smooth and even tube and at the same time hardens it. In general, tubes made by this method have stood the test of time well, but they do have one weakness in that the brazing material (which is usually softer than the body metal) may tear away during subsequent operations, or may form an area favourable to the start of corrosion. More recently, therefore, instrument-makers have taken advantage of tubing made by the 'seamless' drawing process. This, roughly, consists of forming a flat disc of metal into a bowl between male and female dies in a power press; pressing again in stages till a wide closed tube is formed; and finally drawing this down on the mandrel as before. The work-piece is carefully annealed between the stages of pressing and drawing, and of course the thickness of the original blank must be chosen so as to provide sufficient metal to yield a tube wall of the desired thickness when finished. For larger-diameter tubes rolled up from sheet the seams are usually improved by what the trade calls 'dovetailing', a rather different process from that recognised by the woodworker under the same name. In this one of the opposed borders is filed down to a feather edge, while the other is notched with shears and the tabs so formed bent alternately up and down. The feather edge is inserted between the rows of tabs and these are then bent forcibly down upon it. Brazing in the usual manner follows, and then the seam is hammered as flat as possible and finally reduced to wall thickness by fine filing (Fig. 52).

In every brass instrument beyond the very simplest there are curved sections, and shaping these up from straight tubing presents considerable problems. The traditional method, still much used, is to take a piece of suitable length and bore, stop up one end, and, having coated the inside to prevent adhesion, to fill it with molten lead or some low-temperature fusible alloy.[7] When the filling has set the whole mass is held in a jig, or between strong pegs set in a heavy bench, and bent to a predetermined pattern by hand, using a piece of piping or the like as a lever and aided by judicious blows from a soft-headed mallet. It is evident that in the course of bending the metal on the outside of the

Fig. 52   Metal blank notched and 'feathered' for forming a tapered tube by hand methods

curve will be stretched, and that on the inside somewhat compressed, with the possibility of puckering. This must be smoothed out, so the next process is to anneal the bend locally—usually with the blow-pipe flame—and to smooth out any ridges with a light *répoussé* hammer. This is a job calling for great judgment and experience, for it is not a matter of merely knocking down ridges. When properly done the metal will actually 'flow' before the hammer[8] and ultimately a bend which is perfectly smooth results. Such a section as shown in Fig. 53 is typical of the hand work that can be done by a really skilful craftsman.

Fig. 53   Illustrating the complexity of single sections formerly produced by hand methods alone

During the last thirty years or so some manufacturers in a big way of business have eliminated a great deal of laborious hand work by the employment of specially devised mechanical methods, and one of the most remarkable of these is the hydraulic expansion process which can be adapted to the forming of nearly all types of curved tubes. Briefly the method is as follows. A length of tubing of the required gauge, and bent approximately to the desired form, is placed between two heavy metal dies which are hollowed out—half each—to the exact form of the finished part. The dies are locked together in an hydraulic press and one end of the tubing is securely stoppered. Water at a pressure of some 4000 lbs. per square inch is then forced into the other end and this expands the work-piece to an exact fit in the dies, at the same time smoothing out any kinks or ripples due to the preliminary bending. Any number of identical pieces can be produced by these means and each will only require cleaning before it is incorporated into the instrument. The objection to this system is the tremendous initial cost of the presses etc., and particularly of making the dies, which must be accurately finished to a fraction of a millimetre, since every mark or blemish on their surfaces will be reproduced on the work-piece. More-over, a pair of dies will be required for each different curve and tube size it is desired to produce. These factors put the process beyond the reach of all but the biggest firms who can depend on a large and con-tinuing market for standardised instruments. Conservative players have been heard to deplore the reduction of individuality in instruments made largely by mechanical means, but if we look at the matter fairly there can surely be no objection to such repetition work if the original model is really first rate. We may with more justice deplore the dis-placement of specially skilled craftsmen which these machines seem to imply, but it is a sad fact that long before mechanisation reached such a pitch the brass instrument industry was getting short of these men, and the long apprenticeship necessary was not attractive to young talent. It appears, however, that there will be for a long time, if not permanently, a demand for craftsmen of the highest order in the repair side of the business, and this may be increasingly difficult to meet.

The traditional method of forming the bells of brass instruments begins with the cutting of a sheet metal blank somewhat in the shape

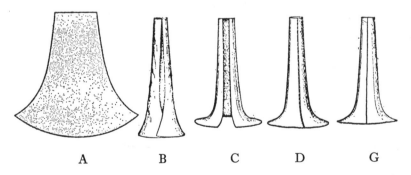

A   B   C   D   G

Fig. 54   Five stages in the formation of a trombone
bell by hand methods

shown in Fig. 54 A. This is first rolled up by hand allowing the 'wings' which will ultimately provide the flare to overlap (Fig. 54 B). The next step is the development of the flare with the 'pegging hammer'—rather like a blunt pick-axe—first against a wooden block, and then on the beak of an anvil, with careful annealing as often as necessary. This brings the work to the shape shown in Fig. 54 C. At this stage the edges of the seam, feathered and dovetailed respectively, are brazed and finished as already described. Also, at this stage, in the case of greatly expanded bells such as that of the French Horn, a wedge-shaped gusset will be fitted in to furnish extra metal. Next the work is placed on a smooth steel mandrel of the exact finished profile, again hammered and annealed, and then drawn through the perforated lead block as far as the root of the flare. The mandrel with the work-piece upon it is then transferred to a heavy lathe where it is rotated at high speed while the flare is 'spun' down into close contact by means of a round-nosed burnishing tool. This spinning very quickly hardens the work, so again annealing is called for, and as many as four or five spinnings may be required before the bell is perfectly shaped. In the last stage on the lathe the bell is trimmed to its final diameter, and the edge is turned up and rolled over its supporting wire ring. (Plate 18 A.)

It need hardly be repeated that such a sequence of operations as out-lined above calls for skill such as only long experience can give, and that the frequency and extent of the different workings will depend on the judgment of the craftsman. They may also be varied somewhat accord-ing to the established custom of a particular workshop, but in any case they are necessarily time-consuming and therefore expensive. It would seem also that machinery can do little to speed the traditional processes. In recent years, however, some manufacturers with plant at their disposal have made an entirely fresh approach to the matter, and they now make excellent trumpet bells in two parts. The bell-pipe proper is formed by the hydraulic expansion process, and the flare is lathe spun or pressed from an annular blank which may itself be stamped from the sheet. The two sections are united at the root of the flare by a single brazed seam (Fig. 55). From the player's point of view there seems to be little difference between the two types of bell, but the second process is obviously the more consistent and economical, and it has the additional advantage that in instruments where the bell expansion begins actually in the bell bow this bend can be formed during the pressing instead of being unavoidably a secondary operation which can only be done after all work on the mandrel has been completed. (Plate 18 B.)

From what has been said in Chapter 8 it will be evident that the manufacture of valves is a tricky and complicated process, particularly in the case of pistons. For rotary valves the rotor is usually formed today from a solid cylinder of metal, turned and fitted to the outer casing

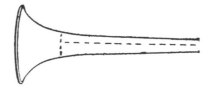

Fig. 55   Two-part built-up bell. Flare 'spun' from a disc

with the utmost nicety. The cross passages are formed by milling grooves of nearly circular section on the periphery of the cylinder with a ball-headed cutter, and where these meet the casing, accurately matching ports are cut to which the various tubes of the instrument are fitted and soldered. It will be noticed that the passages in a rotor made by this method are in fact slots and not actual perforations, and that the windways are completed by the wall of the casing. The section (Fig. 56)

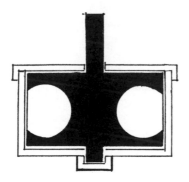

Fig. 56 Vertical section of a rotary valve (through the spindle) showing the inevitable flattening of the passages where a 'milled-out' rotor is used. The clearance between the rotor and the casing is of course exaggerated

will make this construction clear. The cross-section of the windways is evidently not absolutely circular, though in practice this seems to have little effect compared with other lapses from the ideal which are unavoidable in mechanised instruments. Rotors that require more than two passages *in the same plane* can hardly be cut from the solid unless this is made inconveniently large in diameter, so these have usually been built up by methods similar to those used for pistons. (Fig. 57 and Fig 48, p. 171.) The various actuating mechanisms that have been applied to rotary valves need no mention here as they involve no manufacturing processes that are peculiar to the instrument industry.

The construction of modern built-up pistons presents some peculiar and very interesting problems of its own. Although solid rotors are

Fig. 57 Horizontal section through a rotary valve with built-up tubular passages through the rotor. (*From a Patent specification by Gautrot, Paris, c. 1860*)

somewhat heavy in themselves they can be moved with a mere touch of the finger. Solid *pistons* where the whole weight would have to be supported by the return spring are, however, a different matter, as the square Schuster valves proved. The first solution to the inertia problem was to make the piston body of sheet metal or tubing and to use smaller tubing of the correct size for the cross passages also. This was a matter of no special difficulty (though it called for great accuracy) amounting to no more than cutting appropriate holes in the body, passing the smaller tubes either straight through or on the diagonal as required, soldering them in place, cutting off, and smoothing the exterior. When, however, the desirability of completely uniform windways throughout the instrument was fully realised the whole thing became much more difficult and curved passages through the pistons were essential. For the large-diameter Berliner-Pumpen, where there was sufficient room, simple quarter circles cut from preformed loops of tubing could be threaded through and soldered into place, but with the narrower and more complex Périnet-type valves, requiring the windways to be curved in more than one plane, this method could not be used. The curiously twisted little pieces had to be shaped up by hand, fitted meticulously to the holes in the piston body, 'fiddled' in and soldered. Some makers managed to reduce the labour involved by making the passage pieces in two halves which could be produced by pressing between pairs of shaped swage-blocks and then fitted together face to face, rather like the two parts of a mussel shell.[9] It is perhaps from this that the French term 'coquilles' has been applied to the piston passages and corrupted to 'cockades' by English-speaking workers. This procedure certainly reduces the time consumed, but it does introduce a weakness

o

in that each cockade has two lengthwise seams which add to the possibility of leakage. It is evident that in a piston the soldering must be
beyond suspicion, and the less of it the better. To complete a piston the
top and bottom of the body also require to be closed by circular discs
one of which carries the stem, making all together a very complex structure, one in which later error of judgment may well wreck all that has
been done before. To minimise this risk it is sometimes possible to use
different grades of solder, a higher-fusing type first, and then a lower
for the later operations. At the present day cockades are sometimes
produced by an adaptation of the hydraulic expansion process, and no
doubt different manufacturers have also their own carefully guarded
versions of the traditional processes. The final step with some makes of
piston is the fitting of an over-all jacket of very thin tube in which the
side holes are made exactly to match the *bore* of the cross passages. This
protects and gives some extra support to the ends of the cockades which,
of course, pass *through* the wall of the main body. No doubt this arrangement had at one time considerable value and it was regarded as essential in
first-quality valves though it did add somewhat to the weight of moving
parts. In 1864 Henry Distin patented his so-called 'light valve' in which
the jacket was discarded, and the cockades were fixed with hard silver
solder so that they had less need of protection at their ends. Distin's
light valve was continued by Boosey and Co. for some years after they
had acquired his business.

The forming of valve cases, though just as demanding in the matter
of accuracy, is not quite so laborious as the making of pistons, but
here again some very interesting special techniques have been developed.
For piston cases the raw material, rather heavy-walled tubing, is cut to
length, turned, threaded etc. externally as may be required, and the
ports are cut to a most meticulous pattern. The three, four, or five
lengths required to form a group or 'cluster' are placed in a jig which
holds them firmly in exact alignment. The small tubes forming the
connecting passages are then shaped and put in position, together with
any intervening supports and the knuckles which form the connections
for the external tubing of the instrument. Next the assembly is bound
rigidly together with iron wire, the joints are painted with a paste of
powered hard solder and flux (usually borax) and the whole is raised to
soldering temperature at a single heating with a blow-torch. As the
solder fuses it 'flashes' round each junction and forms a solid joint.
Fig. 58 is an 'exploded' drawing of the parts that go to form a cluster
of three piston cases, the commonest form. After soldering, the assembly,

as with the various brazed joints we have already referred to, is 'pickled' in dilute acid to remove any scale or residue of flux. Should any seam show a pin-hole or other defect after cleaning the whole assembly is scrapped, for 'doctoring' a bad joint can never be really

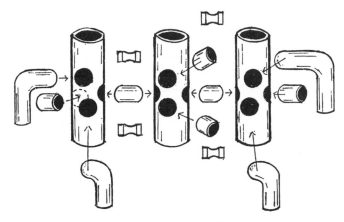

Fig. 58 'Exploded' sketch of a cluster of piston valve cases, with their accessory tube unions and stays. These are nowadays jig-assembled and brazed all at one heating

satisfactory, and any attempt to re-heat one is almost bound to open others. With large manufacturers today the finished diameter of piston or rotor, and the bore of the case, is adjusted by grinding and reaming machines working to micrometer gauges, so the final operation is only to match up individual pairs and lap them together with the very finest abrasives so as to get an air-tight fit with the smoothest possible movement.

The foregoing is, of course, only a sketch of some special processes used in the brass instrument industry, and, as I have indicated, different makers have their own variants and sequences of operation to suit their individual circumstances. The assembly of the various tubes, valves, and bell which make up a modern trumpet or trombone is, however, almost universal. Side tubes for valve slides are joined to the knuckles, and main tubes are united end to end by means of overlapping ferrules (p. 77) and soft solder. The ends of the tubes and the insides of the ferrules are first 'tinned' and then brought together and gently heated till the solder fuses and flows to form a strong and solid joint. In the same way the reinforcing patches, stays, and guards are applied. Finally the whole instrument is cleaned and tested and the chosen finish applied, which may be anything from a simple polish, through silver or gold plating, plain or frosted, to a coloured hard lacquer. The maker's name and any chosen ornamentation is engraved, and the instrument is finished.

It may be asked why soft solder is used for the general assembly in preference to a harder material. The answer is twofold. In the first place tin-based solder applied to an adequate surface is amply strong, and secondly, because of its relatively low melting point it can be used without risk of conducted heat undoing vital joints already made. This is of particular advantage when the question of repairs arises. A soft-soldered instrument can be taken apart just as far as needful without totally wrecking it.

The maintenance and repair of brass instruments is a subject on which no hard-and-fast rules can be laid down. Suffice it to say that the state of dilapidation into which some players allow their instruments to get is quite amazing. One can readily understand a busy soloist being reluctant to give up a cherished instrument even for a short time as long as it will respond, but there is a grave risk in this, for one day it will let him down at the most embarrassing moment. All players should be able to clean and lubricate their instruments properly, and adjust the screws and buffers of a rotary action, if nothing more. Beyond this the art of a skilled repair man should be invoked—*but in good time*—and his advice respected. What he will propose to do in any given case must depend on his judgment and experience, but it will always be based on simple horse sense. The commonest ailment among brasses is bruising and denting, as we see every day. At first this may not inconvenience the player much, but ultimately repeated denting may so distort the bore as to affect the security or the intonation of certain notes. In the end, also, a neglected dent may engender a crack or an open seam and then the instrument will be useless. By local annealing and then careful hammering on a mandrel, a good repairer will easily restore a bruised tube if it be of fairly large diameter, but for narrow tubes he will employ a special technique not known outside his own trade. After a preliminary annealing, he will select an olive-shaped steel 'bullet' of such size that it will pass easily along the bore until obstructed by the dent. He will back this up with two or three more steel balls, and by a gentle rocking of the tube will cause them to hammer the dented part of the tube internally. After some time the olive will pass the obstruction, and then a larger one is substituted. The process is repeated until a ball the exact diameter of the tube will pass through and the bore will have been completely restored. When a fissure of any sort has developed the repairer will most probably apply a patch of very thin soft brass burnished down to the exact contour of the original tube. This may not be beautiful, but it is sound practice, and I have heard magnificent playing on instruments that have been 'soled and heeled' all over. I have even seen a French Horn in which the bell had been worn quite through by repeated hand-stopping, and here a patch had been so well fitted that no roughness was apparent to the touch. Another trouble that may readily be put right is the burring over of the ends of slides, particularly those often withdrawn to empty out moisture. Serious wear of pistons or rotors is not very common with the hard-plated surfaces in use today, but some restoration of older valves can be effected by plating and re-grinding if this should be deemed worth while.

In concluding this necessarily very condensed account, let me say that, though there must be secrets in every trade, I have without exception found instrument-makers and repairers most generous in giving information to anyone interested in their work.

NOTES

[1] The tremendous array of tone-colours imagined by Wagner for his music-dramas was simply not to be found in the average orchestra of his day, with the result that certain enterprising instrument-makers applied themselves to supplying what the Master thought lacking. Thus it is very largely due to Wagner's influence that we have had the revival of the contrabass trombone, the great improvements in the German-style bassoon made by the Heckel family, and the creation of a true bass trumpet, the hybrid Wagner Tubas, and the Heckelphone.

In the third act of *Tristan* Wagner wrote a poignant little pipe tune, ostensibly to be played on-stage by a shepherd boy. In the original score the melody was allotted to an orchestral cor anglais, but in his preface to the opera Wagner wrote that it would be preferable if 'a special instrument of wood be made for it after the model of the alp-horn, which on account of its simplicity, should be neither difficult nor expensive'. To judge by conversations and correspondence quoted by Wilhelm Heckel (*Der Fagott*, Leipzig, 1931) Wagner had something of a romantic obsession with the sound of the alp-horn, and it seems a far cry from a long wooden natural horn to a shepherd's pipe. Nevertheless, a few examples of Wagner's dream instrument have been made in the form of a straight wood trumpet pitched in C, with a spheroidal bell constricted at the mouth. About one-third along from the rather wide trumpet mouthpiece the bore is broken by a short brass section carrying a single whole-tone valve and its supplementary tube. At Bayreuth and one or two other Houses this instrument is to be found today, and it certainly produces an individual tone quality that the composer presumably had in mind, but as a rule it is replaced by anything from a normal trumpet muted with felt, by way of the *tarogato*, to a soprano saxophone, according to the ideas of the conductor or the available player.

[2] A somewhat obscure entry in Talbot's Manuscript refers to the 'Box Trumpet', an instrument of the same dimensions as the common trumpet of the period. It is inferred that 'box' here means box wood, since Talbot refers to 'tenons' which otherwise he mentions only in connection with the woodwind. *Galpin Society Journal*, Vol. I, 1948, p. 22. The term is, however, also applied to a form of trumpet of which a number of 18th-century German examples are known. In these the tubing is closely coiled inside a sort of brass canister with the bell opening at one end.

[3] Maillot and Chorier, two metallurgists of Lyons, devised one of the best-known formulae for a white bronze *c.* 1820; hence the name *Maillechort* sometimes incorrectly rendered as *Melchior*.

[4] I am informed by Mr. H. Fitzpatrick of Wadham College, Oxford, that traditionally Bastard Brass was an alloy prepared by melting together scrap brass with new copper but no calamine, i.e. a very copper-rich brass. This still does not shed much light on Talbot's observations. One may perhaps suppose that his 'copper springy' was in fact copper work-hardened almost beyond the limit of its malleability. The metallurgy of copper alloys *c.* 1840—just the period when satisfactory valves were emerging—is described in much detail in Vol. I of Charles Holtzapffel's *Turning and Mechanical Manipulation*, London, 1843, and is of great interest.

[5] Aluminium bronzes, a comparatively recent metallurgical achievement, have the property of work-hardening in a remarkable degree. Some makers have therefore adopted them for specially vulnerable parts of instruments such as horn bells and trombone slides, though in the latter capacity they have no special low-friction qualities. Quite recently some American firms have begun to advertise super-light valves made, they claim, of aluminium. The material must, in fact, be some alloy, as pure aluminium is much too soft for such use.

[6] The joining of pieces of metal by the application of another metal or alloy of lower melting point is in general termed 'soldering', but there are several recognised variants of the process which go by special names. The brass instrument industry employs three of these—namely, for the heaviest work, *Brazing* in which the binding material is 'spelter', itself a zinc-rich brass which melts at a temperature little below that of the body metal; *Hard* or *silver soldering* in which the fusing point of the solder is considerably lowered by the presence of a large proportion of silver in the alloy; and *Soft* or *tin soldering* where the solder is an alloy of tin and lead only, in varying proportions. Spelter and silver solder make the strongest joints, but they require temperatures beyond red heat and often the naked flame to make them flow. Soft solder can be fused by the application of the soldering 'iron', a heavy copper bolt kept well below red heat although the blowpipe flame discreetly used is sometimes technically more convenient. In each case a 'flux' is applied which has the double effect of assisting fusion and preventing oxidation of the chemically clean surfaces to be joined, so that the solder can form an intimate union with the body metal.

[7] For large-diameter tubes a coarse grade of resin is sometimes used as the filler. Fusible alloys such as 'Wood's Metal' are expensive in the first place, but they have the advantage of speeding work since they melt freely about the temperature of boiling water and so are very easily removed.

[8] The reader who may be interested further is referred to Holtzapffel's book, Vol. I, pp. 389 *et seq.*, where the whole process of metal beating is explained in detail, and the placing of hammer blows for different effects is shown diagrammatically. As an example of the extent to which malleable sheet metal may be formed by hammer and punch alone we may cite the old-fashioned jelly moulds, the best of which were worked up from flat sheet entirely without joining.

[9] This method has been used extensively in making the smaller bows for slides etc., especially in second-class instruments.

CHAPTER 10

Technique and Capabilities

Tone Production, etc.

IN ATTEMPTING to outline the technique and capabilities of a modern brass instrument the first point that demands attention is *embouchure* (in the English sense of that word, i.e. the way of applying the lips to the mouthpiece and so completing the acoustic generator (p. 3)), and it may be said at once that although different expert players may recommend one or other method according to their personal experience, this is really a highly individual matter. A good embouchure is vital to the cultivation of a good tone, in which only the player's ear can be his ultimate guide. The beginner, therefore, will sooner or later develop his individual embouchure, and by his own efforts, though a sympathetic teacher can smooth the way a great deal. The anatomical configuration of a young player's teeth, jaws, and lip muscles are the factors that will determine the particular embouchure which is natural and comfortable to him, and the good teacher should be able to recognise these. In really abnormal cases the mouthpiece expert will be able to help also, but until the student has acquired some considerable experience himself he will do well to be wary of offset rims and such extreme devices. These points are not always fully explained even in some of the most esteemed and authoritative instruction books although the importance of embouchure is continually stressed in the text. This may be because it is assumed that few students would consider taking up a wind instrument without the initial guidance of a qualified instructor, and that in the early stages such considerations might be more of a worry than a help to the novice.

The average student will probably begin by placing the mouthpiece centrally and with about half of the cup against each lip. Fig. 59, which is based on a photograph of an actual trumpeter, illustrates this placing and it is one which many players retain throughout life. On the other hand there are many who believe that the cup is best placed about one-third against one lip and two-thirds against the other, though which lip is to be favoured is a moot point. For example, two celebrated French

professors, Forestier and Arban, disagreed completely, the former
placing his two-thirds on the upper lip and the latter the exact reverse.
While preparing this book the writer has carefully observed a large
number of fine professional players and there appears to him to be
no marked preponderance either way. With the larger mouthpiece of the

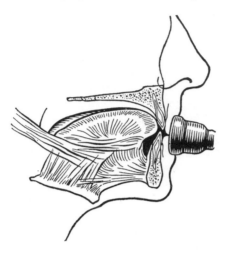

Fig. 59   Relationship of
teeth, tongue and jaws to
mouthpiece in trumpet
playing. Centrally placed
embouchure.
(*After Porter*)

trombone the tendency seems to be to favour the upper lip, but again
this is not very marked. The majority of horn players place two-thirds
of the mouthpiece on the upper lip, and some even go so far as to adopt
what they call the 'set-in' embouchure in which the rim is really bedded
into the vermilion border of the lower lip. This presumably gives a
very firm support but it is condemned by many hornists as reducing
the power of attack and volume of tone. I have never encountered a
trumpeter who uses such a 'set-in', though I believe it is sometimes
done, and I have seen many mouthpieces with rims thin enough to
make it possible. Recently, also, certain American players have adopted
what they term the 'puckered' embouchure where the preparation
consists, not in stretching the lips in a smile as advised by Arban, but
in consciously compressing the lips laterally so as to present as solid
a mass of muscle as possible to the mouthpiece cup. That unorthodox
dispositions of the lips are quite practical has been dramatically shown
by one or two players who, by way of experiment, have placed one lip
right outside the cup, and by setting the tongue against the other
have been able to sound their instrument quite adequately. Though
scientifically interesting this trick is, of course, quite useless for real

playing, the proper function of the tongue being to provide the attack or *coup de langue* which gives the note a clean start.[1]

We have already seen that the higher notes of the harmonic series are elicited by the player by means of increased tension in the lips. Some players habitually foster this by increasing the pressure of the mouthpiece against the mouth. Others believe this to be unnecessary and bad practice. Some years ago there was considerable controversy regarding the so-called 'no-pressure' system—something of a misnomer since obviously there must be *some* pressure, however light, between the mouthpiece and the lips—but no really useful conclusions emerged. It seems likely that in fact every player uses just as much or as little pressure as suits him, and is little concerned by theories.

In Chapters 5 and 6 we have referred to representations of Roman trumpets and medieval buisines sounded with the cheeks inflated, and have taken these as supporting evidence of a primitive blowing technique. It is only fair to add here that some present-day trumpeters, mostly in dance bands, also allow the cheeks to inflate while playing, but careful observation has shown that in spite of this these players manage to maintain great control of the lips themselves. Such relaxation of the cheeks may represent a habit picked up in youth—as a boy bugler perhaps, to whom loudness rather than tone was the first objective—but it does not appear to be really necessary; many object to it on physiological grounds; and the agonised expression which goes with it would hardly commend itself to a Renaissance artist unless perhaps he were a designer of gargoyles.

Compass and Fingering

The compass normally available on the modern valved trumpet (and trombone) extends from the 2nd to the 8th or 9th harmonics. From these, by means of the valves or slide, a chromatic scale of some twenty-six notes is built up, starting a minor fifth below the 2nd harmonic of the natural instrument, as explained in our Acoustics chapter (pp. 1–37). Certain individual players can command much higher partials —on the trumpet the 16th and above, and on the trombone at least the 12th—but these are not to be relied on in the ordinary way. The scale which the composer or arranger may reasonably write for is shown in Fig. 60 overleaf.

Some individual notes, particularly the 2nd harmonic with each valve or valve combination, are more difficult to sound in tune than the rest, but these become progressively easier in the higher-pitched instruments.

The reason for the alternative fingerings for some notes given above has also been explained on p. 12.

Fig. 60 Normal compass of valve-trumpet in C, B♭ or A (written notes). Sounding a whole tone or a minor third lower on B♭ or A instruments respectively.

Similar conditions apply to the slide trombone, where six 'positions' correspond with the use of one or more valves. Fig. 61 shows the notes normally available with the seven positions of the slide and it will be noted that quite a number of them can be obtained in only one position.

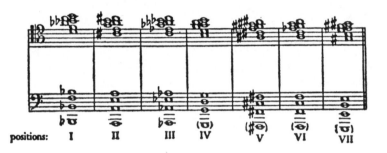

Fig. 61   Compass of B♭ tenor trombone in the seven positions

Composers must therefore take care that notes requiring wide 'shifts' are not written so as to alternate too rapidly. Such a passage as Fig. 62, for example, would be very awkward on the B♭ tenor trombone since it calls for alternating seventh and first positions at some speed. It is in this respect that the valved trombone has its principal advantage,

Fig. 62   Awkward passage on B♭ tenor trombone

but the agility of modern slide technique is now little inferior. Returning for a moment to Fig. 61 we should note one or two further points. The 9th and 10th partials are used chiefly in the first two positions. They are in fact less difficult to sound in the five lower harmonic series, but in practice the actual notes here represented are better taken as lower-numbered partials of higher-placed series. On the trombone the fundamental or 'pedal' tones are excellent notes in the first three positions if the player be given a little time to prepare his embouchure (see also p. 57).

The tenor-bass trombone in Bb–F with the additional E♮ slide provides almost unlimited possibilities throughout both ranges, but with the F tubing switched in the slide is long enough only for six positions. Fig. 63 illustrates the six series available with the F valve

Fig. 63   Series obtainable with the transposing valve
on the Bb-F tenor-bass trombone

and we see that the low B♮ is still missing unless the E slide be pulled out to produce it.

Dynamics

The full power of the brass is capable of dominating, even obliterating, the combined efforts of the rest of the orchestra. This is very generally realised; what is perhaps less appreciated is the absolutely magical effect of brass played *pianissimo*, a quality well understood by the great composers of the Classical period when they brought the old military trumpet into the realm of Art music and imposed a new discipline on it. In present-day performances of the classics it is necessary to bear this in mind. (We ignore here for a moment the achievements of the 18th-century clarinists since their art was forgotten in the Classical period.) As late as 1914, when Cecil Forsyth published the first edition of his celebrated *Orchestration*, the valve instrument in F was still the traditional orchestral trumpet and the higher ones in Bb and C were comparative newcomers. Today the latter are predominant and their brilliant but less weighty tone is not always a perfect substitute in parts conceived for the larger instrument. Mere marking up of the dynamics will not produce a heavier tone and the conductor has a problem on his hands which calls for taste and good judgment. Conversely the F instrument, rich and noble-sounding in the hands of a fine artist, was no doubt often abused by inferior players, but the practice of marking trumpet parts at a lower dynamic than the rest of the movement as a routine is not to be recommended. A good trumpeter is an artist who is perfectly well aware of the relative implication of dynamic markings and his sensibility and judgment should be respected.

Articulation. Staccato and Legato. Trills

Both the trumpet and the trombone are today among the most agile instruments of the orchestra. They permit of a clean and sharp attack in all dynamics from the loudest to a mere whisper, and they respond to double, triple, and flutter tonguing almost as easily as the flute—with this reservation, that the large mouthpiece of the trombone makes long repeated articulations somewhat tiring for the player. *Sforzandi* and *forte-piano* and sharp accents generally are effective on both instruments, but we should be careful to indicate in the part the exact type of accent required. True *legato* playing presents certain problems and indeed a perfect slur can only be obtained between adjacent harmonics of the same series. Where a shift of slide or a change of valves is required between tied notes very skilful co-ordination of tongue and hand is necessary so as not to sound unwanted notes in passing, but when well done the slight break needful to avoid *portamento* is barely discernible. In a flowing melodic passage most trombonists will apply just the slightest attack to every note whether of the same or a different series, the resultant effect being comparable to a well-bowed fiddle passage. This same characteristic which makes some slurring difficult gives the slide trombone one faculty possessed of no other wind instrument, a true *glissando*. It cannot be made over a greater interval than an augmented fourth, that being the relation of the harmonic series of the first and seventh positions, but within these limits it is a useful effect, if one that is nowadays rather often abused. There is more to say about this in a later chapter, as well as about a rather similar effect attempted by the dance band trumpeter. On the trumpet *trills* are usually performed with the valves, though a few between adjacent notes in the high register may be produced by the lips alone. The only problem regarding valve trills arises from the purely mechanical difficulty of certain fingerings.

Fig. 64 shows three trills which may sound awkward for this reason. On the slide trombone only lip trills are of course possible, though some players will produce a sort of *vibrato* with the slide. They are limited

Fig. 64   Examples of valve trills involving awkward fingerings

to the interval of a major second, the widest gap between adjacent notes of the same series.

Breathing

It goes without saying that the brass instruments require more wind than the woodwinds, but this does not imply that they call for *hard* blowing. To keep the lips vibrating so as to energise properly the relatively large air column of the trumpet or trombone a very considerable volume of air must pass, but this does not necessarily take great muscular strength, nor does it require the physique of a giant. Lavoix illustrates a tapestry depicting a German Court ball of *c.* 1560 where in a mixed group a lady is seen playing the sackbut,[2] and in our own day women are playing brass instruments in some of our leading orchestras on equal terms with the men. The justly famous brass section of the Hallé Orchestra comes to mind at once, in which, until a year or two ago, a lady occupied the first trombone desk with the greatest distinction.

The difficulty of most reed players is to relieve the lungs regularly of stale air that has not been expended in playing; with the brass man the problem is to maintain an adequate reserve behind the embouchure, at all times, and this without apparent distress or ugly gasping. Deep and full breathing is therefore necessary with strong control from the diaphragm as in good singing, and the composer or orchestrator should bear this in mind.[3] It is not very usual to find breathing points marked in a brass part, and it might be better if these were indicated more often, since ill-placed breaths can interfere with the intended phrasing. Of course breath indications should be clearly distinguishable from phrase markings or confusion may result. This, however, is another point on which the personal artistry of the player will be the ultimate guide.

Muting

Trumpets and trombones lend themselves very well to muting, and discreetly used the device is very effective. Mutes, and their acoustic behaviour, have already been dealt with on pages 29 and 74. Here it will be sufficient to say that nowadays composers really ought to indicate somehow in the score the type of mute or effect they require. Muting of the brass, be it repeated, is not a dynamic but a *tone modifying* device, though it can sometimes give a spurious impression of reduced loudness by filtering out specific overtones. It is not unknown, even today, for a conductor at rehearsal to say something like, 'Still too loud trumpets. Mute it,' and then be surprised at the altered tone quality. In 1947 a correspondent wrote to the *Philharmonic Post* of London asking if greater homogeneity in the brass could not be assured by requiring all players in a section to use instruments of identical make. The reply was to the effect that even with identical instruments players would to a great extent produce their own individual tones, but the writer was strongly of the opinion that *mutes* used together should be matched, and I believe that the majority of orchestral musicians would endorse this.

NOTES

[1] I am reliably informed that a few players now employ what they call a 'buzzed' attack in which the sound is initiated by the lips alone, but I have not so far had the chance to question one personally.

[2] H. Lavoix, fils, *Histoire de l'Instrumentation*, Paris, Firmin-Didot, 1878.

[3] The reader will find a particularly good note on the subject compressed into only two columns in the American periodical *Crescendo* for April–June, 1952, p. 5.

CHAPTER II

Trumpet and Trombone in the Orchestra

IN OUR GENERAL history sections we have seen something of the circumstances in which the primitive trumpet and trombone developed in Europe, and the particular uses to which they were first put. The small selection we have made from a multitude of references in contemporary pictorial art and literature show that, in addition to doing organised military, ceremonial, and municipal duties, both instruments soon found a place in 'Handschin'—or, as we might say, 'sociable' music making. In this chapter we shall try to survey briefly their vicissitudes during the years when a more specific and self-conscious Art-music was growing up—in so far as this may be done without a comprehensive study of the whole field of Orchestration. It should be understood also that in many cases composers are here named more as convenient landmarks than as the sole originators of any specific trend or technique.

The standardised musical body we recognise as 'The Orchestra' assumed its present form only in the course of the 19th century, though the story of *orchestration* can be traced back some 300 years earlier. By the latter part of the 16th century polyphonic vocal music had reached its culmination in the Mass and the Motet for the Church, and the Madrigal for secular entertainment. Educated musicians then began to explore the possibilities of music written for combinations of string, wind, and keyboard instruments in their own right. They also experimented particularly with the single-voice line with *harmonic* support or contrast supplied by variable groups of instruments as a dramatic method of expression, and so created the first primitive forms of Opera, Oratorio, and Ballet. 'The birth of the orchestra', said Adam Carse, 'is thus connascent with the creation of secular instrumental music as a cultured form of art, and largely arises out of the transition from modal polyphony to monody.'[1] From these unorganised beginnings there finally developed the modern symphony orchestra with its vast expressive ability; but we must not suppose that the process was uninterrupted or that it was equally advanced in all parts of Europe at any one time.

Moreover, it is clear that, even today, finality has not been reached, and composers continue to experiment with new and sometimes surprising resources. This is surely a sign of a living and healthy art.

Looked at broadly, orchestral development divides itself into two main eras; the first ending with the deaths of Bach and Handel, the two great masters of *harmonic* polyphony; the second covering the rise of what we may call 'present-day' orchestration as initiated by Haydn and Mozart and incorporating the successive periods generally labelled 'classical', 'romantic', and 'modern'. The transition is not, of course, in any way rigidly marked, but it corresponds roughly to the life of Gluck (1714–87) and some less important composers of whom C. P. E. Bach is probably the best known. During the initial phase the influences that affected orchestral organisation were many and various. Some were concerned with the advent of new or improved instruments, as for example the violin family, which offered the composer greater brilliance and attack than did the older viols, and in turn stimulated him to make ever greater demands on his string players. Others were connected with the conditions, social or geographical, in which composers worked. The absence of cheap and easy methods of reproducing pages of written music, as well as the lack of ready communication between countries, must have restricted many important innovations to purely local significance for a long time.[2] For an example we need only think of the very small public who heard the music of Bach the Church cantor during his lifetime, and compare this with the opportunities that fell naturally to Lulli the favoured Court musician of Louis XIV of France. Bach also provides an illustration of another sort. A look at scores written at different periods of his career reveals clearly the limited instrumental resources furnished by his different employers, and the use he made of them is a measure of his genius. Bach's surviving records contain many pleas to the Authorities for new instruments, even repairs to existing ones. Compare this situation with that of Haydn as a servant in a Princely household—even if the implication of the Court livery was at times irksome to him. Those minor nobility of the 18th century who were music patrons at all vied with each other in the musical establishments they could afford their *Kapellmeisters*—and Haydn was one of the relatively fortunate ones. His patron, Prince Esterhazy, too, was enlightened enough to give him leave to travel at times, though we are told that even he once needed the 'Farewell' symphony as a reminder that holidays were really necessary.[3] Still other influential factors are illustrated by such a comparison as that of

Handel with Schubert. The one was the true cosmopolitan of the 18th century, and he always wrote music adapted in style and instrumental demands to the town in which he had for the time being settled—were it in Germany, England, or Italy. The other, though born over a century later (he survived just into the age of railway transport), lived in so confined a circle that little, if any, of his orchestral music was published during his lifetime. His marvellous melodic use of the full classical orchestra had therefore little influence on the main stream of progress until virtually rediscovered long after his death. It is against this very varied background that we must look at the trumpet and the trombone as elements in the developing concert orchestra.

Considering first the trumpet, it is not surprising that its appearance in 17th-century oratorio and opera scores was confined to the customary *tutti* which opened the work, and to passages of a jubilant or martial character. Indeed, we might almost apply to it the modern term 'special-effect instrument'. With the trumpets at this time we commonly find their associated drums, and contemporary scores seem to suggest that, more often than not, no special drum part was written, the composer relying on the player as an educated musician for an appropriate improvisation according to the accepted rules. At the beginning of the century it was also the custom to herald dramatic performances with three trumpet fanfares, and no doubt in most cases the players were just left to get on with it. In 1607, however, a most important innovation was made. Monteverdi, evidently not satisfied to accept anything that his trumpeters might choose to offer, incorporated in the overture to *Orfeo* his own fanfare written in five parts, and thus created a fore-piece of great brilliance in itself and directly related to the main work. This is the first example we know of a composer imposing his will on the trumpet body in this way, and it was a landmark in the path of early opera. From the consecutive notes written by Monteverdi it is evident that nothing less than an 8-foot trumpet would serve his purpose, and we note that he marked the upper part *clarino*. At this time clarino playing (p. 106) was already well understood, though not yet carried to the degree of specialisation achieved in the time of Bach.

Following Monteverdi's imaginative though admittedly unregulated innovations—among other things he introduced *pizzicato* string playing —a degree of organisation began to appear in the orchestra. By about 1660 the strings generally had settled down into a coherent body and three- or five-part writing, somewhat allied to the earlier vocal style, was in vogue. Attempts to secure tonal variety now began by contrasting violins with viols, or strings with wind instruments, and among the latter the brass began to be valued for their tone colour and not merely for their associations. These effects were by now common property and many examples could be drawn from operatic composers of the time, but here it will be sufficient to name Cesti (1629–69) as one of the most important. In Cesti's opera *Il Pomo d'Oro* we find two trumpets on an equal footing taking the top line in turn. In one chorus scene also, trumpets alternate with the strings in a manner which anticipates the beginning of the 18th century. Previously such contrast in operatic accompaniment had been almost entirely reserved for distinction between the moods of adjacent scenes. Cesti also made the dubious 11th open note of the C trumpet serve both as f'♮ and f'♯ which gives us some idea of the ability he expected in his trumpeters. It is interesting to compare Cesti's trumpet writing with that of Lulli (1633–87). The latter also used trumpets in pairs, but he confined them exclusively to a martial context, a convention which Cesti sometimes relaxed. Probably Lulli's most significant contribution to the orchestra was the admission of shawms which had formerly belonged entirely to open-air wind bands, and, as the official Organiser of French military music in his day, he had ample resources to do this. From his time on, shawms, or their successors the true oboes, as well as trumpets are rarely absent from any score that contains wind parts at all. Apart from this Lulli's work was mainly to formalise and consolidate; he appears to have been timid in his use of tonal contrast, but when he did employ it, rather stiffly, in eight-bar sections instead of scene by scene, his treatment points towards Handel rather than to any of his predecessors. By reason of his prominence at the French Court, as well as his personal intrigues, Lulli's influence was widespread, and his example stood firm for a considerable time.

The last decades of the 17th century saw another fundamental change in the lay-out of the orchestra, and one that was to become permanent. Even before Lulli had written his last few operas a new generation of composers began to find two tenor parts among the strings unnecessary. It is true that Lulli's pupils and followers adhered to a five-part string section till well into the 1700s, but the majority of younger men soon settled for four clear string parts and this has remained the standard ever since, with *divisi* writing when specially called for. This was the birth period of the string *concerto*, often regarded as the invention of Torelli (d. 1708), with the string body divided unequally into *solo* and *ripieno* sections, and which led in the next century to the solo instrumental concerto on the one hand, and to the classical symphony on the other. Orchestral music was now becoming an expressive art in its own right, and was no longer associated only with oratorio and opera. The tendencies in these years are well exemplified by the work of Alessandro Scarlatti (1659–1725) on the Continent, and of Purcell (1658–95), in England. The latter was somewhat isolated from the main stream, it is true, but he readily absorbed the technical improvements which came to him from abroad and he used them with quite original genius.[4] In writing for wind instruments both Scarlatti and Purcell improved upon Lulli in their use of independent parts though both, like Handel later on, often employed oboes and trumpets merely to double or imitate the violins. This tended to force the trumpets into a florid style, technically possible, but unsuited to their character, and it also obliged trumpeters, willy-nilly, to cultivate the *clarino* register. When 'violin' figuration really got beyond the trumpet's capacity, however, broader, simpler, and more characteristic parts were written, and in this *genre* both composers showed a great advance towards the modern concept of trumpet scoring. It is said that Scarlatti may have been the first to discover the now common device of using detached string chords to reinforce wind instruments playing the accented notes of a theme. In Germany during this period similar influences were at work, particularly in Munich between 1681 and 1688, and thereafter in Hanover, where the Italian-born Steffani had become famous as a composer of opera in addition to his other occupations as a statesman and a dignitary of the Roman Catholic Church. Many judge him to have been the peer of Scarlatti or Purcell, and in one respect he may even have surpassed them. In Hanover it seems that he found an ample supply of wind players, and he used his oboes and bassoons freely to double or alternate with the violin and bass lines respectively. His trumpets and drums he used equally freely, both for characteristic marches and fanfares and in the full *tutti* with chorus voices, woodwind, and strings. Scarlatti and Purcell at times broke the earlier convention of paired trumpets and added a third independent part; Steffani went even farther and frequently wrote in two, three, or four parts as his imagination dictated. Under the influence of Steffani and his like, the main centres of orchestral progress now began to shift from Italy towards Germany, but there was there at the same time an enduring tradition of Protestant Church music which was before long to flower unsurpassedly in the work of J. S. Bach. Pre-eminent among the

Lutheran Church musicians was Dietrich Buxtehude (1637–1707) the organist of Lübeck whom the young Bach so much admired. His instrumental scoring develops naturally via Schütz out of the pattern established at St. Mark's, Venice, in the latter part of the 16th century by G. Gabrielli, of whom we must say more in connection with the trombone. Conservative in all things musical, Buxtehude used paired trumpets in a rather sparing manner, and never as upper voices allied with trombones. For this purpose he is known to have specified *trombette*, i.e. treble trombones, and all in all he seems to have been concerned with a 'vocal' use of instrumental groups rather than with individual qualities or techniques.

The first phase of orchestral development ends, as we have said, with the years dominated by Bach and Handel—roughly the first half of the 18th century—and for this period we are fortunate in having a contemporary account of musical instruments, at least as known in German orchestras. In 1713 Johann Mattheson (1681–1764), a prolific North German composer, published his book *Das neu-eröffnete Orchester* which, for its bearing on 18th-century music, is nearly as valuable to the historian as are Virdung or Praetorius in respect of their periods. Under the heading of 'trumpets' Mattheson quotes the open notes of the 8-foot C instrument but states that for playing at *Kammerton* pitch (note 11, p. 126) the shorter D trumpet is more suitable. He also mentions *Mundstücke*, lowering the pitch by a full semitone, by which he must surely have meant detachable bits rather than actual mouthpieces.

The principal composers who worked during this period fall very roughly into a 'conservative' and a 'progressive' group, a division which today suggests political rather than musical affiliations. Bach and Handel by their musical lineage were both conservatives, and the distinction of their music lies mainly in their brilliant individual use of accepted formulae. To meet their demands the technique of 'clarino' playing reached its zenith. Both adhered to the old practice of imposing string-type figuration on their wind instruments, but Handel also at times divided his orchestra into three contrasted masses: strings, woodwinds, and trumpets with drums, though of course the latter could hardly be a fully melodic section. By different combinations of these groups with each other and with chorus voices in five parts Handel secured great variety and some of his grandest effects. Among the conservative—indeed ultra-conservative—group we must count the entire *galère* of French composers from Lulli to the advent of Rameau (1683–1764), as well as many of those working in and around Vienna.

The characteristics which mark the 'progressive' composers of the mid-18th century are rather difficult to define, since they consist more in the non-observance or bending of the accepted formulae than in any radical innovation. The importance of their work does not become really evident till we look at it beside the mature productions of the next generation who used tone colour, harmony, and rhythm for their own sake, and gave up pure contrapuntal writing as their sole means of expression. Time has shown these composers to have been mostly minor talents, competent certainly, but in the main lacking that personality which makes a man a leader among his fellows—yet to them we owe a debt of gratitude, for by their persistence they kept open a path without which orchestral composition might well have died of sheer stagnation after the passing of the two giants. Among the better known of the progressives we find Telemann, Hasse, Wagenseil, and C. P. E. Bach, all, be it noted, North German composers.

Modern orchestration, as we may call it, really began in the last forty years of the 18th century, the period of Haydn and Mozart as orchestral composers, but we must not suppose that the new system burst suddenly upon a waiting world. There was, as we have seen, a transition, and this, though pivoted about 1750, really covered most of the century, becoming more evident sometimes in one musical centre and sometimes in another. The working period of Gluck coincided almost exactly with the last years of the transition. During a long life he travelled all over the musical centres of Europe, and even before the death of Bach had made an international reputation as an operatic composer. His most important years as such were 1760 to 1780 (*Orfeo ed Euridice* to *Iphigénie en Tauride*) in which he demonstrated his conviction that 'the instruments ought to be introduced in proportion to the degree of interest and passion in the words' and 'instruments are to be employed not according to the dexterity of the players, but according to the dramatic propriety of their tone'. Under the later 'transition composers' in general the trumpets gradually yielded up their high melodic parts, and in Gluck's scores there remain no traces of the clarino technique. Instead trumpets in their lower registers (and drums) are required to play softly and to contribute to the warmth and solidity of the general effect. They are no longer by tradition the loudest voices in the orchestra.

In the time of Haydn, Mozart, and their contemporaries[5] we find the concert orchestra fully established, notably at Mannheim, Dresden, Berlin, and Paris, in addition to specialised opera orchestras in Paris, Naples, and some lesser centres. Their resources had been filled out by the full acceptance of the clarinet, which had been the subject of experiment and technical development for nearly eighty years.[6] At the same time the old cornetts finally disappeared, although their acoustic principle was to survive in the keyed-bugle and the ophicleide until well after Mendelssohn's time. Horns were also by now a regular and valuable constituent of most orchestras, and composers were becoming very skilled in their use of the different crooks. Trumpets, however, still remained intractable with the generally recognised crooks giving only the harmonic series of B♭, C, D, and E♭, and for music outside these keys the range of useful notes was even more restricted. Thus, for example, for movements in G, Haydn employed the C trumpet which gave him tonic, dominant, and sub-dominant but no third. G minor was even worse provided, and Carse has suggested that perhaps it was this inherent poverty that decided Mozart to omit trumpet tone from his famous G minor symphony. The recognised working compass of the trumpet was now from the third to the twelfth open note. The eleventh was as a rule avoided on account of its sharpness in relation to the key, though Haydn did sometimes make it serve for the f'♯ (on the C instrument). There is now little sign of the player being expected to temper the eleventh either way as in many of Bach's scores, and the flat seventh is also usually omitted from both trumpet and horn parts.

The extreme conservatism that this seems to show among trumpeters as distinct from orchestral horn players[7] is interesting and may have been a legacy from Fraternity influence (see pp. 225-27), but we also note that when mechanisation began it was with the horn, already a more complete instrument, which possessed a well-developed technique of hand stopping that never came to much on the trumpet. Prejudice or conservatism notwithstanding, it is in the Haydn–Mozart years that we sense a growing desire to chromaticise the trumpet, throughout its range, and it is from Haydn's pen that we have the famous solo concerto in E♭ clearly intended to demonstrate the possibilities of just such an instrument (p. 118).

With the first quarter of the 19th century we enter what we have already called the Age of Mechanisation, and again we observe the slow acceptance of innovations, however advantageous. For instance, although the Paris Conservatoire had been in existence since 1795, a class for valve horn was not instituted there till 1833, and was dropped again between 1863 and 1896.[8] Long after valves had rendered an armoury of crooks virtually redundant, composers continued to specify them in many different keys, and it was not till near the end of the century that they began to heed the advice of practical players and to write parts in one or two convenient tonalities, regarding the horn as a chromatic instrument. Very similar conditions affected the valve trumpet and specimens with a full complement of crooks are known to have been made as late as *c.* 1870. Players, however, preferred to use one basic instrument and to transpose at sight, and the favoured one proved to be that in F. This remained the standard for orchestral use until about 1910, when a persistent tendency among modern composers to place the trumpet in a high *tessitura* brought the present B♭ or C instrument into favour, albeit with some change in characteristic tone.

The major composers of the 19th century, from Beethoven to Wagner, still form the staple of our average orchestral concerts; their scores are readily available for study, so quite a short reference to their use of the trumpet will serve here. Beethoven and his contemporaries wrote for the natural trumpet, choosing their keys much in the late 18th-century manner and with little technical advance beyond occasionally making it the top voice to a brass group founded on the trombones. They mostly ignored the keyed trumpet, though this enjoyed some vogue in Italian orchestras at the time, and they avoided other than open notes almost entirely. The flat seventh was used fairly freely. Occasionally after about 1830 notes outside the harmonic series were called for, as in Rossini's *Semiramide* Overture, and in some of Mendelssohn's scores, but, as by this time it had become the custom particularly to nominate valve trumpets when they were desired, it seems that some sort of 'faking' was expected. The slide trumpet, which could have taken these notes in its stride, was hardly known outside Britain, and paradoxically, this very ability delayed the full acceptance of valves in England for some time. The usual crooks for the natural trumpet at this period were those in E, F, G, and low A, and supplementary half tone shanks afforded the additional keys of low B♭, D♭, and G♭. Berlioz mentions also a trumpet in high A♭. According to Lavoix[9] valve trumpets made their first appearance in Paris in 1827 in Chelard's *Macbeth*, and from 1831 on such opera composers as Bellini, Meyerbeer, Donizetti, and Halévy began deliberately to write for them in their scores, and treat them as unhampered melodic voices. Berlioz, finding the *cornet-à-piston* complete while natural trumpets were still in the majority in most orchestras, conceived the ingenious idea of using the former to fill in missing notes in trumpet themes. This could not have been altogether satisfactory tonally, we may guess, but perhaps the brilliance of trumpets may have masked the smoothness of cornet tone and given an impression of homogeneity to the mixture.[10] Rather later other French composers exploited the contrast between trumpet and cornet by writing quite independent parts for each. By the mid-century Meyerbeer, a pioneer of lavish though by no means turgid scoring, was employing his brass as a complete chorus in itself and entrusting it alone with essential thematic material; and in this chorus chromatic trumpets formed the top voices. There was but one step farther to go and this was taken by Wagner when he insisted that within the brass section as a whole each tone colour should be available at every pitch. Hence his demand for a true bass trumpet and the revived contrabass trombone.

The story of the trombone as an element in the orchestra is less complicated than that of the trumpet for at least two reasons. In the first place, although it was initially derived from the folded trumpet (p. 132) it somehow escaped annexation by the Fraternity of Trumpeters and Drummers when they began to dominate military music in Europe[11] and had already appropriated the *Clarion* or *Felt Trummet* to themselves exclusively. (See also pp. 225–6.) It was thus freely available to the ordinary people and took part in all sorts of social music-making, from the rich wedding festivity to the popular dance.*

Secondly, the trombone never presented the problems that are inseparable from a 'natural' instrument with an incomplete scale derived from a single harmonic series. It seems curious to us today that its inherent chromatic nature was hardly recognised before the 18th century, and the reason for this must, I think, be sought in a general study of musical thought before that time, which, however, we cannot undertake in the present volume.

The few examples of mid-16th-century social music that have come down to us in actual notation, though usually bearing no more than an indication of suitable instruments, suggest that the trombone of the period was expected to possess considerable flexibility of articulation. Rapid changes of 'position', however, belong to a much later period. In spite of its early secular associations the sackbut was readily adopted by Church composers, on account, we may imagine, of its ability to blend with and support voices, and its warm, rather sombre tone. It would, nevertheless, be a mistake to suppose that 16th-century Church music was itself always sombre. We have many examples to prove the contrary, and it is from this source that we learn most about trombone

* See Appendix 3, p. 256.

writing in these early years. Giovanni Gabrielli, the famous organist at St. Mark's, Venice, could command up to six trombones, according to printed part books published in 1597 and in 1616 (shortly after his death).[12] Antiphonal writing for divided choirs was a feature of vocal music at this time, and Gabrielli experimented with a similar treatment of his instrumental resources, though without any marked attention to tonal contrast. Thus, for example, in the *Sacrae Symphoniae* we find a group consisting of tenor and bass voices, 1st cornett, 1st viola, and tenor trombone opposed by alto voices with 2nd cornett, 2nd viola, two tenor trombones and one bass. Through Gabrielli's pupil, Heinrich Schütz, a similar use of trombones and style of writing reached Germany and was finally reflected in the work of Buxtehude and his contemporaries. Looking at Gabrielli's compositions we see that the highest wind part was regularly allotted to the cornett and not to the soprano of the sackbut family, which in fact did not appear until quite near the end of the 17th century. This situation is not altogether easy to explain, for 16th-century instrument-makers were certainly capable of making a treble sackbut if called upon, and cornett tone was not particularly well matched with that of the trombones. Possibly the existence of the high draw-trumpet, though not itself a very efficient instrument as its meagre history reflects, was yet sufficient to prevent the call being made for nearly another hundred years. On the score of efficiency, too, we must remember that the latent capabilities of the trombone were not fully realised till a much later period. At the time when the Church began to admit the sackbut to its service the association of the latter with cornetts had been established for some time in 'Town Bands', in which, of course, the use of the military trumpet was opposed, if no more, by the powerful Trumpeter Fraternities. Of the soprano instruments available in the circumstances the cornett would seem to be the obvious choice, since it was a 'lip-reed', its tone was penetrating in the *forte*, and its complete scale would have rendered it a useful melodist.[13] Possibly all that the Church composers did was to take over an already recognised partnership and discipline it to their own needs.

In 17th-century opera and oratorio the trombones make rather rare appearances, as do the cornetts, and again Monteverdi and Cesti are the most original users. The former had a relatively huge orchestra for the first performance of *Orfeo* at Mantua in 1607, and among them we find four trombones and two cornetts; but this was a special occasion with special recruitment and is hardly typical of the age. As we have seen in connection with the trumpet, Monteverdi was in advance of most of his contemporaries, and we learn from Praetorius that the common practice of the time was to allot parts with regard to compass rather than to tone colour or technique. Between Monteverdi and Bach the employment of trombones changed little and Mattheson's statement of 1713 that they were then seldom used except in Church and for solemn occasions can be taken to represent a much wider generalisation. With Bach, though he did not employ trombones a great deal,[14] we do find a minor change. In three cantatas he specifies a *discant* trombone, as the top voice in a choir of three or four, though in general he prefers the cornett for this office. Bach's trombone writing is one of the characteristics that most clearly place him among the conservatives of the 18th century; with three exceptions, in Cantatas 25, 118, and 135, his trombones never do more than reinforce the voice parts. With Handel the use of the trombone is rather more 'orchestral' though still infrequent. He may, we suspect, have had some difficulty from time to time in finding competent players, and certainly after his day the instrument was for some long while to be found only in private bands under Royal or noble patronage (see p. 138). It seems very significant that in 1749 Handel revived his Oratorio *Samson*, first produced in 1741, and for the revival replaced the original 'Dead March' with that from *Saul* (1738), transposed up a tone and re-scored *without trombones*. It is also known that complete trombone parts were omitted from some of the earlier printed editions of *Saul* and *Israel in Egypt* (1738) and their appearance in the authoritative *Handel-Gesellschaft* publication is due to the devoted researches of the editor Chrysander. The trombone parts in *Israel* were in fact not found in the autograph full score at all, but in the 'conductor's copy'. The placing of trombone parts in an appendix to the full score, and regarding them as more or less 'ad lib', was apparently not uncommon in the 18th and early 19th centuries, but, as Chrysander pointed out, those provided by Handel for some of his choruses are musically so fundamental as to obviate the need for any other accompaniment.[15] Parallel cases are to be found in the first editions of *The Seasons* and of *Don Giovanni*, though here we can hardly imagine the 'statue' music without its trombones. In general Handel wrote for the group of alto, tenor, and bass trombones, but he seems to have had no special rule about combining them with trumpets, which he employed very freely. The once favoured idea that the *obbligato* to 'The Trumpet Shall Sound' was originally intended for a *soprano trombone* is certainly fallacious.

With the advent of the 18th-century 'transition' composers, and again taking Gluck as representative, we notice a considerable change in the manner of using trombones. They are still only employed occasionally, but the treatment is mainly harmonic with the parts placed close together, and generally higher set than is common today. The bass trombone, too, is no longer rigidly confined to the lowest note of the chord but crosses the other lines freely as required. Trombones in unison also form a feature of some of Gluck's scores, and this we may take as evidence of a new and quieter style of playing, for otherwise these passages would be quite overwhelming.

In the Haydn–Mozart and early Beethoven period we still see comparatively little change in the fortunes of the trombone, except for a more imaginative employment of the accepted formulae. The instrument appears with some frequency in the scores of operas, oratorios, and Masses—those forms of composition whose principal patrons were the Church, and the State or privately subsidised theatres—but from the concert orchestra it remained virtually excluded. Even as late as 1824–25, when Beethoven personally revised an autograph score of the Choral Symphony for the Philharmonic Society of London, he relegated the trombone parts to an appendix in the old manner, so powerful was the influence of custom. Yet Beethoven, years before this, had written trombone parts that were structurally essential in a number of his works. As examples of the capacity of the older trombone in the hands of genius we need only think of the *Funeral Equale*, or the *Miserere* and *Amplius* for four male voices and four trombones published posthumously in 1827;[16] but in spite of examples from a few outstanding composers, we must recognise, I think, that in civilian music from the mid-18th to the first quarter of the 19th centuries, the instrument passed through a phase of stagnation. Only in the mature works of Schubert and Weber do we find much progress; their employment of the mysterious harmonies of brass played *pianissimo* was something new, as was their use of trombones to emphasise detached chords and build climaxes.

About 1820, however, the doldrum period was to some extent offset by the activities of the Military Band reformers already referred to on p. 139. The sackbut had, of course, had a place in outdoor music from the first, and now its function there was to be reviewed. When more or less satisfactory valved instruments began to take over the foundation parts in military music, the trombone (especially the Bass) could give up the largely supporting rôle which had so far been its main occupation, and reveal itself as a melodic voice with power enough for open-air use and a hitherto unsuspected brilliance. This discovery of what was almost a second personality in the trombone soon had repercussions in civil music. Before the mid-century, composers to whom the Weberesque soft harmonies and detached chords had become common currency, welcomed the new brilliance. In the opera house lighter pieces by such as Auber or Lortzing were in public favour, though it must be said that the more serious works of Halévy, Meyerbeer, or Berlioz were equally theatrical and highly coloured. Such were the men who stimulated the new style of trombone playing, though Berlioz, in particular, never neglected the old when it suited what he had to express (see p. 71). It was at this time that French composers, in the search for even greater brilliance, adopted the group of three *tenor* trombones which has remained the standard in that country till quite recently. Only the Germans of this period adhered to a more sober style which, in the next generation, was reflected in the rather heavy trombone writing of Brahms and his followers (see also p. 56). From about 1850 almost all opera scores contained trombone parts as a matter of course, and at long last the instrument found its regular place in the concert orchestra. Curiously enough the lowest part in the brass group there did not go at once to the valved tuba; the keyed ophicleide,[17] in spite of its limitations, held that position quite tenaciously till about 1862.[18] With the trombones fully accepted and the tuba in support the three sections of the orchestra, strings, woodwind, and brass, were each complete in themselves and the modern organisation had come into being. Extensions to each group have been made since, it is true, and over all numbers of players have increased, but the extra instruments have not in any way altered the fundamental structure of the orchestra as consolidated during the third quarter of the 19th century.

It remains only to consider for a moment the valve trombone. The genesis, advantages, and disadvantages of this instrument have already been discussed at some length in the course of Chapters 3 and 8; but how did composers react to it? In certain Continental opera houses it certainly made a considerable impact on account of the surprising agility it showed in comparison with the slide technique of the period. Rossini is perhaps the most important of the composers who were for a time beguiled by this feature, and we can think of passages in the later operas, for example, which probably terrified contemporary slide trombonists. Very soon, however, the novelty wore off—Berlioz wrote in 1848 of the tonal poverty and defective intonation of the valve instrument, and by 1855 German players had in general reverted to the classic trombone, probably with a more developed slide technique in compensation. It is only fair to point out here that the valve trombones now to be found in the Brussels Opéra particularly are built on the 'independent' system (p. 173) and so do not merit Berlioz' strictures.

NOTES

[1] Adam Carse, *The History of Orchestration*, London, Kegan Paul, 1925. Introduction, p. 1.

[2] The operative factors here were undoubtedly the difficulty and hence expense of the processes. The actual printing of music from movable type followed very soon after the discovery of letterpress typography, and some of the earliest examples are attributed with some certainty to Wynkyn de Worde. Music engraving on copper plates seems to have been in very general use by about 1680, and the process of stamping on pewter plates by about 1710, but the cost of such printing on the scale required by a score and set of parts for even a small symphony must have been prohibitive unless the market was assured. See the introduction to Kidson's *British Music Publishers*, London, W. E. Hill and Sons, 1900. Before the 19th century the circulation of large orchestral works depended almost entirely on the transport of sets of manuscript parts, and there is evidence that composers would sometimes even add a specially effective part for the benefit of a known brilliant performer in one centre or another.

[3] Bach also served in noble households, first with the Duke of Weimar (1708–17) and then with Prince Leopold of Anhalt-Cöthen (1717–23). The first of these appointments did not, however, require him to compose until he was promoted *Concertmeister* in 1714, and in the latter his opportunities were much limited by the Calvinistic forms of the Princely chapel.

[4] The appointment of the violin virtuoso Baltasar as leader of Charles II's 'four and twenty fiddlers' must have done much to spread knowledge of Continental string techniques in England at this period, and Purcell freely admitted the benefit he gained by the study of models from abroad. There was also a direct link between Purcell and Lulli in the person of young Pelham Humphrey who, however insufferable he may have been on his return from France (see *Diary of Samuel Pepys*, Vol. II, November 15, 1667), had at least fully absorbed the musical style of his teachers there.

[5] The best known today and their spheres of influence are:

Piccini—Italy, St. Petersburg, London.
Sacchini—Italy, Paris, London, Germany.
Paisiello—Italy, St. Petersburg, Paris.
Cimarosa—Italy, St. Petersburg, Vienna.
Salieri—Italy, Vienna, Paris.
Cannabich—Mannheim, Munich.
Dittersdorf—Vienna and Southern Germany.
Stamitz (the younger)—Mannheim, Paris, London, St. Petersburg.
Gossec—Paris.
Grétry—Paris.

[6] See 'Handel and the Clarinet', R. B. Chatwin, *Galpin Society Journal*, Vol. III, London, March 1950, pp. 3 *et seq.*

[7] There is much ambiguity of nomenclature in the early orchestral use of horns, but the matter seems to resolve into a distinction between the 'jagdhorn',

a true hunting horn played occasionally as a second instrument by trumpeters, and the enlarged and improved 'waldhorn', played with a deep conical mouthpiece, and by specialists. This latter was the parent of the modern orchestral horn.

⁸ The fifty years 1795–1845 saw a growing appreciation of the need for high-grade musical education for composers and orchestral players and the establishment of recognised standards. During this period the great music schools of Paris, Milan, Naples, Prague, Vienna, London, Brussels, and Leipzig all came into being.

⁹ H. Lavoix, fils, *Histoire de l'Instrumentation*, Paris, Firmin-Didot, 1878.

¹⁰ Hector Berlioz (1803–69), regarded by many as the greatest *orchestrator* of the 19th century, devised a great many original and splendid instrumental effects. It seems a pity that the bulk of his music, though much admired in some quarters, has never achieved a universal appeal.

¹¹ The reason may perhaps have been that these organised bodies of highly trained specialists contemned any supposed mechanical aids as beneath their dignity. We note that they do not seem to have interfered with the early draw-trumpet either, and its French name, *Trompette de Ménestrel*, certainly suggests a lower social status than that of the Military Trumpet.

¹² According to the English traveller Thomas Coryat, even larger resources were to be found at St. Mark's in 1608. *Coryat's Crudities*, London, 'W.S.' 1611, pp. 249–52.

¹³ In his *Harmonie Universelle* Mersenne likened the cornett to 'a ray of sunshine piercing the gloom and darkness, when heard among the voices in some cathedral or chapel'. During Bach's lifetime Roger North, in his family *Memoirs*, noted, 'Nothing comes so near or rather imitates so much an excellent voice as a cornett pipe' but adds, 'The labour of the lips is too great and it is seldom well sounded'. On the other hand it is recorded that Benvenuto Cellini's father once begged his son not to abandon 'il tuo lascivissimo cornetto'.

¹⁴ This may have been due to the non-availability of players rather than any reluctance to use the instrument. Even in the relatively music-conscious Leipzig, Bach's predecessor, Kuhnau, reported in 1704 that the trombones belonging to St. Thomas's were battered and useless from old age. (Charles Sanford Terry, *Bach's Orchestra*, London, Oxford University Press, 1932, p. 18.) In contrast, we may note that during the first half of the 18th century *obbligati* for solo trombone formed a prominent feature in the Masses and Church Motets of the Vienna Court composers—evidently a local manifestation which had little influence beyond.

¹⁵ W. F. H. Blandford, 'Handel's Horn and Trombone Parts', *The Musical Times*, London, December 1939, p. 794.

¹⁶ Possibly composed as early as 1812. See Nottebohm's *Thematic Catalogue*.

¹⁷ In some makers' catalogues the term 'Ophicleide' was applied to *valved* basses for a considerable time.

¹⁸ According to Carse, Wallace's *Love's Triumph* contains possibly the first part specifically for *tuba* in place of the customary ophicleide as the foundation of the brass (1862).

CHAPTER 12

The Social and Professional Background

IN READING any account of European music from the Renaissance onwards we cannot fail to encounter references to the various types of professional body into which musicians have formed themselves at different periods. Some knowledge of these is essential to the music historian, for at times they undoubtedly influenced the scope of composers and so the growth of music itself. We can, however, quite easily form a false impression of early professional influence unless we understand something of the circumstances and limitations under which these musicians worked; and of all their instruments the trumpet has been the most subjected to rules and regulations.

In the earliest records of trumpets in Europe we find them consistently the apanages of ceremony, pomp, and pride, and their patrons are kings and nobles. We are told, for instance, that William Rufus at the siege of Rochester in 1087 would not suffer the besieged to quit the City unless to the sound of his triumphal trumpets; and in Queen Elizabeth I's time a ceremonial dinner was ushered in by twelve trumpets with kettledrums. Yet pride was not exclusive to Princes, and quite early on municipal bodies also found trumpets fitted to their dignity. In 1426 the Emperor Sigismund granted the town of Augsburg the privilege of employing municipal trumpeters in exchange for a substantial contribution to his depleted exchequer. This move was much resented by the nobility, and laid the good Augsburgers open to their scorn and lampooning as self-satisfied upstarts. The exclusively noble status of the trumpet had, nevertheless, been breached and in the course of the century several other towns either solicited or took the same rights. The 13th-century charter mentioned on p. 101 does not indicate specifically whether the 'tuba or claro' referred to would be sounded by a municipal servant or perhaps a herald attached to a local nobleman, but it does show that the trumpet was the recognised *signal* instrument of the time. We have, in fact, no evidence of truly *musical* activities among military trumpeters before about the middle of the 16th century. From some time earlier, however, there are abundant records of groups of 'minstrels' (largely wind players) attached to princely households and the more prosperous municipalities, and it is amongst the latter that we see the first evidences of voluntary organisation for the protection of professional interests.[1]

The decline and final disappearance of the troubadours during the 14th century altered greatly the position of the once dependent *jongleur*. No longer a retainer to someone of social position, he became a self-employed man making a living wherever he could find it, and in these circumstances there grew up a large body of itinerant entertainers of all kinds. No doubt some of the ablest musicians of the time were to be found among this heterogeneous crowd, but the majority of them were mountebanks, jugglers, story-tellers, sometimes even college men to whom a wayfaring life appealed more than the cloister; and an unruly lot they seem to have been. With the idea of exercising some control various Governors, as far as their jurisdiction extended, issued edicts of which a typical example is that promulgated at Mainz in 1355 by the Emperor Charles IV. Originally designed for the better ruling of the musicians of the Rhenish Provinces, this order was extended in 1385 by the Bishop of Mainz to include the 'wandering people'. In England the troubadour system never seems to have flourished, but the minstrels appear to have been just as tiresome as elsewhere. In the fourth year of the reign of King Richard II, John of Gaunt, Duke of Lancaster, following French and German examples, created by charter a 'Minstrel King' who had subordinate officers and powers to enforce the regulations which had become necessary due to the increasing number of minstrels on the roads of England.[2] In a very short time this duty had extended to the holding of actual Courts sitting in judgement on the continual disagreements and misdemeanours of these troublesome nomads. Quarrelsome and aggressive as the travelling minstrels were among themselves, they yet found a ready welcome in the homes of the people, for, besides entertaining, they conveyed news, and were indeed almost the only means of long-distance communication among a largely illiterate populace. Some, no doubt, also acted as political spies and traded on their popularity to gain information. With one class, however, wandering minstrels were not popular, and these were the town-dwelling musicians who felt, with some justice, that they had a right to the monopoly of musical employment in their own areas. The fairs and kermesses which contributed to the prosperity of the towns attracted vagrants in great numbers, and their musical activities were much resented by the local players. The picture is not unfamiliar in spheres other than that of music, and at other times, and it was this situation that engendered the first professional associations among musicians. Needless to say neither the military trumpeters nor their municipal counterparts would have anything to do with the wandering players.

The fraternities of military trumpeters and associated drummers were not as ancient as is often supposed. Trumpeters occupied a recognised position in the feudal military system that obtained throughout most of Europe from the Middle Ages onwards. They belonged to the lower order of retainers and waited on their masters in the field and sometimes at table, but they were themselves of officer status, were mounted, and were provided with personal servants or grooms, much as were Dumas' musketeers. Thus they were regarded as of 'knightly kind', and their calling not as a trade but a free and knightly art. It was, however, in these surroundings that the first distinctions appeared between mere field signallers and more accomplished men—'taught trumpeters'—who later on underwent a regular apprenticeship of some years, and among whom the art of 'clarin' playing had its roots. By the early 17th century the separation was complete, and it was only then that the first rather limited Union of trumpeters came into being by virtue of a *privilegium* granted by Frederick II in 1623. This patent was confirmed by several later Emperors up to the time of Joseph II. The organisation was styled a *Kameradschaft* and, to quote Gerald Abraham's translation, was 'an association of public character, with the rights of a corporation, for the exercise of a profession both military and serving the purposes of art, possessed of a privilege for the whole German *Reich* excluding others from this profession.'[3] This mention of the German Reich reminds us of a point that we must keep in mind, viz. that after the Reformation and the Thirty Years War there was little coherence among the various German-speaking States, and no finally united Germany till the time of Bismarck. Rights and privileges granted by the Holy Roman Emperor or his representatives would therefore only be recognised in those States which continued to acknowledge his nominal supremacy. Any 'rights' claimed by military trumpeters before 1623 can only have been based on custom and usage, and their 'legality' was rooted no deeper than in purely local titles. As Arch-Marshal of the Reich, the superintendence and patronage of the Trumpeter Fraternity devolved on the Elector of Saxony, but this duty appears to have had no basis in any specific grant, and its later continuance depended purely on precedent.

Q

In Saxony itself trumpeters, as we might expect, enjoyed very particular favours, and from time to time the scope of their patent was
extended as developments in instrument-making appeared to threaten
their monopoly. Thus we find musicians outside the *Kameradschaft*
prohibited from playing waldhorns or 'trombones of trumpet type' and,
later on, the *Inventionstrompete* or *trompette demilune* also (p. 109). The
latter instrument, which came into rather limited use after 1760, might,
we suppose, have been seen as a threat to the natural trumpet specialist
on account of the hand-stopping technique it permitted, though this
could have had no bearing on the 'mystery' of clarino playing. It is
more probable, I think, that the established trumpeters wished to keep
in their own hands any possible future development of their instrument
at a period when its purely musical capabilities were increasingly
realised. Again, 'trombones of trumpet type' is a curious description and
difficult to interpret, though it might perhaps be applied to the single-
slide draw-trumpet. If so, we can easily understand the growing concern
of the Fraternity at that time with an instrument which they had
formerly ignored although it had been in existence since long before
their first *privilegium* (see p. 114; note 11, p. 126). To be just, however, we
should add that the relatively scanty evidence we have even today
suggests that the draw-trumpet may not at any time have been universally familiar. We must bear in mind the geographical and communication problems outlined at the beginning of Chapter 11 if we seek a
connection between Flanders and Upper Austria, *c.* 1480, Cassel in
1573, Hesse in 1601, and Saxony in 1651.

The enforcement of exclusive privileges, and particularly their
successive encroachments on the field of entertainment music, naturally aroused resentment among civilian players and we hear a good deal
of devices intended to evade the prohibitions. Some of these were no
more than legal fictions such as that quoted by von Gontershausen,
who stated that peasants in Thuringia at one time inserted several
twists in the trumpet tube and claimed that they thus created a different
instrument.[4] Actual brawls between military and civil trumpeters were
not unknown, but the former always had the advantage, and the
brutalities they sometimes committed were condoned as legitimate
defence of their unquestionable rights. By the end of the 17th century
the Fraternity organisation in Germany had reached the fullest development, and had extended its control not only to conditions of performance but to instruction also. Only 'learned trumpeters' who had first
served in the field were permitted to take pupils and train them in the

mysteries of their art, double and triple tonguing, the 'florrey' etc.,[5] and it was with them that the special study of the different registers, *Clarino I*, *Clarino II*, and *Prinzipal*, began. It seems likely that, following the Elector of Saxony, all the Princes of the Reich made sure that the trumpeters attached to their personal regiments were drawn from the ranks of these more notable players.

The reader may perhaps feel at this point that we have been over-concentrating on Germany, but it is from that part of Europe that we have the most complete picture. England, to some extent isolated from the main stream, nevertheless produced notable trumpet players over the period reviewed though she never had such a rigid organisation as the *Kameradschaft* to draw upon. Instead, the records indicate that the duties of control and instruction were mainly vested in the trumpeters attached to the Royal person in pensionable appointments. Even Royal trumpeters, however, had no rights over ordinary musicians except by virtue of common law, as witness the Lord Chamberlain's accounts for December 4, 1668: 'Warrant to the sergeant trumpeter to take his free course at law against certain persons who do . . . refuse to satisfy his Majesty's sergeant trumpeter those fees which are due to him according to his patent . . . and also divers trumpetters and drummes and fifes do sound . . . without lycence of the said sergeant first obtained.'[6] From Italy we have considerable evidence of the use of advanced trumpet techniques in the 16th and 17th centuries (even dismissing Fantini's extravagant remarks) but the musicians concerned appear to have been mainly in private service. France alone provides a curious contrast with the other great European countries, for although the highly organised establishment of the 'Grande Ecurie' had its corps of trumpets certainly as early as 1642, the most advanced techniques, especially clarino playing, seem to have been unknown there. To explain this it has been pointed out that the F trumpet favoured in France was much less amenable to such use than the longer C or D instrument. This is, of course, no more than speculation, but it does suggest that perhaps the initial choice of tonal brilliance may have deprived France of the ultimate brilliance of technique.

We turn now to the non-military side. At the close of the Middle Ages great changes occurred in European life. Developing trade gave rise to closer communities, and the number of towns increased in consequence. The feudal system, which formerly spread over an entire country with the King as its head, broke down into smaller units headed by lesser leaders, lords and barons, many of whom were not content to live off their own lands and who turned to plunder on the slightest pretext. In these circumstances towns of any pretension found it necessary to employ watchmen to keep a look-out from special watch rooms placed in the tower of the municipal building or perhaps some suitably situated church. These Tower-men or *Thurmer* were supplied with trumpets with which to sound the alarm and mark the passing hours—the latter probably as a periodic proof of vigilance. It is again from Germany that we have the fullest information.

The particular instrument regarded as proper to *Thurmer* at the beginning of the 16th century is illustrated by Virdung, and in his woodcut it is specifically labelled *Thurmerhorn*, though it is quite clearly the old S-folded trumpet without stays, and no *horn* at all (see p. 105).

It is a curious fact that there is written evidence of the official employment of musicians by German towns considerably earlier than at the minor princely courts.[7] These men, the *Stadtpfeifer*, were salaried employees whose duties consisted in attendance at all civic festivities, solemn processions, etc., and sometimes in assisting at church services. They could also accept private engagements at weddings and so on, when not on official duty, and it was because of the threat directed at this perquisite in particular that the wandering players were so bitterly resented. The constitution of these Town Bands is typical of Renaissance musical thought, and in them we find the sackbut of major importance. This esteem for sackbuts was not, however, peculiar to Germany although her instrument makers led Europe in their manufacture, for we know that in 1569 François Robillard made a contract with a company of hatters in Paris to provide ten musicians for their celebrations on the feast of St. Michael. These men were to play cornetts and violins if it did not rain, and flutes and trombones if it did.[8] The present-day military bandsman has no such choice of instrument conditioned by the weather forecast. In 1483 the City of Bruges numbered four trumpets among her musicians, and in 1502 the town band of Louvain consisted of trumpet, flute, viol, and harp. At the height of Venetian power the music at the annual 'wedding' of the Doge to the Adriatic was often entrusted to a large choir of trombones alone.

Returning again to the German Stadtpfeifer, it is pretty certain that at first they were quite separate from the Tower Men, although their prescribed duties in certain towns required them also to play from the church towers. According to a document quoted by Fritz Jahn[9] the custom of tower music, as distinct from sounding the alarm, was known at Bautzen in 1584. In Leipzig a twice-daily performance from the balcony of the Town Hall tower was instituted in 1599, and at festival seasons the cornetts and trombones were required to play chorales from the church towers too.[10] No doubt customs varied at different centres according to financial resources, and to the opinions of the local councils. At Lübeck as early as 1474 a tower watchman was expected, in addition to other duties, 'to blow and play the whole year on the Claritte as the custom hath been'. This is particularly interesting as it seems to imply a recognised distinction between mere blowing and artistic playing, and there appears to have been nothing to prevent tower watchmen from relieving their monotony with unofficial music-making from time to time.

The town music of Leipzig was probably little different from that of most well-to-do Continental towns, but it so happens that with the Bach connection the archives have been more fully investigated than most and from them we can build up a fairly typical picture. The Stadtpfeifer office in that town was instituted as early as 1479 with Master Hans Nagel and his two 'sons' (? apprentices) whose instruments were the trumpet, cornett, and trombone.[11] During the 16th century, however, drummers and fifers who had formerly acted only as town criers etc., began to rival the Stadtpfeifer, and in 1550 a civic ordinance permitted 'a drummer and his fifer' to play at weddings. Open conflict between the two bodies was averted by an agreement concluded in 1581. The Stadtpfeifer were, however, evidently the superior musicians, and when public taste veered towards the new *Hausmusik* it was the drummers and fifers who succumbed. In 1595 the council licensed two fiddlers to play at weddings, and by 1607 there were three definitely recognised as *Stadtgeiger* with the privilege of participating in the official church music, though only in an inferior capacity. Thereafter the two classes of civic musicians were accepted though the Stadtpfeifer retained the socially superior engagements. In 1626 the fiddlers gained a new official title as *Kunstgeiger*—presumably to distinguish them from the less refined players of the itinerant class—but even so we often read outspoken criticisms of their ability.

When Bach came to Leipzig in 1723 the two civic bodies supplied the professional backbone of his church orchestras, though their combined strength was insufficient to meet even his modest demands and he had to draw on amateurs and students as well. Bach's brilliant clarinist Gottfried Reiche was a Stadtpfeifer who also played the Zug-trompete and Waldhorn as required. In the first years of the 18th century the requirements of Church music changed so much that the old division of wind instruments for Stadtpfeifer and strings for Kunstgeiger was no longer practical and both bodies had to extend their scope. Thus, during quite half of his service in Leipzig, Bach had a Stadtpfeifer as his leading violinist. Although the numbers of 18th-century civic musicians were small according to modern ideas, these men were expected to be both competent and versatile. Because of the better social position, emoluments, and perquisites, transfer from the Kunstgeiger to the Stadtpfeifer was eagerly sought, and the promotion was supposed to be dependent on a practical examination.[12] In fact this requirement was often relaxed. In 1745 Bach gave one C. F. Pfaffe a testimonial of competence on the standard instruments expected, namely 'violin, oboe, transverse flute, trumpet, horn, and other wind instruments', although at the same time another candidate was excused examination on the grounds that he had already proved himself while a Kunstgeiger. Five years later another applicant failed his test on trumpet, wald-horn, and oboe, the three *principal* instruments, without which, said his examiners, no one could qualify as a Stadtpfeifer however many others he professed. It seems probable that the need to study so many different instruments may have given birth to a 'Jack-of-all-trades' type of performer, and that a really high general standard was attained by few. We notice the absence of any specific reference to the trombone in the above two entries, but it is recorded that in 1769 J. F. Doles, Bach's second successor in the Leipzig Cantorate, required candidates to play simple chorales on all four trombones and either a horn or a flute and oboe concerto. The difference in the two styles of music clearly reflects the place of the trombone in the German scheme of things at that time; an instrument characterised by solemn dignity.

We have already remarked that in the course of the 1700s the trom-bone, in other than German-speaking countries, suffered a gradual decline in general popularity until it was resuscitated by the military band performers in the very last years of the century (p. 138). There is little to add to that in this chapter, except to say that during the period of its eclipse the preservation of the trombone lay almost entirely in the hands of Court musicians, and when the revival did come the social status of military music itself had undergone some change. In the precarious 'peace of exhaustion' that followed on the Thirty Years War a number of European sovereigns found it expedient to maintain considerable standing armies, instead of disbanding the greater part of their troops as formerly after a campaign. In consequence a new concept of full-time professional soldiering grew up during the later 17th and early 18th centuries. Under the new system the need to discipline and drill much larger groups of men, and, above all, the different sorts of *marches* which then became an essential part of field exercises, increased greatly the importance of pace markers—the drums attached to each troop, with perhaps a fife or two added. This type of organisation was known in England certainly as early as 1622,[13] though we must admit that it had little real musical significance, especially as the average fifer could command no more than eight or nine chromatic tones. It was, nevertheless, the beginning of a military music more closely integrated with the rank and file and not just the prerogative of high-born commanders, and within a decade or two of the peace in Europe, favoured regiments were already being granted a larger establishment. In 1684 Charles II, probably competing with Louis XIV of France, granted a warrant 'authorising the entertaining of twelve Hautbois in the Companies of the King's Regiment of Foot Guards in London, and that fictitious names should be borne, on the strength of each of the other Companies of the Regiment quartered in the country, with a view to granting the musicians higher pay.'[14] This 'fiddle' is perhaps the first indication we have of military musicians' pay becoming a charge on the State instead of a private expense.

Just a century after Charles II, in 1783, the establishments of the three regiments of Foot Guards had progressed to two oboes, two clarinets, two horns, and two bassoons, and this was the type of band that became the subject of reform during the next thirty years. In 1781, we are told, a celebrated Viennese military band had the same constitution with the addition of one *trumpet* and drums, but we note that neither in England nor Austria were trombones added, although they had always been well known in the Austrian town bands. The rapid growth of professionalism that we notice in 18th-century soldiering does not, of course, imply any decline in the pride of aristocratic commanders regarding their personal contingents, but now the officers of line regiments too were becoming concerned with prestige. This applied no less in their music than in other matters, and the formation of a good band could become a heavy expense. In France, for instance, even as late as 1820 the number of musicians per regiment allowed officially by the Minister of War was only eight, and the British War Office imposed similar limits on the number of private soldiers who might be trained in music. In the latter case, too, the cost of professional training, as well as the purchase of music and instruments, was left to the officers. When these were men of means the strength of the band was sometimes increased unofficially and the standard of playing attained was often a great credit to their taste and devotion, but it is no wonder that there was little uniformity among army bands in general. It was in such circumstances that the trombone found its new vocation (p. 140).

One final observation on what some historians have called the 'Trumpeter Band'. Near the beginning of this chapter we made an oblique reference to the mid-16th century as marking the earliest efforts we know to use the trumpet in a truly musical fashion. From this period quite a number of pieces survive, some without any indication of suitable instruments, but others either expressly or implicitly intended for trumpets, as proved by the scale used. Three or four independent trumpet parts were usual in these compositions, and sometimes the lowest part was given to tuned drums and so limited to the tonic and dominant of the key. In the absence of kettledrums a trumpet would take this part also which was then designated 'toccato' in reference to the style of attack called for. For such performances, then, a group of at least three musicians was required—perfectly feasible in the average princely household of the time. In the post-Thirty Years War period, however, things became rather different. The one or two trumpets attached to a cavalry squadron clearly could not tackle three or four independent parts, so when set pieces were requisitioned for special occasions it became the custom to assemble the trumpets of an entire regiment and constitute them a Trumpeter Band, the instruments being, of course, the ordinary duty trumpets. This remained the recognised cavalry music organisation long after foot regiments had been granted additional instruments. From time to time

Fig. 65   Melody divided between trumpets in
different pitches

attempts were made to increase the scope of Trumpeter Bands by combining instruments in different keys, as in the foregoing example (Fig. 65), but the crooks (or even duplicate trumpets) called for were hardly welcome in service conditions. Pitch standards were also variable, and made almost insurmountable difficulties when 'massed bands' were wanted. The traditional music of mounted regiments therefore remained much as it had been from the mid-17th century to well on in the 19th when Wieprecht began to introduce valved instruments in the Prussian cavalry (p. 141) and so paved the way for the modern military band, both mounted and infantry.

NOTES

[1] It is recorded that John of Gaunt had among his retainers two 'trumpours' and eight minstrels. At a New Year gathering at Kenilworth in 1380 there appeared, in addition to the household men, the herald and four minstrels of the Earl of Cambridge, the herald and eleven minstrels of the Earl of Nottingham, three minstrels attached to Sir Baldwin Freville, and one unattached minstrel. All these had money from their host, the heralds twenty shillings each, and the minstrels six and eight pence. Noble entertaining in those days must have been an expensive matter, and it is not to be wondered at that in a later century the Royal Progresses of Queen Elizabeth I nearly ruined some of her enforced though loyal hosts.
See *John of Gaunt's Register*, 1379-83, Vol. I., edited by E. C. Lodge and R. Somerville (Camden, 3rd ser. Vol. LXI), Royal Historical Society, 1937.
On the municipal side records prove the existence of similar though usually smaller musical establishments. The magistrates of Basle, for example, in the 14th century retained three salaried pipers who were required to play in one of the public squares at stated hours for the pleasure of the citizens, as well as to take part in Town functions.
See Kappey, *A Short History of Military Music*, London, Boosey and Co., undated. This work contains many picturesque and useful references, but is unfortunately very badly documented.
In 1469 Edward IV granted a charter empowering his 'beloved minstrels' to form themselves into a Guild, and we learn from records of the reign that their duties included praying 'particularly for the departed souls of the King and Queen when they shall die'. The minstrels were then beholden to the monastic schools for the practical knowledge of music which they later secularised.
[2] Ibid., p. 14.
[3] Quoted in W. Menke, *History of the Trumpet of Bach and Handel*, London, William Reeves, 1934 (English translation by Gerald Abraham), p. 27. For much detail see also Caldwell Titcomb, 'Baroque Court and Military Trumpets and Kettledrums', *Galpin Society Journal*, Vol. IX, 1956, pp. 56 *et seq.* Also D. L. Smithers, 'The Hapsburg Imperial *Trompeter* and *Heerpauker* Privileges', *G.S.J.*, XXIV, 1971, pp. 84 *et seq.*
[4] H. Welcker von Gontershausen, *Magazin Musikalischer Tonwerkzeuge*, p. 155. Frankfurt, 1855.
[5] The *florrey* or *flurry* was what we now call 'flutter-tonguing'. It was employed particularly at the end of the 'Tusch' or flourish, a sort of *ad lib* arpeggio on the chord of C played by all the brass together, with a long-held

note to close. The effect is both noble and exciting. The Tusch is still sometimes sounded in Continental opera houses, notably at Copenhagen, as a tribute from the orchestra to an outstanding artist at the close of his curtain calls.

[6] See H. C. de Lafontaine, *The King's Music*, London, Novello and Co. Ltd., 1909, p. 206. From these invaluable records we learn much of the organisation and customs of Royal music in England. Musicians in ordinary, it seems, held their offices for life, though they were permitted to surrender them voluntarily. They did not, however, have the right to bequeath their appointments by will as was at one time customary in France. In the late 17th century, the widow of a Royal musician dying in the service enjoyed for a fixed period a portion of the emoluments of her husband's successor. De Lafontaine's book contains an exhaustive list of all Royal musicians and their instruments from 1460 to 1699. For an account of the duties of Royal trumpeters in France from 1464 to 1594 see *Le Cérémonial de France*, by Théodore Godefroy, published in Paris in 1619.

[7] See note 2, above.

[8] F. Lesure, 'La facture instrumentale à Paris au seizième siècle', *Galpin Society Journal*, Vol. VII, London, 1954. The discrimination between instruments that would or would not suffer from getting wet is interesting. Presumably *straight* cornetts turned from the solid would have been as safe as the transverse flutes.

[9] Fritz Jahn, 'Die Nürnberger Trompeten und Posaunenmacher im 16 Jahrhundert', *Archiv für Musikwissenschaft*, Vol. VII, 1925.

[10] A. Schering, *Musikgeschichte Leipzigs—von 1650 bis 1723*, Leipzig, 1926, pp. 271, 278, and 285.

[11] R. Wustmann, *Musikgeschichte Leipzigs—bis zur Mitte des 17 Jahrhunderts*, Leipzig and Berlin, 1909, pp. 31–33.

[12] The musical customs of Leipzig in the early 18th century are most lucidly discussed by Sanford Terry in Chapter I of his *Bach's Orchestra*, London, O.U.P., 1932.

[13] '*The Military Art of Trayning* with a description of all Martiall Officers, their places, Duties and Hon-ble: ceremonie from a General to an Inferior Souldier etc', London, 1622.

Under the heading 'Drums and Phife' we read, 'There is commonly two Drums to every Company, and one Phife to excite cheerfulness and alacrity in the Souldier.'

[14] Hamilton, General Sir F. W., *Origin and History of the First Grenadier Guards*, London, John Murray, 1874.

CHAPTER 13

Trumpet and Trombone in the Jazz Idiom

BEFORE WE TOUCH on this subject we require to ask a question. What do we personally understand by 'Jazz'? We may say at once that the music served up today by the average dance band, whatever the layman may call it, is by no means jazz as the committed student understands it. Yet a negative statement like this is of very little help, and for thirty years jazz enthusiasts and music historians alike have sought without success for a concise and positive definition. Volumes have been written on this form of music, and on the different manifestations which the student recognises at once as belonging to jazz; and still the comprehensive description remains elusive. Some 'straight' musicians have suggested, for instance, that the definitive characteristic of jazz lies in the shifting of the normal accents of a basically simple beat pattern. Others point to the distortion of the intervals of an accepted scale. Still others hold that the most important feature of jazz playing is the element of collective improvisation which is denied to the symphonic player. This may be nearer the mark, though all these views tend to oversimplify the matter since none of the above factors is invariably and necessarily present in any one jazz performance. Moreover, syncopation has been known in conventional music for hundreds of years, and string players have been adjusting intervals according to mood or tonality for as long. Again, although many (probably the majority) of the early jazz instrumentalists were musically unlettered, the arrangements that emerged from long ensemble rehearsals tended very soon to be remembered *in toto*, and these so-called 'head arrangements' could become quite as binding as the later written ones. The opportunity for improvisation was then limited to the solo player who came in at a predetermined point for a predetermined number of bars. There may be some analogy here with the *cadenza* in classical concerto form, but of course in jazz the soloist is also a member of the ensemble, and during his improvisation the basic rhythm continues to be marked by other members of the band. The sole exception to this is found in the 'break'[1] where the basic rhythm is indeed momentarily suspended, but here

235

the exploitation of thematic material is primitive in comparison with the conventional cadenza. There is nothing that the average jazz man does today which is technically beyond the capacity of the symphony player if he so desires—allowing for the fact that there have always been exceptional men in both categories. The difference appears to be one of mental approach to ensemble playing. Even when working to a detailed written score the true jazz man presents something of an individual interpretation, and very few players have been equally successful in both *genres*. To anticipate a little, we may cite as the perfect example the case of Bix Beiderbecke who became famous as a white cornet player in small true-jazz combinations, but who, in spite of his admirable capability, was deeply unhappy in later life as a featured soloist in the 'style-bound' large band of Paul Whiteman.[2] It is not, however, our object here to embark on yet another attempt to define jazz, but to examine how the trumpet and trombone have been employed in this particular musical idiom, and to what extent their characteristics may have influenced its growth. For this a brief summary of the historical origins and the social influences that have affected jazz will make the best foundation.

It is generally agreed that instrumental jazz began in New Orleans about the year 1900, and that its two 'tap roots' were on the one hand the native melody, and on the other the innate rhythm sense of the African Negro. Even before the American Civil War these elements had appeared, first in the work songs of the slaves in the Deep South, and then rather later in the original Blues which (with some influence from the imported English ballad and a good deal more from the hymns of Moody and Sankey) was able to express a much wider and deeper-ranging gamut of emotion. Indeed some authorities find in the Methodist hymnals the roots of the simple chordal progressions of early jazz. After the War the situation of the bulk of the Negro population was tragic indeed. They had no longer even the certainty of the old Slave Code, evil and degrading though that had often been, and under so-called emancipation there was no security of any kind. Very many, in their resentment of the past, refused absolutely to work as free employees of their former masters and preferred to accept whatever Fate might send them. In these conditions the Blues[3] became not only an emotional outlet, but also something of a binding force among a rootless people. Gradually, however, some sort of *modus vivendi* developed among them, and the easy-going New Orleans, situated in a bend of the Mississippi, the great communication artery of the country, became almost automatically their metropolis. At the same time Negroes and Mulattos from the Antilles, where a more tolerant form of slavery had been practised, began freely to enter the area bringing with them a degree of culture hitherto utterly denied to the mainland slaves. Thus the drums of the Caribbean Negroes found an avid welcome among these intensely rhythm-conscious people, and it is at this point that we find the first signs of an instrumental synthesis.

The population of New Orleans in the last decades of the 19th century fell broadly into four distinct and self-conscious communities. These were: (1) White Americans of various social classes; (2) the aristocratic Creoles, intensely conservative and proud of their French or Spanish descent; (3) 'Creoles of Colour', a group of mixed blood; and (4) the Negroes. Each of these occupied their own more or less exclusive section of the town, and indeed there still remained some distinction between the French and Spanish parts of the mainly Creole area. Among the aristocracy of New Orleans at this period music was much as we might expect in any European community of similar cultural background (with perhaps some stress on French or Spanish sources among the Creole element) but this is of little significance in the present context.[4] The Creoles of Colour,[5] however, are important for they represented a socially inferior class who, nevertheless, could have the advantage of musical education, and who played the piano or stringed instruments in their own homes. Outside the domestic circle these men were the principal source of the discreet string orchestras provided by the better-class pleasure-houses of the notorious Storeyville area, and some were musicians whose attainments even gained them a welcome in the opera or symphony orchestras. The full-blooded Negroes had no such advantages and when they first began to fuse into a community they possessed no musical heritage save their vocal Blues. It was, however, inevitable that such naturally musical people in urban conditions should assimilate and improvise on the melodies and methods of their more sophisticated neighbours and bend these to their own use. Thus there arose the desire for instruments which was at first met by any improvisation from comb and paper to the cigar box banjo or the bum-bass made from a keg, a broomstick, and a single string.[6] The next phase was the acquisition of proper instruments which for many must have entailed tremendous sacrifices, and on this Rex Harris[7] makes some important observations. He writes—'In what manner did they acquire such expensive things as clarinets, cornets, and trombones? It is highly probable that the ending of the Civil War in 1865 must

have seen many an old band instrument discarded throughout
Louisiana, Mississippi, Alabama, Georgia, and South Carolina. These,
rescued and treasured by Negroes, must have been doubly sacred in
that many of them were relics of the emancipating Union army . . . . The
very instruments that went "Marching Through Georgia" went marching along Canal Street.' No doubt the first band instruments to get into
Negro hands were certainly war relics, but it seems hardly possible that
this source could have supplied all that were to be found in New
Orleans in the next fifteen years.

There are in the paragraph just quoted two points that are of great
importance to us here, but we shall consider them in the reverse order.
In the life of the Creoles and White Americans of New Orleans, as in
many other essentially Latin cities, public celebrations and parades
with music had always been a prominent feature, and their emotional
impact soon found an echo in the mind of the growing Negro community. The result was that by about 1880 many Negro 'Marching
Bands' of more or less military conformation were in being, and there
was great rivalry among them. They appeared at virtually every Negro
activity of a public nature, and they were the object almost of hero
worship. The repertoire of the marching bands was drawn largely from
that of the Whites, but again this material was adapted and 'bent'.
At a Negro funeral the cortège would be led to the graveside by a band
playing orthodox marches; but after the service the same music would
be relaxed, and improvisation, both solo and collective, would creep in.
These bands would also vary formal march rhythms by transferring
accents to the weak beats of the bar—both ideas that were later to be
recognised as characteristics of fully developed jazz. The second
point relates to the instruments themselves, and here we may recognise
a dual significance. Cornet, clarinet, and trombone have been mentioned, and the derivation of this group from the usual military band
organisation of the period is surely evident. These were the three
melody instruments of the Marching Bands, as they were later in the
specialist jazz bands. Indeed we might well say that the early New
Orleans jazz combination was the original and authentic

> '. . . band with the curious tone
> of the cornet, clarinet and big trombone.'

But many historians go farther, and suggest that, quite apart from
the question of taking over a ready-made group from those available,
these instruments individually would be an obvious choice to the Negro

long conditioned to 'think' his music in vocal terms. They would represent to him the high, medium, and low voices; and in support of this idea we may note that in modern standard military band scoring they have become (with the euphonium) the preferred solo voices.

This vocal concept of American Negro music goes far to explain many features which are not always recognised by the conventional musician, and which are sometimes distasteful to him. The voices of African Negroes are, on the whole, guttural but not unmelodious, and their original languages make great play with consonants. Their words often sound to us harsh and clipped. When the African has to contend with a Latin language with mainly terminal stresses he does not, as a rule, change its rhythms much; but with English he meets greater difficulties. He tends to weaken unstressed sounds even further and to over-accent strong syllables. Had New Orleans remained a predominantly French-speaking city it seems probable that immigrant Negroes would have assimilated the Creole dialect without much modification, but after the Louisiana Purchase in 1803 English became more and more the common language. Thus, when freed slaves flocked into the city after 1865 their language, whatever it had been before, came under English influence and consequently developed syncopated rhythms and a characteristic 'swing' which, transferred to their music, presaged jazz. The glissandi, 'smears' and 'growls' so much deplored by some 'straight' musicians come also from this source, and we must admit that they do sound startling to the conventional ear. So do the modified intervals to which we have already alluded (see note 3) but, to be just, we should recognise that all these devices have too often been torn from their proper context and cheapened as mere 'stunts' by commercial men who have no idea of the significance of true jazz and whose playing bears no resemblance to it. Incidentally, it should be pointed out that the word *Jazz* did not become a definitive term till some time near the end of the First World War.

Reverting to instruments, the slide trombone, by its construction, lends itself naturally to both glissandi and modified intervals, but there is no evidence that this had any particular influence on its adoption by the marching bands. The well-known jazz critic Steve Race once told the writer that he felt that had the abandoned Union army stores afforded a wider selection of instruments more would certainly have found their way into the Negro bands, but this view is in no way incompatible with the concept of an underlying vocal influence. The cornet, as a valved instrument, is, of course, less amenable to such handling, although its relatively wide bore and deeper mouthpiece make it more 'vocal' than the trumpet. Presumably trumpets as well as cornets could have been found as relics of the Civil War, but we do not see evidence of them in the early Negro instrumentation, and of course the natural instrument with its limited scale would have had little appeal. There is here, by the way, some confusion among musical writers, and many men referred to as trumpeters, including the great Louis Armstrong himself, are known to have been cornet players—at least until influenced by commercial jazz in the 1920s. Perhaps also we detect a touch of snobbery here, for at this period certain well-known instrument firms were supplying 'long' model cornets deliberately designed to resemble orchestral trumpets. Verbal accounts from surviving players are unreliable in this matter for in a certain class of American parlance today all brass instruments, more or less, are 'horns'.

It is the greatest pity that we have so little evidence as to how the early New Orleans men really played. Contemporary writers can hardly be expected to have foreseen the growth of what they took to be a local and socially inferior manifestation, and the gramophone, later so valuable, was hardly in the field. Moreover, when recording did become more advanced many players felt their music to be too personal a thing to be broadcast beyond their immediate and sympathetic circle. Many of the pioneers are therefore today no more than names revered by those who remember their playing, and who can perhaps imitate their style. We do know certainly, however, that most of these men were necessarily self-taught. Many developed methods and techniques that were quite unorthodox, and indeed some of these techniques were copied by admirers who could have had formal tuition. In later days some of the unorthodox players, though acknowledged masters, tended to be self-conscious when sitting beside formally trained musicians. More than one celebrated trumpeter is known habitually to have draped his handkerchief over the valves at public performances. Blowing techniques particularly seem to have been acquired by trial-and-error methods, and it is perhaps to the example of such as Armstrong, who picked up the rudiments of cornet playing before the age of thirteen, that we can trace the relaxed cheeks of some present-day jazz trumpeters. Armstrong, though born in the poor district of Perdido, was, in fact, more fortunate than many. When placed in a reform school in 1913 as the result of a prank that would probably have been excused in a white boy, he was befriended by a guard who taught him to read music. Few of his contemporaries had this advantage even under such sad circumstances. Armstrong remained exclusively a cornet player till some time in the 1920s.

Among the New Orleans Negroes professionalism came first to those who could get access to pianos, probably because of the amount of concentration and practice demanded. Round these men the other players gathered and thus the first coloured entertainment bands began. The pianists played mainly 'ragtime' (not synonymous with jazz but an element in its growth) and their music soon found a demand in the lower-grade dance halls, saloons, and brothels of Storeyville, for that accommodating area catered for all classes. There also a White imitation of Negro music began, but this is not to be confused with the true White jazz of later years. In 1917 the U.S. Navy brought strong pressure to bear in Washington and, in spite of the protests of interested parties, Storeyville as a 'pleasure' area was closed down. As a consequence many musicians were forced to seek employment elsewhere, and the majority settled in Chicago which appeared to offer the best livelihood. This large exodus is often regarded as marking the entry of jazz into the world at large, but in fact the expansion of trade and all that went with it had tempted a considerable body of musicians to move up-river some years earlier. These had settled in St. Louis, Memphis, etc., and some even as far away as Minneapolis. The Mississippi river boats, too, had traditionally carried their own orchestras to entertain voyagers, and as their tastes changed so enterprising proprietors began to employ New Orleans coloured bands. Still, 1917–18 was the great turning point and from then on commercial exploitation really began. The story of jazz and its ramifications (some would say debasement) after 1918 is far too complicated to set out here, but for the interested reader we reproduce a detailed chart devised by Rex Harris, and this will also be useful as a framework upon which to relate certain aspects of brass playing that we find in modern popular music outside the strict concept of jazz. A word of warning however; the boundaries of areas of influence as shown on any printed chart must obviously be too rigid and we should interpret them with discretion. Moreover, jazz is a living expressive medium that has progressed far since the 1940s as we shall shortly see.

We have already stated that in classic jazz the cornet and not the trumpet came first and we have offered some explanation for this. The trumpet in jazz really came into its own about 1920 and seems to have been taken up by certain traditional players when they came under the influence of conventional music in Chicago. Even so, the performance

R

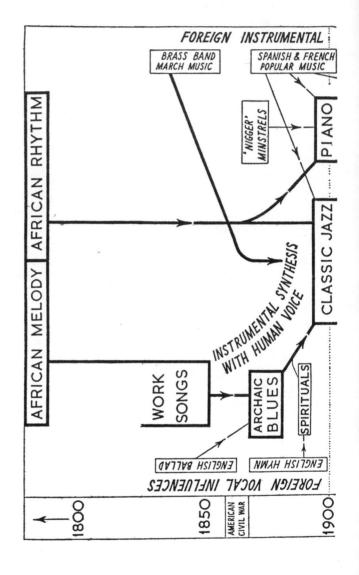

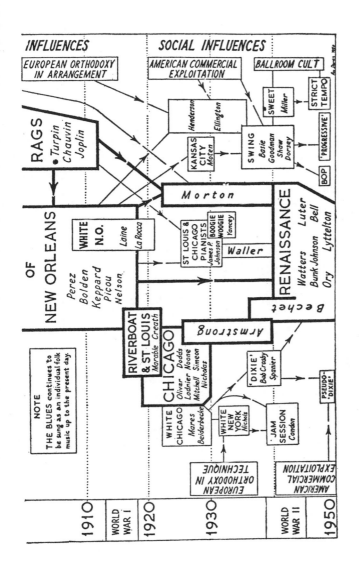

of these men remained quite unlike that of the symphony players for the obvious reason that their chosen instrument, whatever it may have been, was to them a vehicle of intensely personal expression. Although tone colour in symphonic playing is, as we have admitted (pp. 56, 70), to some extent a personal matter, style and musical approach in that field can hardly be so. Among idiomatic jazz men, however, the personal element developed to a quite extraordinary degree, particularly in respect of tone quality, and the best of them could make the trumpet triumph, laugh, or weep at will, as we can hear from gramophone records of the period. It was this sense of personal 'message' that led some players to alternate trumpet and cornet, and indeed in present-day jazz there are some who find that the fuller tone of the flügelhorn suits them best. On the other hand some jazz men find a harsh and strident tone best fitted to what they have to say. In the Chicago period the circumstances affecting *style*, however, began to change somewhat, and when commercial interests began to demand big bands for dancing or for stage presentations some curbing was inevitable as written arrangements became increasingly necessary. This is not to say that the best arrangers did not appreciate the individual qualities of the great trumpeters and trombonists and try to give them opportunities, but it is hardly possible for a natural extemporiser to be equally at home in the show band 'front line' of three or four identical instruments. The point is clearly illustrated by the careers of Armstrong and Beiderbecke, one coloured, the other white, and both using true jazz as their medium of expression. Armstrong, after his stormy youth, found employment on the river boats with Fate Marable and with Kid Ory's band. His real training in band work came, however, when King Oliver, himself a cornettist, took him to Chicago. Armstrong has always acknowledged his debt to Oliver, but before very long he severed the connection for he could not find self-realisation as an ensemble man or as his leader's shadow. Only when he was able to select his own supporting musicians (and these had to be individually first-rate) could he reveal his superlative gifts. At his best his tone is strong, clear, and noble, and his command of the upper register of the B♭ trumpet is remarkable, though his technique remains in some respects unorthodox to this day. Though imitated everywhere he is not, perhaps, the best model for young players. Beiderbecke, in contrast, began with a formal musical education in a middle-class family. He taught himself the cornet (later the trumpet too), and then, against some family opposition, found his métier as the bright star of a semi-professional small group who called themselves the Wolverines. These men played in what is now recognised as the 'Dixieland' manner, by which we understand a style based on an intensive study and enthusiasm for the original New Orleans jazz, but animated by a purely white *ethos*.[8] After the break-up of the Wolverines Beiderbecke for a time found congenial surroundings in several other bands, but circumstances soon forced him to accept 'big band' work and he ended up with Paul Whiteman. Here, in a combination of almost symphonic proportions and discipline, he felt nervous and seldom revealed himself fully, although Whiteman and his arrangers valued Beiderbecke's quality and reputation and did their best in commercial conditions to make him opportunities. This, however, was not enough and Beiderbecke, lacking Armstrong's resilience, fell into chronic alcoholism and died at the age of twenty-eight. The most interesting thing about him compared with Armstrong was the limited range he explored. Most of his melodies and improvisations were confined to about one octave, and he rarely ventured into the extreme high range. In his free solos a falling cadence with wide intervals is almost as characteristic as it is in the melodies of Elgar. It has been said that his technique was in fact rather meagre, but, be that as it may, it proved sufficient for what he had to say and he became a legend in his own time. His tone was warm and rounded, and his gift for subtle phrasing was unsurpassed.

Mention of Beiderbecke brings to mind another important aspect of jazz in the earlier days, if only because it is a matter in which he seems so often to have been unfortunate—the personal artistic relationship between trumpet, trombone, and clarinet. In the most successful small combination jazz we find the three instruments working together as complementary voices. This does not necessarily imply identity of style, and sometimes it appears more like mere rivalry in performance, but at its best it does suggest a special measure of mutual sympathy. Some enthusiasts have, however, tended to sentimentalise the situation and make a *mystique* of it when in fact a practical and inescapable bond was imposed on the players by the very nature of jazz improvisation. Unlike the concerto soloists' *cadenza* which might depart from the main key of the movement, pass through several remote keys, and then return for the *tutti*, jazz improvisation was always limited by the chord sequence and structure of the piece.

The reader will have remarked that so far we have made no mention of the saxophone in jazz. Certainly it had no part in the early stages, but as bands grew larger and began to feel their way beyond the simple polyphony of three contrasted voices it commended itself, first as an alternative to the clarinet (as with the New Orleans clarinettist Sydney Bechet) and ultimately as the principal instrument of a three-, four-, or five-man reed section. The development of the Big Bands, some of them preserving the essence of true jazz, others losing sight of it in an orgy of almost academic arranging, is a phase of musical history that we can only mention here before passing on to the present day.

The revolution of the mid to late 1940s, known first as 'Be-bop', then as 'modern jazz' and now accepted as part of the main stream of development, changed the function of virtually all instruments in jazz. It also brought new names to the forefront. The main architects of the new style were four in number: Charlie Parker (alto saxophone), Dizzy Gillespie (trumpet), Thelonius Monk (piano), and Kenny Clarke (drums), though they were supported by other players, notably the trombonist J. J. Johnson.

The new jazz was melodically and harmonically more complex, infinitely more challenging (and therefore to the player more rewarding) from the technical point of view; while socially speaking it marked the first determined breakaway from the 'Uncle Tom' concept of Negro music, bitterly resented ever since the Coon Songs and Minstrel Shows of the old days. It is significant that the four pioneers—Parker, Gillespie, Monk, and Clarke—represented between them the four divisions which had in the course of time become standardised in the jazz instrumental combination—reeds, brass, 'tuned rhythm', and percussion—and as we might expect with any 'new wave', their reforms were at first extravagant. In its attempt to be 'cool' the music became fevered; soloists began and ended their contributions at an arbitrary point in the chorus structure; the closing chord of every piece became a suspension rather than a full-close. As the melodic and harmonic complexity grew the old concept of collective improvisation fell into disuse. Even the evergreen tunes which served so long as a basis for improvisation became neglected, and to suggest playing them marked one down as a 'square'.

Gillespie brought to jazz trumpet playing a technical facility and an extended upward range that was far beyond the powers even of Armstrong; and his followers Clifford Brown, Fats Navarro, Kenny Dorham, and Miles Davis were almost his technical equals. On the trombone J. J. Johnson copied the rapid articulation of Gillespie and Parker and developed a staccato style which was dictated by the instrument's construction but which called for a virtuosity at least equal to theirs. Johnson's principal follower was Kai Winding, a white trombonist who was later to become his partner in a memorable series of recorded duets.*

As the new movement lost its novelty value (and the ludicrous name of be-bop) much of its bizarre, extravagant quality disappeared, though the challenge to the performer remained as strong as ever. There are few young jazz musicians today whose work does not reflect the influence of Gillespie and Parker.

Of the pioneer modern jazz brass players, Gillespie is still at the peak of his powers. Navarro and Brown are dead; Dorham has slipped into an undeserved obscurity. Miles Davis, once as fiery and flamboyant as Gillespie, has developed a muted style described by the cognoscenti as 'ultra-cool' and is greatly admired. As throughout the history of jazz, the Negro concept has again been welcomed and adapted by white musicians, and notable among these—at least in point of technique— was the Canadian trumpeter Maynard Ferguson. His extraordinary facility in playing clean, sharply-defined chromatic passages on the higher leger lines of the treble clef can be heard in many records of the Stan Kenton band made in the 1950s, and now regarded as historic.* In Ferguson we may perhaps find a parallel to the clarinists of the 18th century (p. 127 note 18). Similarly J. J. Johnson's trombone technique was extended by Frank Rosolino who may also be heard in Stan Kenton recordings.

For a time, in discussing jazz, it became necessary to use qualifying adjectives. It was not enough to mention 'jazz'; one had to specify Traditional jazz (Armstrong, King Oliver, etc.), Mainstream jazz (middle-period music exemplified by Buck Clayton and Humphrey Lyttleton) or Modern jazz (Gillespie, etc.). Today the single word 'jazz' has come to mean the music currently being played and this through the sheer passage of time inevitably implies music of the post-Parker/Gillespie type. The early music of New Orleans is historically and ethnologically important, but in the very nature of things it is a dying art. Every year there are fewer genuine traditional jazzmen, and many of those still living are finding it pathetically hard to get an audience. To the brass-playing jazz musician of the 1960s Dizzy Gillespie is the father-figure, just as Armstrong was in the 1920s and 30s. Time marches on, and for jazz it is a quick march.

As we have seen, the basic instruments of jazz, apart from drums, were borrowed in the first place from the *armamentarium* of conventional music, and it only remains to enquire what effect jazz techniques

* See Appendix 3, p. 257.

may have had on present-day orthodox brass playing. The influence of the jazz idiom on many composers, modern and not so modern, is recognised and needs no comment, but has there been any 'feedback', as it were, among players?

As regards the trombone most young instrumentalists, and many of an older generation, freely acknowledge a debt to the great jazz players. In respect of slide technique they will mention the names of Jack Teagarden and Tommy Dorsey (the latter published a series of studies that many orthodox players recommend) and in articulation generally J. J. Johnson commands the greatest admiration. Orchestral trumpet playing seems on the whole to have assimilated less from the special techniques of jazz. The phenomenal excursions of Ferguson into the extreme top register of the B♭ trumpet have found no echo in orthodox playing, nor do composers show signs of imperatively demanding them. This is probably because symphony trumpeters are already accustomed to sounding these notes as lower harmonics of higher pitched instruments, and moreover, the tone of the B♭ (and smaller) trumpets at these altitudes is inevitably meagre and lacking in harmonic content. Nevertheless, Ferguson has shown beyond dispute that it *can* be done by a gifted and determined trumpeter.

Glissandi and 'smears', as the jazz man calls them, have been part of legitimate trombone technique for many years, but many regard them as foreign to the valve trumpet. The majority of modern orchestral trumpeters can, however, essay them if demanded. Here we touch on a point of jazz technique which, I believe, has no counter-part in orthodox playing—the 'half-valve'. In this some players, in addition to progressively modifying successive notes with the lips, deliberately half depress a valve in passing, thus opening two alternative windways at the same time. The acoustics of this process could, no doubt, be investigated mathematically, but one rather doubts the value of such a proceeding.

Finally there is one benefit deriving from the 'Big Band' phase from which orchestral music has not profited as much as it might— the identification of different sorts of mutes. Although many of these still appear in makers' lists under fancy names, the characteristics of the main types are now clearly defined, and the composer can, if he will, specify and secure the effect he desires (see also pp. 29 and 74).

If the reader can get access to a copy of the very remarkable Swedish film *Bolos*, an entry in the 1964 Italia Prize Competition, he will find it most rewarding. The first section demonstrates very clearly the tonal characteristics of various standard trombone mutes, as well as the natural resonances, etc., of the body tube.

NOTES

[1] Defined by André Francis in 1960 as 'An imaginative flight of melody or rhythm which is generally at the end of a phrase (or often in the Blues at the beginning of a chorus) wherein the regular rhythmic accompaniment is momentarily stopped.'

[2] In spite of the unfortunate title 'King of Jazz' conferred on Paul Whiteman by certain film interests, his band was never in the true sense a jazz combination. Rather was it a large light orchestra depending for its effects on luscious and skilful arrangements as demanded by the entertainment industry of the time. Whiteman himself no doubt understood jazz and from time to time he employed famous jazz players and tried to fuse their idiom with a more or less orthodox symphonic style. His efforts led no less a critic than the late Ernest Newman to prophesy that therein lay the ultimate future of jazz, but subsequent history has shown that the two styles are quite incompatible. As Steve Race puts it, 'The marriage did not take place'. See Burnett James, *Bix Beiderbecke*, London 1957, Cassell and Co. Ltd.

[3] For an admirably clear and full explanation of this form of American Negro folk song see André Francis, *Jazz*, translated by Martin Williams, London, Evergreen Books Ltd., and New York, Grove Press Inc., 1960, pp. 166 *et seq.* The famous 'blue note' associated with this style is a deliberate flattening by about half a tone of the third and seventh of the scale, and is traceable to ancestral African roots.

[4] These people did in fact look to Europe for much of their musical fare, and maintained a considerable traffic with the European music industry.

[5] Some historians do not stress the distinction between these two groups which, however, appears to be useful in a condensed account such as the present. The reader should note that some of the social boundaries were no doubt less clearly marked than our brief summary necessarily suggests. Today the word Creole *tout court* has largely lost its original and specific meaning and usually implies 'of mixed blood'.

[6] Galpin points out that this instrument, in various degrees of improvisation, has been known from the time of the *jongleurs* to the present day, see *Old English Instruments of Music*, London, Methuen and Co., 3rd. edn., 1932, pp. 85 and 97. The most recent manifestation has been among the first 'skiffle' groups in Britain, where a ply-wood tea chest was used as the resonator.

[7] Rex Harris, *Jazz*, Penguin Books Ltd., London, 1952, p. 56.

[8] *Op. cit.*, pp. 71 and 197. See also André Francis, *op. cit.*, p. 178.

A List of the Principal Nürnberg Brass Instrument Makers of the 16th, 17th, and 18th Centuries, as known from Surviving Specimens of their Work

THE MOST VALUABLE paper on this subject is Willi Wörthmüller's 'Die Nürnberger Trompeten—und Posaunenmacher des 17 und 18 Jahrhunderts', *Mitteilungen . . . der Stadt Nürnberg*, Vol. 45 (1954) and Vol. 46 (1955), and from this the following material is mainly drawn. Examples of Nürnberg trumpets and trombones are to be found in most major European and American musical collections, but a comprehensive account would be far too long to insert here. For notes on both public and private collections the reader is referred to Lyndesay G. Langwill's *Index of Musical Wind-instrument Makers*, privately issued from 19 Melville Street, Edinburgh, 3. Second edition (revised and enlarged) 1962.

In the following tables dates of birth and death are inserted when known, failing which working periods as shown by surviving specimens are quoted.

The recurrence of family names in this list clearly indicates the close organisation and family apprenticeship system of the Nürnberg makers. An excellent article which sheds much light on the subject, as well as on working conditions in Nürnberg, has appeared in the *Galpin Society Journal*, No. XVIII, 1965: see 'The Trumpets of J. W. Haas, a Survey of Four Generations of Nürnberg Brass Instrument Makers' by Don Smithers. For comparison, names from Langwill's Index for Vienna and Prague for the same period have been extracted, and it is notable that there are comparatively few from these centres before the 18th century when the 'player-manufacturer' system of Nürnberg began to loosen and break up. England, in her relative isolation, produced few brass makers, but examples of their work are of the highest quality by any standards, and show certain unmistakable national characteristics. Five important names are quoted.

NÜRNBERG

Bauer, Jacob, d. 1612.
Birckholtz, Wolfgang, worked *c.* 1650, d. 1701.
Doll, Hanns, *c.* 1582–1668.
Drewelwecz, Anton, d. 1603.
Droschel, Conrat, 1596–1645.
Ehe, Isaac, 1586–1632.
Ehe, Georg, 1595–1668.
Ehe, Johann Leonard I, 1638–1707.
Ehe, Johann Leonard II, 1664–1724.
Ehe, Friedrich, 1669–1743.
Ehe, Johann Leonard III, 1770–
Ehe, Johann Leonard, junior ?
Ehe, Martin Friedrich, 1714–1779.
Ehe, Wolf Magnus I, 1690–1722.

Ehe, Wolf Magnus II, d. 1794.
Frank, Johann Christopher, 1754–1818.
Haas, Johann Wilhelm, 1649–1723.
Haas, Wolf Wilhelm, 1681–1760.
Haas, Ernst Joh. Conrad, 1723–1792.
Hainlein, Hanns, 1596–1671. (The first of the Nürnberg 'dynasty'.)
Hainlein, Michael, 1659, d. pre 1725.
Hainlein, Paul, 1626–1686.
Hainlein, Sebastian I, d. 1631.
Hainlein, Sebastian II, 1594–1655.
Kodisch, Daniel, 1686–1714. (Son of J. C. K. below, and son-in-law of Michael
    Hainlein. He used the latter's mark and was presumably his apprentice.)
Kodisch, Johann Carl, 1654–1721.
Linczer, Cunrat, fl. 1568–1609.
Linczer, Elias, 1572–1626. ⎫
Linczer, Bonifatius, 1578–1616. ⎬ Sons of the above.
Müller, Hans, d. post 1661.
Nagel, Michael, 1621–1664.
Neuschel, Hans, senior, d. 1503.
Neuschel, Hans, junior, d. 1533. (Court Musician and Trombonist to the
    Emperor Maximilian I. Portrayed in 'The Triumph of Maximilian', 1512.)
Neuschel, Jörg, d. 1557.
Ochsenkun, Jörg, c. 1515.
Reichard, Simon, b. 1580.
Schmidt, Jakob, 1642–1720.
Schmidt, Johann Jakob, 1686–c. 1756.
Schmidt, Paulus, c. 1719. (Son of J. J. Schmidt. Both became Nürnberg Town
    Musicians. See pp. 223 and 227.)
Schnitzer, Erasmus, d. 1566.
Schnitzer, Anton, the elder, d. 1608.
Schnitzer, Anton, the younger, b. 1654. (According to Wörthmüller the work of
    these two is indistinguishable. Anton the younger married and set up in
    business in 1591, so specimens of an earlier date may presumably be ascribed
    to Anton the elder.)
Schnitzer, Jobst, 1576–1616.

The following members of the Schnitzer family are also recorded though so
far no specimens of their work are known to survive.

Schnitzer, Hans, the elder, d. 1608.
Schnitzer, Veit, c. 1540.
Schnitzer, Albrecht. (Known to have attained the status of Master-Craftsman
    in 1573.)
Schnitzer, Hans, c. 1571–1609.
Schnitzer, Eberhard, 1600–1634.
Starck, Hieronymus, 1640–1693.
Steinmetz, Georg Friedrich, 1668, d. post 1740.
Steinmetz, Cornelius, 1702–1780.
Steinmetz, Christof Wilhelm, 1736–1786.
Wagger, Georg, c. 1596.

VIENNA

Ferber, Adam, c. 1745.
Geier, Hans, c 1800.

Geyer, Hans. Working 1676–1698.
Glier, I. A., *c.* 1800.
Hofman, I. G., late 18th century?
Huschauer, Joseph, 1748–1805.
Kerner, Anton, 1726–1806?
Kerner, Anton, junior ⎫
Kerner, Ignaz, 1768–1813. ⎬ Sons of the above.
Körner, Joseph, *c.* 1755.
Leichamschneider, Johannes. Working 1710–1725.
Leichamschneider, Michael, 1709–1741.
Leichamschneider, Franz, *c.* 1746.
Leichamschneider, Erasmus, ?
Liebel, M. J. G., *c.* 1791.
Mazogato, Franz, 1779–1832.
Purggraf, Franz Anton, *c.* 1728.
Startzer, Carl, *c.* 1770.

PRAGUE

Fratisch, J. J., *c.* 1752.
Umlauff, Wenzel, *c.* 1770.
Wolf, Joseph, early 18th century.

LONDON

Beale, Simon, *c.* 1660–1680.
Bull, William, *c.* 1680.
Dudley, Augustine, *c.* 1651.
Harris, John, fl. 1716–1717.
Shaw, William, 1775–1817.

Draw-trumpet and Trombone— A Comparative Experiment

AMONG THOSE musicologists who in the past have found themselves unable to accept the idea that Bach's *tromba-da-tirarsi* was indeed a single-slide draw-trumpet, the commonest objection seems to be the presumed lack of agility in that instrument. This has persisted in spite of Sanford Terry's quite convincing argument that such an instrument could compass the parts Bach wrote at the tempi implied in the scores, and with a total 'shift' length of some 17 inches, which is about the same as the distance between first and fifth positions on a modern B♭ tenor trombone. While this book was in preparation the need was felt for some up-to-date evidence, so a short study was made.

In the absence of a genuine old *Zugtrompete* Canon Galpin's experiment was reproduced (p. 113) using a J. W. Haas D trumpet of the late 17th century as the basis. It was very soon found that practically no support could be given to the body of the instrument with the left hand which was fully occupied in keeping the mouthpiece with its extension tube up to the lips. The full weight of the body, 21 ozs., was therefore carried entirely by the right hand, and although the 'positions' could be reproduced accurately time after time with a little practice, the inertia was considerable. With the slide extended the forward distribution of the weight, together with almost unconscious efforts to keep the slide moving as freely as possible, resulted in a natural playing position with the instrument sloping downwards like a woodwind, as can be seen in many paintings of early draw-trumpet and sackbut players.

The marked difference between the sloping position imposed by the improvised draw-trumpet and the nearly horizontal carriage now adopted by many slide trombone players suggested an enquiry into the distribution of weight with this instrument. Assistance was sought from a well-known English professor of trombone, and for comparison from an amateur player as well. Both the B♭ tenor (counter-weighted permanently to the taste of the player) and the B♭–F tenor-bass instruments were investigated. It was clear that in both cases a large part of the dead weight of the instrument was borne on the left shoulder, and again the left hand did little beyond keeping the mouthpiece to the lips with the requisite pressure. The weight carried by the right hand was measured by the following method. The slide was opened to each position in succession, and when the player had settled comfortably and 'played himself in', a sensitive spring balance was hooked under the cross bar of the slide and sufficient force applied just to lift the slide from the supporting hand. An average of three or four readings was taken as a measure of the actual weight carried by the hand. Results are tabulated below.

(A) Wide-bore B♭ tenor (8-inch bell)—
    Total Weight: 3 lb. 8 oz.
    Weight on right hand:

1st position: 17 oz.
2nd position: 16 oz.
3rd position: 15 oz.
4th position: 10 oz.
5th position: 9½ oz.
6th position: 8 oz.
7th position: 7 oz.

(B) B♭–F tenor-bass (9 inch bell)—
Total weight: 4 lb. 6 oz.
Weight on right hand:
    1st position: 12½ oz.
    2nd position: 11 oz.
    3rd position: 10½ oz.
    4th position: 9 oz.
    5th position: 5½ oz.
    6th position: 3½ oz.
    7th position: 3 oz.

It is notable that of the two, the tenor-bass, though heavier, appeared to be the better-balanced instrument, since less of the total weight in any position fell on the supporting hand. There is a marked break in each series of readings, in one case between the 3rd and 4th positions, and in the other between the 4th and 5th. This is not explained by our experiment unless it may represent some twisting force applied by the left hand at a point where a change of embouchure takes place.

At first sight it appears paradoxical that the force required from the right hand to maintain a horizontal playing position gets progressively less as the slide is extended, but this is, of course, explained if we regard the whole instrument as a first-order lever in a state of balance. Readers will recall that in these circumstances the turning moments on either side of the point of balance are equal and appear as *force* × *distance*.

A Short List of L.P. Gramophone Records Illustrating Certain Points in the Foregoing Text

Reference.
Chap. *Page*

3   55   'Pop' Concert. (*H.M.V. Concert Classics XLP 20030*. Side 1, Band 2)
'España', Chabrier.
Orchestre de l'Association de Concerts Colonne, conducted by Pierre Dervaux.

3   55   *Twilight Concert No. 2 (Philips Favourite Music Series SLB 5230*. Side 1, Band 3)
'España', Chabrier.
The Philadelphia Orchestra conducted by Eugene Ormandy.
With the increasing use of the wide-bore trombone in all parts of the world it is difficult to find good recorded examples of the older narrow-tubed instrument. Comparison of the *forte* trombone passages about 2 min. 35 sec. in on the two above recordings will give some indication however of the difference between French and German-American ideas at the time of writing. If the reader can get access to the deleted 78 r.p.m. recording of the Band of the Garde Républicaine playing the same work (*Col. D 11019*) he will find an excellent and typical example of narrow-bore trombone tone in the *forte*.
Another interesting deleted 78 r.p.m. record is *Col. D.B. 1923*. In July 1940 the Band of H.M. Grenadier Guards recorded on this disc 'España' arranged by Hughes as a military march. In the arranging the original character of the piece is completely lost, but the corresponding trombone passage gives a splendid example of the light, brilliant tone of the 'pea-shooter' instrument when well played.

3   55   *In The Mood (Ace of Hearts AH. 12) (The Glenn Miller Story)*
Band 5—the diminuendo passage at the end of the band particularly. This illustrates the suave tone combined with clean attack for which the Glenn Miller trombone section was at one time famous. In listening to this and other modern recordings of light music we must recognise that dynamics and reverberation are now frequently 'doctored' as a routine part of recording technique, but in this case the essential tones are not in any way

Chap.   Page   modified. The Glenn Miller Orchestra was a notable 'sweet' combination of the Second World War period.

3   55   *'Afrikaan Beat'* from *A Swingin' Safari* (*Polydor International Production. 46 384 B*, Band 1)

Bert Kaempfert and his Orchestra

An interesting example of 'dialogue' between trumpet and trombone in the middle dynamic, the two players matching their tone.

5   84   *The Land of the Morning Star* (*H.M.V. O.C.1.p. 7610*. Side 2, bands 7 and 8)

Two excellent examples of solo playing on the didjeridu. The harmonics mentioned can readily be heard. Other bands on this disc record the didjeridu as an accompanying instrument.

6   119   *Deutsche Grammophon. 'Archive Production'* (*ARC 3252*)

Concerto for Trumpet and Orchestra in E♭ major. Joseph Haydn. Adolf Scherbaum, Trumpet, and The Munich Chamber Orchestra, conducted by Hans Stadlmair.

6   119   *Vanguard* (*PVL 7012*)
Concerto for Trumpet and Orchestra in E♭ major. Joseph Haydn. George Eskdale, Trumpet, and the Vienna State Opera Orchestra, conducted by Franz Litschauer.

These two recordings of the Haydn Concerto provide a most interesting comparison. Scherbaum, using an E♭ trumpet by Heckel of Dresden, produces a tone that is almost flute-like but perhaps somewhat lacking in character, though his execution is brilliant. George Eskdale used an E♭ trumpet specially made by Besson of London. His tone was more virile than that of Scherbaum, though without a trace of harshness in this recording, and there appears to have been no difficulty in the matter of balance. Both examples show what can be done with a modern valve trumpet in the hands of a specialist. According to a contemporary account in the *Historisches Taschenbuch* of Vienna (1802) the tone of Weidinger's keyed trumpet approached 'more the sound of a strong oboe' so probably neither of these recordings can be taken to represent the Haydn concerto as originally heard.

6   256   *Munchen—Die Hofkapelle unter Orlando di Lasso* (*Columbia C. 91 108*. Side 1 'Aufzug' by an unknown composer. Begins 6 min. 50 sec. in)

Walter Holy and Helmut Finke playing Steinkopf-Finke trumpets. Helmut Schmitt and Wilhelm Wendland playing Sackbuts (Renaissance-Posaunen).

7   216   Side 2. Pavane 'La Bataille' by Tilman Susato, published in Antwerp 1551. Begins 12 min. in.
Harry Barteld—Tenor-Posaune.
Kurt Federowitz—Bass-Posaune (with Krummhorns).

This extremely interesting recording contains a selection of music of *c*. 1530–1600 sung and played on contemporary instru-

Chap. *Page* ments (or reconstructions from contemporary descriptions) at a
truly professional standard. It is probably the best evidence of
the real sound of these instruments that we have at present. The
second example chosen demonstrates the degree of articulation
expected of trombones of the period.

11   217   *Brass-counter-Brass. Westminster X.W.N. 18887*
Music of Andrea and Giovanni Gabrielli. Brass Ensemble of the
Vienna State Opera Orchestra, conducted by Sayard Stone. This
record presents an interesting selection most beautifully played on
modern Brass. The purist may perhaps query in some cases the
choice of modern instruments selected to replace obsolete ones,
e.g. *cornets-à-piston* to represent cornetts, though in fact this
proves to be an agreeable working substitute. The sleeve notes
tend to be a little misleading as the writer has adopted the same
spelling—*cornet*—to indicate both the old and the very different
modern instruments. This, however, does not affect the value of
the record in most respects.

13   247   *'Reflections' (Realm Jazz. Savoy Series. Rm—167)*
J. J. Johnson and Kai Winding, solo trombones with various
supporting artists.
      Beautiful trombone playing by two superb artists. In spite
of the jazz idiom of the music the listener may well sense in some
of these recordings (especially Side A, Band 2, 'Lament' by J. J.
Jones) a full circle return to the 'vocal' sackbut playing of the
16th century.

13   247   *'A Trumpet'* from *This Modern World (Capitol LC. 6667.* Side
2, Band 2)
Stan Kenton and his Orchestra with Maynard Ferguson, solo
trumpet.

APPENDIX 4

A Selective Bibliography–Short Title

IN ADDITION to the specific references included in the foregoing text, this general bibliography is offered. It makes no claim to completeness, but I have included all publications that I have found most useful or informative. The specialised literature of the trumpet and the trombone is not very extensive and a large part of it is necessarily to be found in the pages of comprehensive musical works—encyclopædias, treatises on orchestration, catalogues of musical collections, etc. Much of the most important material appears in correspondence published in periodicals, and the discovery of this is often a matter of chance or informed guesswork. Such published letters as have come my way have been recorded, and reference to the most valuable has been made in the main text.

Those readers who may have a closely specialised interest in one or another aspect of Brass lore are recommended to see *Brass Quarterly*, a remarkable periodical published since 1957 from Durham, New Hampshire, U.S.A., under the editorship of Mary Rasmussen. Quarter by quarter, this journal has carried instalments of a 'Brass Bibliography' which is probably the fullest now available to the student. It covers all aspects of Brass literature and is specially valuable in its references to such works as university theses which are difficult of access in the ordinary way.

In the following list comparatively few tutors, methods, and instruction books have been included, since these tend to duplicate each other. Those mentioned have been selected either because they refer to special types of instrument, or because they indicate clearly the scope of an instrument at their period. With this in mind these books have been listed in order of publication; otherwise the customary alphabetical arrangement is used.

The playing literature of the trumpet and the trombone is not touched on here for reasons that have been explained in the General Introduction.

A. Tutors and Instruction Books

Trumpet

Fantini, Girolamo. *Modo per imparar a sonare di tromba.* D. Vuastch, Frankfurt, 1638. (Facsimile, Bolletino Bibliografico Musicale, Milan, 1934.)
Altenburg, Johann Ernst. *Versuch an einer Anleitung der Trompeter und Pauker-Kunst.* Halle, 1795. (Facsimile, R. Bertling, Dresden, 1911). Translated into English and reprinted in *Brass Quarterly*, 1958–59.
Hyde, John. *A New and Complete Preceptor for the Trumpet and Bugle-Horn.* Thompson's Warehouse, London, *c.* 1800.
Noblet. *Nouvelle Méthode de Bugle ou Trompette à clef.* (*Klapp-horn-schule.*)
Roy and Muller. *Tutor for the Keyed Trumpet.* London, *c.* 1835.
Harper, Thomas, sen. *Instructions for the Trumpet.* London, 1836. (English slide trumpet.)
Dauverné, aîné. *Méthode de trompette.* Paris, pre 1848. (Natural trumpet.)
Dauverné, F. G. A. *Méthode complète de trompette à cylindres.* Paris, pre 1848.
—— *Méthode pour la trompette.* Paris, 1857.

Harper, Thomas, jun. *Harper's School for the Trumpet*. Rudall, Carte & Co. London, 1875.

Arban, J. B. *Complete Method*. Paris, pre 1889. (Reprinted and translated many times since its first publication, this is a standard work used probably by the majority of French and English speaking teachers today.)

Langey, Otto. *Tutor for the Trumpet*. Riviere and Hawkes, London, *c.* 1885. (One of a series of Tutors for various instruments which appeared over Langey's signature. Revised editions were issued by Hawkes and Son from about 1911, and these are still much used for elementary teaching.)

Franquin, M. *Méthode pour trompette, cornet à pistons et bugle*. Paris, post 1916.

Trombone

Nemetz. *Neueste Posaun-schule*. Vienna, *c.* 1830.

Cornette, V. *Méthode de trombone ordinaire ou à coulisses*. Richaud, Paris, pre 1848.

Vobaron. *Méthode de trombone*. Paris, *c.* 1833. (A work of no particular merit which is, however, still sometimes used for elementary teaching.)

Dieppo (with Beer). *Méthode complète pour le trombone*. Troupenas et Cie. Paris. (The official instruction book in the Paris Conservatoire during its author's period as professor there after 1836. About 1866 Dieppo, under pressure from Military Authorities, began teaching the Sax six-valve trombone which was also obligatory in the Opéra. This for a time greatly damaged slide trombone playing in France and caused much poverty and distress among the older players.)

Kastner, G. *Méthode élémentaire de trombone*. Troupenas et Cie. Paris, *c.* 1840.

Langey, Otto. *Tutor for the Trombone*. (*See* Trumpet, above.)

From the above dates the reader will see that the majority of Tutors devoted exclusively to the trombone date from the revival of that instrument towards the beginning of the 19th century. See p. 140, above.

B. HISTORICAL AND DESCRIPTIVE

Agricola, M. *Musica Instrumentalis deudsch*. Wittemberg, 1528, 1532, 1542, 1545.

—— *Musica Instrumentalis deudsch*. (Reprint in facsimile.) Breitkopf, Leipzig, 1896.

Apel, W. *The Harvard Dictionary of Music*. Cambridge, Mass., 1945.

Arnold, Denis. *Brass Instruments in the Italian Church Music of the Sixteenth and Early Seventeenth Centuries* (ex *Brass Quarterly*), 1959.

Bonanni, F. *Gabinetto armonico*. Rome, 1722.

Brancour. *Histoire des Instruments de Musique*. H. Laurens, Paris, 1921.

Burney, Dr. C. *A General History of Music*. London, 1776.

—— *The Present State of Music in France and Italy*. London, 1771.

—— *The Present State of Music in Germany and the Netherlands*. London, 1773.

Carse, A. *The History of Orchestration*. Kegan Paul, London, 1925.

—— *Musical Wind Instruments*. Macmillan, London, 1939.

—— *The Orchestra in the 18th Century*. Heffer, Cambridge, 1940.

—— *The Orchestra from Beethoven to Berlioz*. Heffer, Cambridge, 1948.

Catrufo, J. *Traité des Voix et des Instruments*. Paris, 1832.

Cobbett, W. W. *Cyclopedic Survey of Chamber Music*. Oxford, 1929.

Comettant, O. *Histoire d'un Inventeur* (*Ad. Sax*). Paris, 1860.

Cucuel, G. *Etudes sur un orchestre au 18ᵐᵉ siècle*. Fischbacher, Paris, 1913.

Dalyell, J. G. *Musical Memoirs of Scotland.* Pickering, London, 1849.
Diderot and d'Alembert. *Encyclopédie.* Paris, 1767, 1776.
Donington, R. *The Instruments of Music.* London, 1949.
Doppelmayr, J. *Historische Nachtricht von den Nürnbergischen Mathematicis und Kunstlern.* Nürnberg, 1730.
Ehmann, W. *New Brass Instruments Based on Old Models* (ex *Brass Quarterly,* Vol. 1, No. 3), 1958.
Eichborn, H. *Girolamo Fantini, ein Virtuos des 17 Jahrhunderts und seine Trompeten-Schule* (ex *Monatscheft für Musikwissenschaft,* xxii, Leipzig), 1890.
—— *Das alte Clarinblasen auf Trompeten.* Breitkopf, Leipzig, 1894.
Euting, E. *Zur Geschichte der Blasinstrumente in 16 and 17 Jahrhundert,* Berlin, 1899.
Farmer, H. *Rise and Development of Military Music.* W. Reeves, London, 1912.
Fétis, F. J. *Biographie Universelle des Musiciens.* Firmin-Didot, Paris, 1868.
Francoeur, L. J. *Diapason général—des instruments à vent.* Paris, 1772.
—— *Traité général—des instruments d'orchestre.* (Revised by A. Choron.) Paris, 1813.
Galpin, F. W. *European Musical Instruments.* Williams and Norgate, London, 1937.
—— *Old English Instruments of Music.* (3rd edition.) Methuen, London, 1932.
Gerber, E. L. *Historisch—biographisches Lexikon.* Breitkopf, Leipzig, 1792.
Gevaert, F. A. *Nouveau traité d'instrumentation.* Lemoine, Paris, 1885.
Grove, G. *Dictionary of Music and Musicians.* (5th edition.) Macmillan & Co., London, 1954.
Hawkins, C. *A General History of Music.* London, 1876.
Heckel, W. *Der Fagott.* Merseburger, Leipzig, 1899.
—— English translation by L. G. Langwill. 1931. (Typescript.)
—— Ex. *Journal of Musicology,* Vol. 11. Ohio, U.S.A., 1940.
Hipkins and Gibb. *Musical Instruments, etc.* A. and C. Black, Edinburgh, 1888, 1921.
Jahn, F. *Die Nürnberger Trompeten und Posaunenmacher im 16. Jahrhundert* (ex *Archiv für Musikwissenschaft,* VII), 1925.
Junker. *Musikalischer Almanach.* 1782.
Kappey, J. A. *Short History of Military Music.* Boosey & Company, London, c. 1890.
Kastner, G. *Manuel Général de Musique Militaire.* Firmin-Didot, Paris, 1848.
Kinsky, G. *A History of Music in Pictures.* Dent, London, 1930-37.
Kircher, A. *Musurgia Universalis.* Corbeletti, Rome, 1650.
Koch, H. *Musikalisches Lexikon.* Offenbach, 1802.
Koch-Dommer. *Musikalisches Lexikon.* Heidelberg, 1865.
Laborde, J. B. de. *Essai sur la Musique.* Paris, 1780, 1781.
Langwill, L. G. *Two Rare Eighteenth-century London Directories.* (Ex. *Music and Letters.*) London, January 1949.
—— *London Wind-instrument Makers—17th and 18th Centuries.* (Ex. *The Music Review,* Vol. VII.) Heffer, Cambridge.
Lavoix, H. *Histoire de l'instrumentation.* Firmin-Didot, Paris, 1878.
Lucinius, O. *Musurgia.* Joan Schott, Strassburg, 1536.
Majer, J. *Neu eröffneter Musik Saal.* (2nd edition.) Kremer, Nürnberg, 1741.
Mattheson, J. *Das neu-eröffnete Orchester.* Hamburg, 1713.
Mersenne, M. *Harmonie universelle.* Baudry, Paris. 1636.
Miller, G. *The Military Band.* Boosey & Co., London, 1912.
Norlind, T. *Musikinstrumentenhistoria i ord och bild.* Dordish Rotogravyr, Stockholm, 1941.

Parke, W. *Musical Memoirs*. Colburn and Bentley, London, 1830.
Pierre, C. *Les facteurs d'instruments de musique*. Sagot, Paris, 1893.
—— *La Facture Instrumentale*.
Pontécoulant, L. G. le D. *Organographie*. Castel, Paris, 1861.
Praetorius, M. *Syntagma musicum*. E. Holwein, Wolfenbüttel, 1619.
—— Reprint. Trautwein, Berlin, 1884.
Prestini, G. *Notizie intorno alla storia degli strumenti, etc.* Bongiovanni, Bologna, 1925.
Profeta, R. *Storia—degli strumenti musicali*. Florence, 1952.
Rasmussen, Mary. *Gottfried Reiche, and his 'Vierzwantig Neue Quatricinia', Leipzig, 1696.* (ex *Brass Quarterly*.) 1960.
Redfield, J. *Music, a Science and an Art*. Knopf, New York, 1928.
Riemann, H. *Musik—Lexikon*. (Various editions.) Mainz, Leipzig, Berlin, 1882–1922.
Sachs, C. *Handbuch der Musikinstrumentenkunde*. Breitkopf, Leipzig, 1930.
—— *Real-Lexikon der Musikinstrumente*. Berlin, 1913.
Schering, Adolf. *Zu Gottfried Reiches Leben und Kunst*, in *Bach-Jahrbuch*. Leipzig, 1918.
Schlesinger, K. *Modern Orchestral Instruments*. W. Reeves, London, 1910.
Schmidl, C. *Dizionario universale dei musicisti*. Milan, 1928–38.
Schneider, W. *Historisch-Technische Beschreibung, etc.* Hennings, Leipzig, 1834.
Speer, D. *Grund-rightiger Unterricht der Musikalischen Kunst*. Ulm, 1687, 1697.
Sundelin. *Die Instrumentirung—Militar Musik-Chöre*. Wagenfüht, Berlin, 1828.
—— *Die Instrumentirung für das Orchester*. Berlin, 1828.
Tans'ur, William. *The Elements of Music Displayed*. London, 1772.
Terry, C. S. *Bach's Orchestra*. O.U.P., London, 1932.
Teuchert, E., and Haupt, E. *Musik-Instrumentenkunde in Wort und Bild*. (Vol. II.) Breitkopf, Leipzig, 1911.
Virdung, S. *Musica Getutscht*. Basle, 1511.
—— Reprint in facsimile. Trautwein, Berlin, 1882. Kassel, 1931.
Weckerlin, J. B. *Nouveau Musiciana*. Paris, 1890.
Wright, R. *Dictionnaire des instruments de musique*. Battley Bros., London, 1941.
Zacconi, L. *Prattica di Musica*. Venice, 1596.
Zedler. *Universal Lexikon*. 1735.

C. TECHNICAL

Ancell, J. F. *Sound Pressure Spectra of a Muted Cornet* (ex *Journal A.S.A.* 27, p. 996). Menasha, 1935.
Andries. *Aperçu theorique de tous les instruments de musique*. Ghent, 1856.
Barton, E. H., and Browning, Mary. *Sound Changes analysed by Records— Trumpet and Cornet* (ex *Philosophical Magazine*, 50, pp. 951–67). 1925.
Berlioz, H. *Traité de l'instrumentation*. Schonenberger, Paris, 1844.
—— *Instrumentationslehre. Erganstz u. revidiert von Richard Strauss*. Leipzig, 1905.
Buck, Percy. *Acoustics for Musicians*. O.U.P., London, 1918.
Bonavia-Hunt, N. A. *What is the Formant?* (ex. *Musical Opinion*.) London, December 1948, January 1949.
Forsyth, Cecil. *Orchestration*. Macmillan, London, 1922.
Hague, B. *The Tonal Spectra of Wind Instruments* (ex. Proc. Roy. Mus. Ass. Session LXXIII) 1947.
Helmholtz, H. L. F. von. *The Sensations of Tone*, trans. A. J. Ellis. (2nd edition.) Longmans, Green & Co., London, 1885.
Hopkins and Rimbault. *The Organ*. (3rd edition.) Robert Cocks, London, 1877.

Lloyd, Ll. *The Musical Ear.* O.U.P., London, 1940.
Mackworth-Young, G. *What Happens in Singing.* Newman Neame, London, 1953.
Mahillon, V. *Eléments d'acoustique.* Mahillon, Brussels, 1874.
Miller, D. C. *The Science of Musical Sounds.* The Macmillan Co., New York, 1922.
—— *Sound Waves.* The Macmillan Co., New York, 1937.
Richardson, E. G. *The Acoustics of Orchestral Instruments.* Arnold, London, 1929
Smith, Robert. *Harmonics.* T. and J. Merrill, Cambridge, 1757.
Webster, J. C. *Measurable Differences among Trumpet Players* (ex *Proc. of the Music Teachers' National Association.* Series 43. Pittsburgh). 1951.
Wood, Alexander. *The Physics of Music.* Methuen, London, 1944.

PERIODICALS

Acoustical Society of America. Journal. Menasha, 1929.
Allgemeine Musikalische Zeitung. Leipzig, 1798–1849, 1863–1882.
Brass Quarterly. New Hampshire, 1957.
Cæcilia. Mainz, 1824–48.
Royal Musical Association, Proceedings, London. London, 1875.
Galpin Society Journal. London, 1948.
Monatsheft für Musikwissenschaft.
Musical Opinion. London, 1877.
Woodwind Magazine. New York, 1948.
Zeitschrift für Instrumentenbau. Leipzig, 1880.
Zeitschrift für Musikwissenschaft.
Sitzungberichte der Preuss, Akad. der Wissenschaft, Berlin, 1882.

D. CATALOGUES OF COLLECTIONS AND EXHIBITIONS (INCLUDING COMMENTARIES)

AMSTERDAM. Rijksmuseum—Musiekinstrumenten uit het Rijksmuseum te Amsterdam, 1952. (Exhibition in The Hague.)
BASLE. Historisches Museum, Basel. *Katalog* No. IV, KARL NEF, 1906.
BERLIN. Sammlung der Staatlichen Hochschule. *Beschreibender Katalog.* CURT SACHS, 1922.
BOLOGNA. Esposizione internazionale di Musica in Bologna, nel 1888. *Catalogo ufficiale.* (Parma 1888.)
BOSTON, MASS. Boston Museum of Fine Arts, Boston, Massachusetts. *Ancient European Musical Instruments, An Organological Study of the Musical Instruments in the Lesley Lindsey Mason Collection at the Museum of Fine Arts, Boston.* N. BESSARABOFF, Harvard University Press, 1941.
BRESLAU. Schlesisches Museum. *Catalogue.* EPSTEIN–SCHEYER, 1932.
BRUSSELS. Musée instrumental du Conservatoire Royal. *Catalogue descriptif et analytique.* V. C. MAHILLON, 5 vols., 1893–1922.
BIRMINGHAM. Birmingham and Midland Institute. *Catalogue,* 1953 (cyclostyled).
COLOGNE. Musikhistorisches Museum von Wilhelm Heyer in Cöln. *Kleiner Katalog.* GEORGE KINSKY, 1913.
COPENHAGEN. Music History Museum. *Das Musikhistorische Museum, Kopenhagen.* ANGUL HAMMERICH, 1911. German translation of Danish text, Erna Bobe, pub. Breitkopf, Leipzig. (179 illustrations.)
—— Claudius Collection. *Catalogue* 1900 and enlarged edition Danish and German texts, 1921.
GLASGOW. Kelvingrove Art Gallery and Museum. *The Glen Collection of*

Musical Instruments. HENRY GEORGE FARMER, 1943. (Ex *The Art Review of the Glasgow Gallery and Museums Association.*)

FLORENCE. *Catalogo de Instrumentos antigos de Leopold Francolini.*

—— R. Istituto L. Cherubini. *Gli strumenti raccolti nel Museo* etc. LETO BARGAGNA, 1911.

—— Collezione Etnografico-Musicale Kraus. *Catalogo Sezione Instrumenti Musicali.* A. KRAUS FIGLIO, 1901.

GHENT. Collection d'Instruments de Musique Anciens ou Curieux formée par C. C. Snoeck. *Catalogue*, 1894. (This collection was subsequently divided between the Berlin Hochschule and the Brussels Conservatoire Museums but certain specimens mentioned in the Catalogue are no longer to be found in either of these.)

HAGUE. THE. D. F. Scheurleer Collection. *De Muziek-Historische Afdeling.* Gemeente-Museum, 's-Gravenhage. DIRK J. BALFOORT, 1935.

HAMBURG. Museum für Hamburgische Geschichte. *Verzeichnis der Sammlung alter Musikinstrumente.* HANS SCHRÖDER, 1930.

INNSBRUCK. Museum Ferdinandeum. *Catalogue.*

LEIPZIG. Instrumenten-Sammlung von Paul de Wit. *Perlen aus der I–S etc.* German, French and English texts in parallel columns and 16 plates in colour. 1892.

LISBON. Museu Instrumental em Lisboa. *Catalogo summario.* MICHEL'ANGELO LAMBERTINI, 1914.

—— Collecções Keil. *Breve noticia dos instrumentos de musica antigos e modernos.* ALFREDO KEIL, 1904.

LIVERPOOL. Rushworth and Dreaper Collection. *General Catalogue*, 1923.

LONDON. Exhibition 1852. *Exhibition Lecture on the Musical Department.* W. W. CAZALET.

—— *Douze jours à Londres. Voyage d'un mélomane à travers l'Exposition Universelle.* COMTE AD. DE PONTÉCOULANT, 1862 (Paris).

—— South Kensington Museum. *Descriptive Catalogue of the Musical Instruments.* CARL ENGEL, 1870.

—— South Kensington Museum. *Catalogue of the Special Exhibition of Ancient Musical Instruments* (1872), published 1873.

—— International Inventions Exhibition, 1885. *Guide to the Loan Collection and List of Musical Instruments, etc.*

—— Royal Military Exhibition, 1890. *Descriptive Catalogue of the Musical Instruments.* C. R. DAY, 1891.

—— Crystal Palace Exhibition. *Catalogue*, 1900.

—— Loan Exhibition, Fishmongers' Hall, 1904. *Illustrated Catalogue.* Various contributors, published Novello, London, 1909. (This and the R.M.E. are probably the most important of all English catalogues.)

—— The Horniman Museum. *The Adam Carse Collection of Musical Wind Instruments.* A list published by the London County Council, 1947.

—— As above a *Catalogue*, illustrated. Published by the L.C.C. 1951.

—— The Galpin Society. British Musical Instruments, an Exhibition by arrangement with the Arts Council of Great Britain, *Catalogue* 1951.

—— Boosey and Hawkes Collection. *Catalogue* 1939. (Typescript, privately circulated.)

LUTON. Luton Museum. Exhibition 1947. 'Growth of Music.' *Catalogue* (cyclostyled 1947.)

MILAN. Museo del Conservatorio. *Gli strumenti musicali nel Museo.* EUGENIO DE GUARINONI, 1908.

MILAN. Esposizione musicale, sotto il patrocinio di S.M. la Regina. Atti del congresso dei Musicisti italiani, riunito in Milano dal 16 al 22 Giugno, 1881.

MICHIGAN. University of Ann Arbor. The Frederick Stearns Collection. *Catalogue.* A. A. STANLEY, 1921.

MUNICH. Baiersches Nationalmuseum. *Catalogue.* K. A. BIERDIMPFL, 1883.

NEW YORK. Crosby Brown Collection. The Metropolitan Museum of Art. *Catalogue* 1902.

PARIS. Musée du Conservatoire National. *Catalogue raisonné.* G. CHOUQUET, 1884. Supplements 1894, 1899, 1903.

—— Conservatoire des Arts et Métiers. *General Catalogue* in course of reprinting in 1948.

—— *Catalogue du Musée instrumental de M. Adolphe Sax,* 1877.

—— L'Industrie. *Exposition de* 1834. STEPHEN FLACHAT.

—— *Histoire illustrée de l'Exposition Universelle, par catégories d'industries, avec notices sur les exposants.* 1855. (Vol. I refers to the musical section.) CHARLES ROBIN.

—— *La Musique à l'Exposition Universelle de* 1867. COMTE DE PONTÉCOULANT. Published 1868.

—— *La Musique, les Musiciens, et les Instruments de Musique . . . Archive complètes . . . l'Exposition Internationale de* 1867. OSCAR COMETTANT. Published 1869.

—— *Exposition Universelle de Paris, en* 1855. *Fabrication des Instruments de Musique, rapport.* F. J. FÉTIS. Published 1856.

—— *La facture instrumentale à l'Exposition Universelle de* 1889 *. . . etc.* CONSTANT PIERRE. Published 1890.

—— Exposition universelle internationale de 1878 à Paris. *Les instruments de musique etc.* G. CHOUQUET. Published 1880.

—— Exposition universelle internationale de 1900 à Paris. *Instruments de musique. Rapport.* E. BRIQUEVILLE.

PRAGUE. National Museum. An exhibition of musical instruments. *Catalogue.* ALEXANDER BUCHNER, 1952.

SALZBURG. Museum Carolino Augusteum. *Catalogue.* C. GEIRINGER (Leipzig), 1931.

STOCKHOLM. Musikhistoriska Museet. *Catalogue.* J. SVANBERG, 1902.

VERONA. *Catalogo de Instrumentos do municipio de Verona.*

VIENNA. Die Sammlung Alter Muskinstrumente. *Beschreibendes Verzeichnis.* J. SCHLOSSER, 1920. (A most important work with many magnificent illustrations.)

—— Sammlung der K. K. Gesellschaft der Musikfreunde in Wien. *Catalogue.* E. MANDYCZEWSKI, 1921.

—— *Rapport sur les Instruments de Musique à l'Exposition de Vienne en 1837.* LISSAJOUS. Published 1895.

YORK. The Castle Museum. Musical section. *Catalogue.*

Condensed Subject Index

(Principal References)

Index of Names

Proper names in the following table are arranged alphabetically. Celebrities are indicated by surname only. In other cases where pre-names are known, these are either printed at length or represented by initials, according to whichever is the commoner usage in conversational reference.

Index of Instruments

The following list is confined to first references and principal ones in the text.

Printed offset in Great Britain by
The Camelot Press Ltd., London and Southampton